Cooking by the Calendar

A FAMILY WEEKLY COOKBOOK

JANUARY	FEBRUARY
MAY	JUNE
SEPTEMBER	OCTOBER

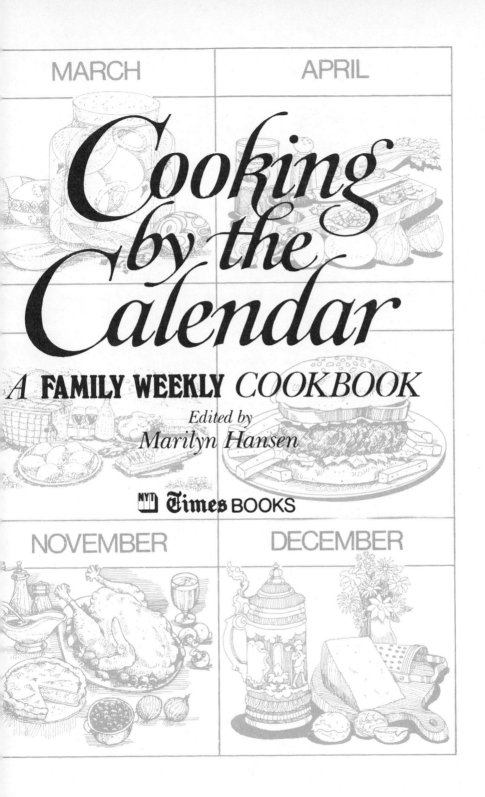

MARCH

APRIL

Cooking by the Calendar

A FAMILY WEEKLY COOKBOOK

Edited by

Marilyn Hansen

NYT **Times** BOOKS

NOVEMBER

DECEMBER

Published by TIMES BOOKS, a division of Quadrangle/The New York Times Book Co., Inc., Three Park Avenue, New York, N.Y. 10016.

Published simultaneously in Canada by Fitzhenry & Whiteside, Ltd., Toronto.

Library of Congress Cataloging in Publication Data

Main entry under title:
Cooking by the calendar.
    Includes index.
    1. Cookery. I. Hansen, Marilyn. II. Family
Weekly magazine.
TX652.C73   641.5   78-58167
ISBN 0-8129-0786-8

Manufactured in the United States of America.
Designed by Beth Tondreau

Dedicated to all the *Family Weekly* readers, young and old, who throughout our twenty-five years of publishing have become loyal friends of and active participants in the food pages. It is due to their continuing interest in a *Family Weekly* Cookbook that this book came into being.

Acknowledgments

It is a clear, sunny June afternoon in New York. The air has a special brilliance that comes when there is low humidity and almost no pollution.

I have come to the welcome finishing touch of composing my list of acknowledgments.

First of all, I'd like to thank the persons at *Family Weekly*: Mort Frank, our long-time Publisher, who had the faith in me to edit this cookbook; Leonard S. Davidow, *Family Weekly* Chairman Emeritus, who encouraged and inspired me; Scott DeGarmo, our *Family Weekly* Editor, who graciously gave me the time I needed and who left me alone; Tim Mulligan, *Family Weekly* Managing Editor, who encouraged me and gave words of praise along the way: Hal Landon, Senior Editor, for his many kindnesses; the *Family Weekly* Art Department; and Kate Gallagher, my attentive, energetic secretary, who gave unhesitatingly of her time.

The business and public relations firms who have cheerfully supplied much information and editorial material are many across our country. I would like to especially credit the following organizations for outstanding service: N. W. Ayer Public Aelations: Souzen Deavers; American Lamb Council: Donna Hamilton; American Meat Institute: Jane Anderson; Maidie Alexander Associates: Maidie Alexander; Bordens Inc.: Karen Johnson; Burson Marsteller: Gloria Marshall and Saralie Slonsky; Botsford, Ketchum Inc., San Francisco: Bee Marks; Carol Ashimine and Maggie Waldron; California Iceberg Lettuce Commission: Caryl Saunders; Campbell's Soup Co.: Charlotte Ruf; Creamer, Dickson, Basford: Wendy Burrell; California Almond Advisory Board: Keith Thomas and Jeanne Bauer; Corn Products Corporation: Diane Kline; Carnation Company: Virginia Piper; Castle & Cooke Foods, Inc.: Rowena Hubbard; Diamond Walnut Growers: Dennis Bruner; Dudley-Anderson-Yutzy: Anita Mizner; Del Monte Corporation: Donna Higgins; Foote, Cone and Belding: Arlene Wanderman; Food Communications: Tom Arsenault and Howard Helmer; General Foods: Martha Kelley; General Electric News Bureau: Barbara Parsky and Charlene Corenman; General Mills, Inc.: Mercedes Bates; Howlette and Gaines: Roxie Howlett; Harshe, Rotman & Druck: Laura Weill and Kay Berger; Kraft Foods: Jae Haeslep; Lewis Neale, Inc.: Anita Fial; Manning, Selvage and Lee, Inc.: Pat Mason; Carol Moberg, Inc.: Linda Taber; Nabisco: Eleanor Crozier; Newman, Saylor and Gregory: Nancy R. McLeod; National Livestock and Meat Board: David Stroud; Nestles: Ann Dries; Pepperidge Farm: Mary McGrath; Pacific Kitchen: Shirley Mack; Pillsbury Co.: Catherine Hanley; The Quaker Oats Co.: Lois Ross; Rice Council: Rae Hartfield; Reynolds Metals: Judy Moore; Smith Bucklin & Associates: Sheila Sandy; Niki Singer, Inc.: Constance English; Standard Brands, Inc.: Virginia Schroeder; Sunkist Growers, Inc.: Barbara Robison; J. Walter Thompson: Margaret Spader; Western Foods Associates: Dorothy Canet and Helen Tobias.

Photographers whose work I admire and couldn't do without: Gus Francisco/Alan Baillie; Walter Storck; Fred Lyon; Elmer Moss; Willard Purvis; Lubeck; Bill Margerin; Bill Holland; and Rupert Callendar.

A special commendation goes to our artist, Tom Cavanaugh, whose light-hearted approach and adaptability made him especially valuable with the illustrations.

My introduction to the world of book publishing was made easier by working with Leonard Schwartz, Vice-President, Director of Marketing, Times Books; Beth Tondreau, Art Director; and Jim Fitzgerald, Managing Editor. Rosalyn Badalamenti, Production Editor, and I worked closely together on many details of the book form, and I especially thank her for her understanding and good will.

In closing, I would like to mention two of my mentors. A tribute to Melanie DeProft, *Family Weekly* Food Editor for eighteen years before I came on the scene, whose wide knowledge of food and enthusiasm about *Family Weekly* were contagious. And Mary Eckley, Food Editor of *McCall's* magazine, whose standard of taste in food is a constant inspiration.

Also, I would especially like to thank my daughters Carla, Ardeth and Ava for their own special words of encouragement and sensitivity while the book was taking shape.

MARILYN HANSEN
New York City
June, 1978

Contents Introduction

To every thing there is a season and a time to every purpose under the heaven:

A time to be born, and a time to die; a time to plant and a time to pluck up that which is planted.*

And also that everyman should eat and drink, and enjoy the good of all his labor, it is the gift of God.*

Those timeless passages from Ecclesiastes form the philosophy of the Family Weekly Cooking By The Calendar Cookbook.

We take our readers through the changing spirit of the seasons, month by month. To sense and be in touch with the ebb and flow of the year and how it relates to life-giving food is our purpose.

* The Bible: Ecclesiastes—Chapter 3, verses 1, 2 and 13.

Contents

January

It's a brand-new year, so let's celebrate. Ring out the old, ring in the new; it's a time for new beginnings. .

The cold air whirling about our homes makes us conscious of pulling inward toward the home hearth, and we are eager for ways to trim the family food budget after the excesses of the holiday season.

Our feature chart spotlights quick rice skillets and rice casseroles. Both are handy practical ways to use leftovers.

Thrifty main dishes and favorite pasta dishes are our answers for many of the meals this month.

We can also enjoy the bounty of the tangy sweet citrus fruits now: grapefruits, oranges, lemons and tangerines.

The Vegetable of the Month is the robust onion which warms and fills out the corners of this stark time.

Speedy Rice Skillets

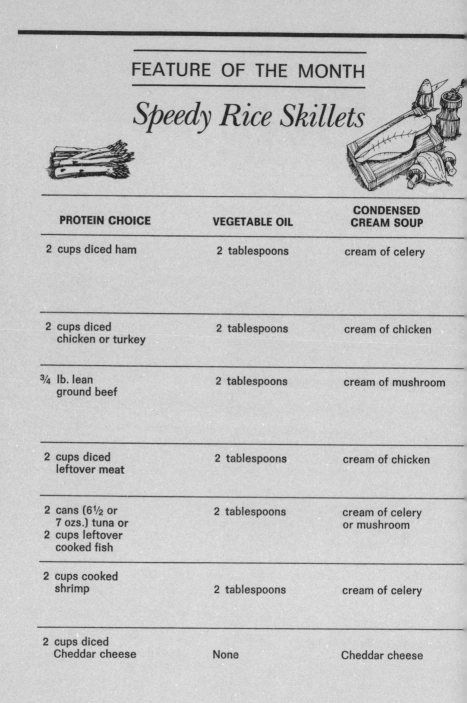

PROTEIN CHOICE	VEGETABLE OIL	CONDENSED CREAM SOUP
2 cups diced ham	2 tablespoons	cream of celery
2 cups diced chicken or turkey	2 tablespoons	cream of chicken
¾ lb. lean ground beef	2 tablespoons	cream of mushroom
2 cups diced leftover meat	2 tablespoons	cream of chicken
2 cans (6½ or 7 ozs.) tuna or 2 cups leftover cooked fish	2 tablespoons	cream of celery or mushroom
2 cups cooked shrimp	2 tablespoons	cream of celery
2 cups diced Cheddar cheese	None	Cheddar cheese

HOW TO MAKE SPEEDY RICE SKILLETS

MAKES 5 SERVINGS

In skillet saute protein choice (except cheese) in oil until lightly browned. Stir in 1 can (10¾ ozs.) condensed soup, 1 cup water, and 1 package (10 ozs.) frozen vegetable. Bring to boil. Add rice and seasonings, return to boil. Cover and simmer 5 to 8 minutes or until rice is tender. Stir lightly with fork before serving. If using cheese simply add to skillet with rice.

WATER	VEGETABLE	QUICK COOK-ING RICE	SEASONING
1 cup	peas/carrots	1½ cups	1 teaspoon salt 1 teaspoon prepared mustard ⅛ teaspoon freshly ground pepper
1 cup	peas	1½ cups	1 teaspoon salt 1 teaspoon curry powder ½ cup chopped apple
1 cup	peas	1½ cups	½ teaspoon salt 2 teaspoons Worcestershire sauce ⅛ teaspoon freshly ground black pepper
1 cup	grean beans	1½ cups	2 tablespoons soy sauce 1 cup sliced celery ½ cup sliced onion
1 cup	broccoli spears, sliced	1½ cups	½ teaspoon salt 2 tablespoons lemon juice ¼ teaspoon celery salt
1 cup	broccoli spears, sliced	1½ cups	½ teaspoon salt ⅛ teaspoon freshly ground black pepper ½ cup sliced celery
1 cup	green beans or peas	1½ cups	½ teaspoon salt 1 teaspoon prepared mustard ⅛ teaspoon freshly ground black pepper

FEATURE OF THE MONTH

Speedy Rice Casseroles

QUICK COOK-ING RICE	BOILING WATER	PROTEIN	SOUP
1½ cups	1¾ cups	2 cups diced cooked beef	cream of potato
1½ cups	1¾ cups	2 cups diced cooked ham	cream of celery
1½ cups	1¾ cups	2 cups diced cooked pork	cream of onion
1½ cups	1¾ cups	2 cups diced cooked chicken	cream of chicken
1½ cups	1¾ cups	2 cups cooked medium shrimp	cream of mushroom
1½ cups	1¾ cups	2 cans (6½ or 7 ozs.) tuna	cream of celery
1½ cups	1¾ cups	2 cups diced cooked turkey	cream of chicken

HOW TO MAKE SPEEDY RICE CASSEROLES

MAKES 6 SERVINGS

Combine quick cooking rice, boiling water, protein choice, soup, 1 package (10 ozs.) frozen vegetables, and seasonings in 2 quart casserole; mix well. Sprinkle with garnish or topping; cover and bake at 400°F. for 15 to 20 minutes until rice is tender and casserole is bubbly. Stir lightly with fork before serving.

VEGETABLES	SEASONINGS	GARNISH
green peas	1 teaspoon Worcestershire sauce ⅛ teaspoon freshly ground black pepper	cheese croutons
broccoli spears, sliced	1 teaspoon prepared mustard dash hot pepper sauce	grated sharp Cheddar cheese
cut green beans	⅛ teaspoon freshly ground black pepper ½ cup chopped onion	French fried onion rings
peas and carrots	1 teaspoon curry powder ⅛ teaspoon freshly ground black pepper ½ cup chopped onion	salted peanuts
broccoli spears, sliced	1 teaspoon salt ⅛ teaspoon freshly ground black pepper 2 tablespoons lemon juice	
green beans	¼ cup sliced stuffed olives or pickles ¼ cup chopped onion 1 teaspoon salt ⅛ teaspoon freshly ground black pepper	crushed potato chips
peas	1 teaspon salt ⅛ teaspoon freshly ground black pepper 1 teaspoon chili powder ½ cup chopped onion	crushed corn chips

Thrifty Main Dishes

THREE CHEESE NOODLE CASSEROLE

MAKES 8 SERVINGS

1 lb. medium egg noodles (about 8 cups)
1 tablespoon salt
4 to 6 qts. boiling water
½ cup butter or margarine
2 cloves garlic, crushed
¼ cup all-purpose flour
1 teaspoon salt
½ teaspoon ground mustard
¼ teaspoon freshly ground black pepper
½ teaspoon Worcestershire sauce
1 qt. (4 cups) milk
2 cups (8 ozs.) grated natural Swiss cheese
1 cup (4 ozs.) grated sharp Cheddar cheese
½ cup grated Romano or Parmesan cheese
½ cup fine dry bread crumbs
2 tablespoons butter or margarine, melted

1. Gradually add noodles and 1 tablespoon salt to rapidly boiling water so that water continues to boil. Cook, uncovered, stirring occasionally until tender. Drain in colander. Rinse with cold water.

2. Prepare cheese sauce: melt ½ cup butter in Dutch oven or large saucepan over low heat. Add garlic and sauté ½ minute.

3. Stir in flour, 1 teaspoon salt, mustard, pepper and Worcestershire sauce.

4. Gradually stir in milk; bring mixture to a boil. Simmer 1 minute, stirring constantly.

5. Add cheeses; stir mixture constantly over low heat 1 to 2 minutes or until cheeses melt.

6. Add noodles; toss until well coated with cheese sauce. Turn into lightly greased 2½- or 3-qt. baking dish.

7. Mix crumbs with melted butter; sprinkle over noodles. Bake in preheated 350°F. oven for 30 to 40 minutes until bubbly.

CHEESE STRATA

MAKES 6 TO
8 SERVINGS

1 lb. loaf enriched sliced white bread
1 package (8 ozs.) process American cheese, sliced, or ½ lb. Cheddar cheese, sliced
5 large eggs
1 can (13½ ozs.) evaporated milk
1½ cups water
2 tablespoons finely chopped onion
1½ teaspoons salt
1 teaspoon prepared mustard
¼ teaspoon freshly ground black pepper
Dash hot pepper sauce
¼ cup grated Parmesan cheese

1. Grease a 13- x 9- x 2 inch baking pan.
2. Trim crusts from bread. Layer bread and cheese in pan.
3. Beat together eggs, evaporated milk, water, onion, salt, mustard, pepper and pepper sauce.
4. Pour half of mixture over bread and cheese. Wait 5 minutes, pour remaining half of mixture over all.
5. Sprinkle with Parmesan cheese. Cover and refrigerate 1 hour or overnight.
6. Preheat oven to 350°F. Bake 60 to 70 minutes, or until well puffed up and golden.

SWISS BAKED FISH FILLETS

MAKES 6 SERVINGS

2 lbs. frozen fish fillets, thawed
1 cup sour cream
½ cup slivered Swiss cheese
¼ cup finely chopped scallions or onion
¾ teaspoon salt
⅛ teaspoon freshly ground black pepper
1 teaspoon prepared mustard

1. Preheat oven to 425°F. Lightly grease a 2½-qt. shallow baking pan.
2. Arrange fish fillets in baking pan. In small bowl combine rest of ingredients. Spread over fillets.
3. Bake for about 20 minutes, until fish is opaque and flakes easily with a fork. To brown surface, place baking pan under broiler 1 to 2 minutes.

SWISS-TUNA NOODLE BAKE

MAKES 6 SERVINGS

1 package (8 ozs.) wide
noodles
Salt
Boiling water
2 tablespoons butter or
margarine
½ cup chopped onion
¼ cup finely chopped parsley
½ teaspoon salt
¼ teaspoon ground nutmeg
⅛ teaspoon freshly ground
black pepper

2 tablespoons sherry
2 cans (6½- or 7-oz. size) tuna
in vegetable oil, undrained
1 package (10 ozs.) frozen
peas, thawed
1 cup shredded natural Swiss
cheese
4 eggs, slightly beaten
1 cup milk
½ cup grated Parmesan cheese

1. Preheat oven to 350°F. Grease a 2-qt. baking dish.
2. Cook noodles in salted boiling water according to package directions; drain.
3. In large skillet, melt butter. Add onion and parsley; cook. stirring until onion is tender. Remove from heat, stir in noodles and remaining ingredients, except Parmesan, mix well.
4. Turn mixture into baking dish; sprinkle with Parmesan. Bake, uncovered, 50 to 55 minutes or until set. Let stand 10 minutes before serving.

SAUSAGE-BEAN POLENTA

MAKES 6 SERVINGS

Sauce:
½ lb. pork sausage or ground
beef
1 cup chopped onion
1 can (16 ozs.) red kidney
beans, undrained
1 can (16 ozs.) tomatoes
1 can (8 ozs.) tomato sauce
½ teaspoon crushed oregano
leaves
½ teaspoon salt

¼ teaspoon garlic salt
⅛ teaspoon freshly ground
black pepper

Polenta:
1 cup enriched cornmeal
1 teaspoon salt
1 cup cold water
3 cups boiling water
¼ cup grated Romano cheese

1. First make sauce: In large skillet, cook sausage and onion together. Stir sausage to break it up and cook it until meat is cooked through. Drain off excess fat if necessary.

2. Add beans, tomatoes, tomato sauce, oregano, salt, garlic salt and pepper; stir to combine the ingredients. Heat sauce to boiling. Reduce heat; simmer uncovered about 20 minutes, stirring occasionally.

3. For polenta: Combine cornmeal, salt and cold water. Slowly add to boiling water, stirring constantly. Cook until thickened. Cover; reduce heat and continue cooking 10 minutes. Stir in grated cheese.

4. To serve: Spoon polenta onto large platter, making a ring. Fill center of ring with ½ of sauce. Serve rest of sauce separately.

MACARONI CHILI

MAKES 3½ QUARTS,
10 TO 12 SERVINGS

2 lbs. lean ground chuck
3 tablespoons vegetable oil
1 can (28 ozs.) plum tomatoes
1 qt. tomato juice
2 cups chopped onion
3 cloves garlic, crushed
1 tablespoon salt
3 tablespoons chili powder
1 teaspoon ground cumin seed
1 teaspoon oregano leaves

½ teaspoon freshly ground black pepper
1 bay leaf
1 can (15 ozs. or 1 lb.) red kidney beans, drained
1 tablespoon salt
3 qts. boiling water
2 cups elbow macaroni (8 ozs.)
1 jar (8 ozs.) sweet mixed pickles, drained and coarsely chopped

1. In 6-qt. Dutch oven, brown beef in hot oil, stirring frequently, until it is no longer pink.

2. Stir in tomatoes, tomato juice, onion, garlic, 1 tablespoon salt, chili powder, cumin seed, oregano, pepper and bay leaf. Bring to boiling, reduce heat and simmer, covered, 1 hour. Stir occasionally.

3. Stir in kidney beans, bring back to boiling, reduce heat and simmer, uncovered, 30 minutes. Remove bay leaf.

4. Meanwhile cook elbow macaroni: in 6- to 8-qt. kettle add 1 tablespoon salt to the 3 qts. of rapidly boiling water. Gradually add macaroni so that water continues to boil.

5. Cook uncovered, stirring occasionally, until just tender, 10 to 12 minutes. Drain in colander.

6. Stir macaroni and pickles into chili. Serve in bowls.

Pasta Favorites

CHICKEN TETRAZZINI

MAKES 6 SERVINGS

1½ tablespoons salt
5 qts. boiling water
12 ozs. spaghetti (¾ of 1-lb. pkg.), any variety
¼ cup margarine or butter
2 cups chopped onion
¼ cup all-purpose flour
1½ cups chicken broth
½ cup milk
½ cup evaporated milk, undiluted

½ teaspoon salt
⅛ teaspoon freshly ground black pepper
½ cup dry vermouth or chicken broth
1 can (6 ozs.) sliced mushrooms, undrained
½ cup grated Parmesan or Romano cheese
3 cups cooked, boned chicken or turkey

1. In 8- to 12-qt. kettle add 1½ tablespoons salt to rapidly boiling water. Gradually add spaghetti so that water continues to boil.
2. Cook uncovered, stirring occasionally, until just tender, 12 to 15 minutes. Drain in colander. Set aside.
3. Meanwhile make Tetrazzini Sauce: slowly heat margarine in 2-qt. saucepan. Add onion and sauté over medium heat for 10 minutes, stirring occasionally.
4. Remove from heat; stir in flour smoothly. Gradually add chicken broth, milk and evaporated milk; over medium heat, bring to boiling, stirring. Reduce heat; simmer uncovered, 1 minute.
5. Stir in ½ teaspoon salt, pepper, vermouth, mushroom liquid, and ¼ cup Parmesan cheese; set aside.
6. Preheat oven to 375°F. Lightly grease a 2½-qt. shallow casserole.
7. Arrange spaghetti, mushrooms and chicken in casserole. Pour sauce on top, poke gently with spoon here and there to allow sauce to spread.
8. Sprinkle with remaining Parmesan cheese; bake 40 to 45 minutes until bubbly and cheese is golden brown.

MANICOTTI AMERICAN STYLE

MAKES 6 SERVINGS

1 lb. ground chuck or sausage meat
1 cup finely chopped onion
½ cup chopped green pepper
2 cans (6-oz. size) tomato paste
2 cups water
Salt
2 teaspoons sugar
1 teaspoon oregano leaves
½ teaspoon freshly ground black pepper
1 package (8 ozs.) manicotti shells
1 tablespoon salt
6 qts. boiling water
1 lb. fine-curd creamed cottage cheese or ricotta
2 cups (8 ozs.) grated mozzarella cheese
½ teaspoon freshly ground black pepper
2 tablespoons chopped parsley
¼ cup grated Parmesan cheese

1. In large skillet or Dutch oven, cook beef until it is no longer pink, breaking up with spoon as it cooks.
2. Add onion and green pepper; cook until tender, stirring occasionally. Drain off fat if necessary.
3. Stir in tomato paste, 2 cups water, 2 teaspoons salt, sugar, oregano, ½ teaspoon pepper; bring to boiling. Cover and simmer 1 hour, stirring occasionally.
4. Meanwhile, gradually add manicotti and 1 tablespoon salt to rapidly boiling water so that water continues to boil. Cook, uncovered, stirring occasionally, until barely tender. Drain in colander. Keep shells in cold water until ready to fill.
5. Combine cottage cheese, mozzarella, ½ teaspoon pepper and parsley. Using small spatula, fill shells with cheese mixture.
6. Pour a thin layer of meat sauce in bottom of shallow baking pan. Arrange filled shells side by side in single layer in pan.
7. Cover with remaining meat sauce. Sprinkle with Parmesan cheese. Bake, uncovered, in preheated 350°F. oven 30 to 40 minutes until bubbly.

LASAGNE DELIZIOSO

MAKES 16 SERVINGS

4 tablespoons olive or
   vegetable oil
1½ cups finely chopped onion
1 tablespoon finely chopped
   garlic
1½ lbs. ground chuck
1 teaspoon oregano leaves
1 teaspoon basil leaves
1 bay leaf
2 teaspoons sugar
1 teaspoon salt
½ teaspoon freshly ground
   black pepper
2 cans (28-oz. size) plum
   tomatoes
1 can (15 ozs.) tomato sauce
1 can (6 ozs.) tomato paste
1 cup water
2 lbs. ricotta cheese

1 egg
1¼ teaspoons salt
¾ teaspoon freshly ground
   black pepper
½ cup chopped parsley
1 package (8-oz. size)
   mozzarella cheese
4 tablespoons grated
   Parmesan or Romano
   cheese
6 qts. boiling water
2 tablespoons salt
2 tablespoons grated
   Parmesan or Romano
   cheese
1 package (8 ozs.) mozzarella
   cheese
1 lb. curly edge or plain
   lasagne

1. In 6-qt. Dutch oven, heat oil, add onion and garlic. Sauté over medium heat 5 minutes, stirring occasionally.

2. Add meat and cook over medium heat until meat is no longer red. Break up large clumps of meat with spoon.

3. Stir in oregano, basil, bay leaf, sugar, 1 teaspoon salt and ½ teaspoon pepper. Add tomatoes, tomato sauce, tomato paste and water. Break up tomatoes with a potato masher.

4. Heat to boiling, reduce heat and simmer uncovered, 45 to 60 minutes. Stir occasionally.

5. Meanwhile, make ricotta filling: In large bowl combine ricotta, egg, 1¼ teaspoons salt and ¾ teaspoon pepper. Beat with spoon until smooth.

6. Stir in parsley, 1 package mozzarella diced and 4 tablespoons grated Parmesan. Set aside.

7. In large 8- to 12-qt. kettle bring 6 qts. water to boil, add 2 tablespoons salt.

8. Add lasagne strips, one at a time, keeping water boiling as you add. Boil rapidly, uncovered, for 15 minutes, or until just tender. Drain in colander.

9. Preheat your oven to 350°F. Lightly grease two 7- x 11- x 2-inch baking dishes. Spoon a little tomato-meat sauce in the bottom of each.

10. Layer noodles, cheese mixture, sauce in dishes, ending with sauce.
11. Sprinkle with remaining grated cheese and top with 1 package mozzarella cheese, sliced.
12. Bake 45 to 50 minutes, until bubbly. Remove from oven and let "rest" 5 minutes, to make cutting easier. Cut each pan into 8 squares.

NOODLES ROMANOFF

MAKES 8 TO 10 SERVINGS

1½ tablespoons salt
5 qts. boiling water
12 ozs. ½-inch-wide noodles or fettucine noodles (about 6 cups)
3 cups cottage cheese
2 cups sour cream

6 tablespoons butter or margarine, melted
1½ cups chopped green onions
1 clove garlic, crushed
¼ teaspoon freshly ground black pepper
½ cup fine bread crumbs

1. Preheat oven to 350°F. Lightly grease 2½-qt. casserole.
2. In 8- to 12-qt. kettle add salt to rapidly boiling water. Gradually add noodles so that water continues to boil.
3. Cook uncovered, stirring occasionally, 7 minutes, until just tender. Drain in a colander, set aside.
4. In large bowl combine cottage cheese, sour cream, 4 tablespoons butter or margarine, green onions, garlic and pepper.
5. Add noodles and toss lightly with fork to combine. Turn into casserole.
6. Stir crumbs into remaining 2 tablespoons melted butter, toss lightly with fork. Sprinkle crumbs on top of casserole.
7. Bake for 25 to 30 minutes, until piping hot.

Citrus Sampler

UNCOOKED CRANBERRY-APPLE RELISH

MAKES ABOUT 1½ QUARTS

1 large orange, quartered and seeded
1 lb. (4 cups) fresh or frozen and slightly thawed cranberries
1¼ cups firmly packed light-brown sugar
¼ teaspoon ground cinnamon
1 large apple, finely chopped
1 tablespoon lemon juice
½ cup chopped walnuts

1. Put orange and cranberries through the coarse blade of a food grinder. Or chop orange and cranberries coarsely; mix. Put about ¼ of the mixture at a time in electric blender container; blend until very finely chopped.
2. Stir in all remaining ingredients. Cover and refrigerate.

QUICK ORANGE MARMALADE

MAKES ABOUT 7 (6-OUNCE) JARS OR 5 CUPS MARMALADE

4 large oranges
1½ cups water
5 cups sugar
½ bottle (3 ozs.) liquid pectin
Paraffin

1. To prepare slivered orange rind: remove the thin outer rind, using a vegetable peeler. Use scissors to cut the strips of rind into slivers.
2. To section orange: with a sharp knife, cut slice from top. Cut off peel in strips from top to bottom, cutting deep enough to remove white

membrane, then cut slice from bottom. Or remove peel by cutting round and round, spiral-fashion. Cut off any remaining white membrane. To remove each section, cut along dividing membrane from outside to core of orange, then cut section from membrane on the other side. Repeat with remaining 3 oranges, holding over bowl to retain juice.

3. To cook marmalade: place slivered orange rind and water in large saucepan; bring to a boil. Reduce heat, cover and simmer 20 minutes. Add orange sections and juice from sectioning. Add sugar. Cook over medium heat, stirring constantly until sugar dissolves. Bring to a full rolling boil that won't stir down. Boil hard for 1 minute, stirring constantly. Remove from heat; stir in pectin. With metal spoon, skim off foam. Stir and skim for 5 minutes. Meanwhile, melt paraffin in a jar set in pan of simmering water.

4. To seal marmalade in jars: sterilize jars by placing for a few minutes in boiling water. Remove from water with tongs and drain well. Quickly ladle hot marmalade into hot, sterilized jars, leaving a 1/4-inch head space. Adjust lids. Place in hot water in water bath canner, covering by two inches. Process 10 minutes in boiling water bath. Cool on rack.

MAPLE BROILED GRAPEFRUIT

MAKES 4 SERVINGS

2 seedless grapefruit, halved and sectioned

4 teaspoons butter or margarine

4 tablespoons maple-blended syrup

4 Maraschino cherries, with stems

1. Dot each grapefruit with a teaspoon of butter. Drizzle 1 tablespoon syrup over each.

2. Place on baking pan. Place 4 to 5 inches from source of heat in preheated broiler and broil 10 to 15 minutes, until hot and bubbly. Garnish each with a Maraschino cherry.

LEMONY LAMB SHANKS WITH NOODLES

MAKES 4 TO 6 SERVINGS

2 teaspoons salt
½ teaspoon freshly ground black pepper
1 teaspoon paprika
½ teaspoon thyme leaves
4 to 6 lamb shanks (1-1½ lbs. each)
2 to 3 tablespoons all-purpose flour
3 to 4 tablespoons vegetable oil
1 cup thinly sliced onion
2 cloves garlic, minced

4 peppercorns
1 bay leaf
2 sprigs parsley, chopped
2 tablespoons grated lemon rind
½ cup lemon juice
½ cup water
1 tablespoon flour, optional
2 tablespoons water, optional
12 ozs. noodles, cooked
2 tablespoons capers, optional
1 lemon, thinly sliced

1. Combine salt, pepper, paprika and thyme on sheet of waxed paper. Rub seasonings well over all sides of lamb. Coat lightly with flour.

2. Heat vegetable oil slowly in large heavy skillet or Dutch oven. Brown shanks, a few at a time, very slowly on all sides. Remove from pan.

3. Sauté onion and garlic in remaining oil about 5 minutes, until limp and transparent.

4. Return shanks to pan. Add peppercorns, bay leaf, parsley, lemon rind, lemon juice and water.

5. Bring to boiling. Cover; reduce heat and simmer 2 hours, or until tender. Turn shanks once or twice for even cooking. Add small amount of water if necessary.

6. Place meat on warm serving platter and keep warm. Blot up surface grease from pan gravy with paper towel; discard.

7. Heat gravy and stir briskly. Thicken if desired with mixture of 1 tablespoon flour and 2 tablespoons water. Bring to boiling, stirring. Let simmer 2 to 3 minutes.

8. Arrange cooked, drained noodles on platter, top with lamb shanks. Sprinkle with capers if desired and pour some of gravy over lamb. Pass remaining gravy in sauce boat. Garnish platter with lemon slices.

ORANGE-TOMATO PORK CHOPS

MAKES 4 SERVINGS

4 pork chops, about ¾-inch thick
1 tablespoon butter or margarine
½ cup chopped onion
1 tablespoon flour
1 cup chopped fresh tomatoes or 1 cup chopped canned tomatoes
1 cup orange juice
½ cup water
1 chicken bouillon cube
½ teaspoon salt
½ teaspoon thyme leaves
½ avocado, sliced
2 oranges, peeled and sliced

1. Place large skillet over medium heat. Stand pork chops on end in skillet, and cook until enough fat to coat pan cooks out of chops.
2. Place chops flat in skillet and brown on both sides over high heat.
3. Remove; add butter if there is very little fat from chops. Add onion and cook, stirring until tender.
4. Sprinkle in flour; stir to mix well. Add tomatoes, orange juice, water, bouillon cube, salt and thyme. Add pork chops; cover and simmer 50 to 60 minutes. Add sliced avocado and oranges. Heat.

EASY FRESH LEMON ICE CREAM

MAKES ABOUT 3 CUPS

2 cups heavy cream or half-and-half
1 cup sugar
1 tablespoon freshly grated lemon peel
⅓ cup freshly squeezed lemon juice
7 to 10 lemon shells or boats,* optional

1. In large bowl, combine cream and sugar; stir until sugar dissolves.
2. Blend in lemon peel and juice. Pour into shallow pan. (An 8- x 8-inch square pan is fine.)
3. Freeze until firm, about 4 hours. Serve in dessert glasses, lemon shells or boats.

* To Make Lemon Shell: Cut ⅓ off end of large lemon. Carefully clean out pulp; reserve. Scrape shell clean with spoon. To Make Lemon Boat: Cut large lemon in half lengthwise and, with shallow V-shape cut, remove white center core. Carefully ream out pulp; reserve. Scrape shell "clean" with spoon.

Vegetable of the Month:
Onions

FRENCH ONION SOUP

MAKES 2¾ QUARTS,
8 TO 10 SERVINGS

2 tablespoons butter or margarine
2 tablespoons vegetable oil
6 to 7 cups (2 lbs.) thinly sliced yellow onions
½ teaspoon sugar
2 tablespoons all-purpose flour
5 cans (10½-oz. size) condensed beef bouillon
3 soup cans water
1 teaspoon salt
Several twists freshly ground black pepper
1½ cups Burgundy or dry red wine
¼ cup Madeira or port wine
8 to 10 slices toasted French bread
2 cups grated natural Gruyère, Swiss or Parmesan cheese

1. In 4- to 6-qt. Dutch oven or kettle, heat butter and oil until hot. Add onions and sugar. Cook over medium heat for 20 to 30 minutes, stirring frequently until onions are lightly browned and bottom of pan is lightly glazed.

2. Scrape glaze from bottom of pan and blend with onions. Stir in flour and cook 1 minute.

3. Stir in beef bouillon, water, salt and pepper. Bring to boiling. Reduce heat and simmer, covered, for 30 minutes.

4. Stir in Burgundy and Madeira. Taste for seasoning. Pour into tureen or ladle into soup bowls over rounds of bread. Pass grated cheese separately.

Editor's Note: To serve gratine, preheat oven to 450°F. Pour hot soup into ovenproof tureen or casserole. Place 8 to 10 slices toasted French bread on surface of soup and sprinkle thickly with 1½ to 2 cups grated

18

Gruyère or Swiss cheese. Bake for 15 minutes, then place under broiler for a few minutes to brown top lightly. Ladle into soup bowls in front of guests, serving a slice of bread and melted cheese in each bowl. Or you may prepare individual ovenproof bowls as directed above.

PARMESAN ONION THINS

MAKES 48 APPETIZER SERVINGS

48 (2-inch) bread rounds, cut from firm, thinly sliced white bread
1 cup mayonnaise

1 cup grated Parmesan or Romano cheese
1 cup very thin white onion slices

1. Preheat oven to 375°F.
2. Toast bread rounds on one side; use your broiler rack and broiler, but watch carefully so bread does not burn. ·
3. Blend the mayonnaise and grated Parmesan cheese. Put a thin slice of onion on the untoasted bread side and top with a generous spoonful of mayonnaise mixture, spreading to edges.
4. Bake 10 to 12 minutes, until puffed and golden.

ONION FRITTERS

MAKES 6 SERVINGS

1 cup unsifted all-purpose flour
1 teaspoon baking powder
½ teaspoon salt
½ teaspoon ground mace
¼ teaspoon paprika
1 teaspoon sugar

Dash freshly ground black pepper
1 large egg, beaten
⅔ cup water
¾ lb. (3 medium) onions
¾ teaspoon salt
Shortening or oil for deep-fat frying

1. Sift together into a large bowl flour, baking powder, ½ teaspoon salt, mace, paprika, sugar and pepper.
2. Beat egg with water and add to flour mixture, making a smooth batter.
3. Peel onions, rinse and drain. Cut into ¼-inch-thick crosswise slices. Toss with ¾ teaspoon salt.
4. Dip onions into batter and fry in fat about 2 inches deep, heated to 360°F., until they are browned and float to the surface. Drain on paper towels; serve hot.

BAKED ONIONS VINAIGRETTE

MAKES 4 TO 8 SERVINGS

8 medium onions, unpeeled
½ cup red wine vinegar
¾ cup olive oil
1 tablespoon sugar
½ teaspoon salt

Several twists freshly
ground black pepper
½ teaspoon ground mustard
1 bay leaf

1. Preheat oven to 400°F. Line shallow baking pan with foil. Arrange onions in pan. Bake, uncovered, 60 to 70 minutes or until fork tender.
2. Carefully slip off outside skins and discard. Place onions in serving dish.
3. Heat vinegar, olive oil, sugar, salt, pepper, dry mustard and bay leaf, stirring until sugar dissolves. Pour hot vinaigrette over onions. Serve warm or cold as an accompaniment to hot or cold meats.

CHICKEN WITH SAUCE SOUBISE

MAKES 4 SERVINGS

4 whole chicken breasts,
boned, split and skinned
2 cups water
1 rib celery with leaves,
broken
1 onion stuck with 2 whole
cloves
1 bay leaf
3 peppercorns
½ teaspoon salt
Sauce Soubise:
¼ cup butter

1 cup finely chopped onion
¼ cup water
¼ cup all-purpose flour
2 cups milk or half-and-half
Dash ground nutmeg or
mace
Dash freshly ground black
pepper
½ teaspoon salt
Chopped parsley
Hot cooked rice

1. In large skillet or Dutch oven, place chicken breasts, water, celery, onion, bay leaf, peppercorns and salt. Heat to boiling; reduce heat and simmer 10 to 15 minutes until chicken is done. Remove chicken breasts from broth, drain, and keep warm. Reserve broth for another use.
2. In medium saucepan, heat butter until melted. Add onion and water. Heat to boiling, stirring until water evaporates.
3. Stir in flour smoothly. Add milk; heat to boiling, stirring until mixture thickens and boils.
4. Season sauce with nutmeg, pepper and salt.
5. Place drained chicken breasts on serving platter. Cover with Sauce Soubise. Sprinkle with parsley. Serve with rice.

February

We are really into winter now. It's time to use the treasures we put by at harvest time—all the varied foods we canned, preserved, and put by in the freezer.

February is the month we celebrate the birthdays of Presidents Lincoln and Washington. It seems appropriate, too, to enjoy the foods served in the White House.

Valentine's Day graces this month, and we give special attention to those sweet things for sweethearts.

Our best recipes for hearty pot roasts, vegetabled stews and savory simmered slow-cooker recipes seem the best answers to what to have for dinner on these cold February nights.

The humble cabbage is our stalwart friend, and with its many changes of face is our Vegetable of the Month.

Frozen Fruit Assets

FRUIT	DRY PACK	SYRUP PACK
Apples	Apple slices for pie: 1 quart apple slices 1 teaspoon ascorbic acid powder ½ to 1 cup sugar	Apple slices: 3 cups sugar 1 quart water ½ teaspoon ascorbic acid powder
Pears, canning best		
Peaches	Peach slices: 1 quart peach slices 1 teaspoon ascorbic acid powder ½ to 1 cup sugar	Peach slices: 3 cups sugar 1 quart water ½ teaspoon ascorbic acid powder
Plums		pitted halves or quarters 3 cups sugar 1 quart water
Prunes, fresh	Whole prunes, no syrup, no sugar	pitted halves 3 cups sugar 1 quart water
Melon		Melon balls or cubes 2 cups sugar 1 quart water

FRUIT FREEZING GUIDE

Select firm ripe fruit. Wash and remove any discolored spots or blemishes. Prepare according to use.

Prepare syrup just before using in proportions given, stirring until sugar is dissolved.

Slice fruit directly into syrup in freezer container. To keep fruit submerged, crumble a square of waxed paper under lid. Cover, label, date and freeze.

For dry pack, toss prepared fruit with sugar and ascorbic acid powder as directed, spoon into freezer container, label, date and freeze.

BAKED GOODS	MAIN DISHES	OTHER DISHES
Apple Pie Fruit Kuchen Apple Cake Tea Bread	Apple Pot Roast	Applesauce
Freezin' Season Pies Fruit Kuchen Tea Bread	Chicken with Peaches Roast Duck with Peaches	Fresh Tart Fruit Soup Spiked Peach Jam Upside Down Cake
Freezin' Season Pies Fruit Kuchen Tea Bread	Roast Duck with Plums	Plum Leather Upside Down Cake
Freezin' Season Pies Fruit Kuchen Tea Bread		Prune Leather Fresh Tart Fruit Soup Stewed Prunes Upside Down Cake
		Use in Fruit Cups Salads

BOULA-BOULA
One of Jackie Kennedy's Favorite Soups

MAKES 6 SERVINGS
---

3 cups frozen peas, cooked
¼ cup liquid from peas
1 tablespoon butter or
   margarine
¼ teaspoon salt
   Dash freshly ground black
   pepper

3 cups canned green turtle
   soup or beef bouillon
1½ cups dry sherry
½ cup heavy cream, whipped

1. Using electric blender, purée peas with ¼ cup liquid from peas until very smooth.
2. Heat pea purée in medium saucepan, add butter, salt and pepper. Stir until butter melts.
3. Add green turtle soup and sherry; heat just to the boiling point.
4. Ladle soup into serving cups and top each with a little plain whipped cream. If desired, quickly place cups under the broiler to lightly brown the cream.

GLAZED ONIONS
Washington's Favorite Vegetable

MAKES 6 SERVINGS
---

12 medium onions, peeled
 4 tablespoons butter or
   margarine
½ teaspoon salt

¼ teaspoon freshly ground
   black pepper
12 teaspoons honey

1. Preheat oven to 450°F.
2. Cut onions in half crosswise, dot with butter and arrange in a shallow baking dish. Sprinkle with salt and pepper.
3. Pour 1 teaspoon honey over each onion. Bake uncovered for 45 minutes, until tender.

SALAD OF MIXED GARDEN GREENS
Jefferson Was Famous for His Interest in Fresh-Grown Foods

MAKES 4 TO 6 SERVINGS

1 head Bibb or Boston lettuce
1 bunch watercress
1 small head endive
1 small head iceberg lettuce
1 small head chicory

2 cups fresh young spinach leaves
1 tablespoon chopped chives or scallions
Monticello Dressing (recipe below)

1. Make sure all greens are washed and crisp. Then tear leaves into bite-size pieces and combine in large salad bowl.
2. Add chopped chives and toss with dressing.

MONTICELLO DRESSING
MAKES 1 CUP

1 small clove garlic, crushed
1 teaspoon salt
1/2 teaspoon freshly ground black pepper

1/3 cup olive oil
1/3 cup sesame or vegetable oil
1/3 cup tarragon or wine vinegar

1. Place all ingredients in jar, cover tightly and shake well.
2. Serve with mixed greens.

DELMONICO POTATOES
One of Lincoln's Favorites

MAKES 6 SERVINGS

8 medium all-purpose potatoes
Boiling water, salted
6 tablespoons butter or margarine
6 tablespoons flour
2½ cups light cream or half-and-half
½ teaspoon salt
Few twists freshly ground black pepper
1 cup grated sharp Cheddar cheese
2 tablespoons butter or margarine
½ cup fine dry bread crumbs

1. Preheat oven to 400°F.
2. Wash, peel and dice potatoes. Boil in lightly salted water until just done, but not mushy.
3. Drain potatoes and place in a 2-qt. lightly greased casserole or baking dish.
4. In medium saucepan, melt 6 tablespoons butter, and blend in 6 tablespoons flour. Gradually add cream, stirring.
5. Heat to boiling, stirring constantly. Season with ½ teaspoon salt and a bit of pepper. Pour over potatoes. Top with grated cheese.
6. Melt remaining 2 tablespoons butter; stir in bread crumbs, mixing until coated. Sprinkle buttered crumbs over casserole.
7. Bake until cheese melts and casserole is bubbly, about 20 to 30 minutes.

CHICKEN SUPREME
Rosalynn Carter

MAKES 4 TO 8 SERVINGS

4 (3 lbs.) whole boned chicken breasts, split
1½ teaspoons ground cardamom
3 teaspoons chervil or tarragon leaves
3 teaspoons salt
1 teaspoon freshly ground black pepper
1 egg
¼ cup milk
1 cup fine dry bread crumbs
8 tablespoons margarine
2 tablespoons brandy
¼ cup Burgundy, or a dry white wine, such as Chablis
1½ cups chicken broth
2 tablespoons all-purpose flour

1. Preheat oven to 350°F.
2. Season chicken breasts with cardamom, chervil, salt and pepper.
3. Beat egg and milk together. Dip chicken into egg-milk mixture, then coat with fine bread crumbs.
4. Heat margarine, about 4 tablespoons at a time, until hot but not smoking. Add chicken breasts, several at a time, and brown on both sides. Add additional margarine as needed until all chicken is browned.
5. Place chicken in shallow baking dish; pour brandy, Burgundy and 1 cup of chicken broth over chicken.
6. Bake about 30 to 40 minutes until chicken is done. Pour broth off into 1-qt. saucepan.
7. Blend smoothly 2 tablespoons flour with ½ cup chicken broth. Stir into reserved broth. Heat, stirring until boiling. Arrange chicken in serving dish; pour some of gravy over chicken and serve remainder separately.

STRAWBERRY BLITZ TORTE
One of Betty Ford's Favorite Desserts

MAKES 1 (8-INCH) TORTE,
8 TO 10 SERVINGS

1 cup sifted cake flour
1 teaspoon baking powder
¼ teaspoon salt
½ cup shortening
½ cup sugar
4 egg yolks

3 tablespoons milk
1 teaspoon pure vanilla extract
Meringue (recipe below)
Filling and topping (recipe below)

1. Preheat oven to 350°F. Grease two 8-inch layer-cake pans.
2. Sift flour, baking powder and salt together.
3. In large bowl, with electric mixer set at medium speed, beat shortening until creamy. Gradually add sugar and continue beating until light and fluffy.
4. Beat egg yolks in separate bowl and add to creamed mixture. Stir in milk and vanilla.
5. Add dry ingredients at low speed and beat until batter is smooth. Pour batter into cake pans.
6. Lightly pile half of the meringue mixture over the batter in each pan, spread evenly. Bake in 350°-oven until cake tests done and meringue is pale gold, about 35 minutes.
7. Remove from oven, loosen sides of tortes from pans and remove them to wire racks, keeping the meringue side up. Add filling and topping.

MERINGUE

4 egg whites
½ teaspoon salt
½ teaspoon cream of tartar

1 cup sugar
½ teaspoon pure vanilla extract

1. Beat egg whites, salt and cream of tartar until they stand in soft peaks.
2. Add sugar, 2 tablespoons at a time, beating very thoroughly after each addition. Then add vanilla.

STRAWBERRY FILLING AND TOPPING

1 cup heavy cream, whipped
4 tablespoons confectioners' sugar

2 cups sliced strawberries
8 strawberries for garnish

1. Combine whipped cream and confectioners' sugar. Fold in sliced strawberries.
2. Spread half between layers of Blitz Torte (meringue side up) and use remaining as topping. Decorate with whole berries. Refrigerate if not serving immediately.

SCRIPTURE CAKE
Dolley Madison

**MAKES 1 LARGE TUBE
CAKE OR 2 LOAF CAKES**

---

1 cup Judges 5:25 (last clause: butter or margarine)
1¾ cups Jeremiah 6:20 (sugar)
¼ cup Proverbs 24:13 (honey)
6 Job 39:14 (eggs)
1st Kings 10:2 (spices: 1½ teaspoons ground cinnamon, ½ teaspoon ground cloves, 1 teaspoon ground allspice, 1 teaspoon ground nutmeg)
3 teaspoons Amos 4:5 (baking powder, plus 1 teaspoon baking soda)

1 teaspoon Leviticus 2:13 (salt)
3¾ cups 1st Kings 4:22 (unsifted all-purpose flour)
1 cup Genesis 24:11 (water; we substituted 1 cup cold buttermilk)
2 cups 1st Samuel 30:12 (second clause: raisins)
2 cups Revelation 6:13 (cut up dried figs)
1 cup Numbers 17:8 (chopped almonds)

1. Preheat oven to 300°F. Heavily grease and flour a 10-inch tube or bundt pan or two 9- x 5- x 3-inch loaf pans.

2. In large bowl, with electric mixer at medium speed, beat butter until smooth. At low speed, add sugar gradually; beat in well. Clean beaters. Blend in honey at low speed.

3. Add eggs one at a time, beating at medium-high speed after each addition.

4. On large sheet of waxed paper combine cinnamon, cloves, allspice, nutmeg, baking powder, baking soda, salt and 3¼ cups flour.

5. Add blended dry ingredients to batter alternately with buttermilk. Toss reserved ½ cup flour with raisins, figs and almonds. Gently fold fruit and nuts into batter.

6. Pour batter into pan. Cut through batter with knife to distribute evenly. Bake for about 1½ hours, or until a cake tester poked into center comes out clean. Let cool in pan 30 minutes, then turn out on rack to cool completely.

MILLION-DOLLAR FUDGE
Eisenhower Named This Fudge Recipe of Mamie's

MAKES 30 SQUARES
---

1 can (13½ ozs.) evaporated milk	1 bar (12 ozs.) sweet chocolate, broken into pieces
4½ cups sugar	
2 tablespoons butter or margarine	1 jar (8 ozs.) marshmallow whip
Dash salt	2½ cups chopped walnuts
1 package (12 ozs.) chocolate bits	

1. Mix evaporated milk, sugar, butter and salt in a saucepan and bring to boiling. Stir and boil for 7 minutes.

2. Combine all remaining ingredients in large bowl, mix well. Pour boiling evaporated milk mixture over all. Beat until fudge is creamy.

3. Pour into buttered 9- x 9-inch square pan to cool. Cut into squares when cold.

Valentine Favorites

BEST-EVER CHERRIES JUBILEE

MAKES 4 SERVINGS

1 package (10 ozs.) frozen
  sweet Bing cherries,
  thawed
2 tablespoons currant jelly

1 teaspoon cornstarch
2 tablespoons water
¼ cup brandy, rum or kirsch
1 pt. vanilla ice cream

1. Drain cherries, reserving syrup.
2. In small saucepan or top of chafing dish, heat cherry syrup and currant jelly, stirring until jelly melts.
3. Combine cornstarch and water smoothly, add to sauce. Heat, stirring, until mixture thickens and boils.
4. Heat brandy in separate pan. Ignite brandy with match at table. Pour into sauce.
5. Ladle flaming sauce over ice cream in dessert dishes.

STRAWBERRY CHIFFON PIE

MAKES 1 (9-INCH) PIE

Coconut Cereal Crust:
  3 cups crisp, ready-to-eat rice
    cereal
½ cup margarine, melted
¼ cup sugar
  1 cup flaked coconut

Strawberry Filling:
  1 envelope unflavored gelatin
½ cup cold water
½ cup sugar

⅛ teaspoon salt
1 teaspoon grated lemon rind
1 tablespoon lemon juice
1 package (10 ozs.) frozen
  strawberries in syrup,
  thawed and puréed
2 egg whites
¼ cup sliced fresh strawberries
  or flaked coconut for
  garnish

1. Make cereal crust: In large bowl lightly crush rice cereal to make 1½ cups. Stir in melted margarine, sugar and coconut.
2. Press mixture evenly over bottom and sides of 9-inch pie plate. Bake in preheated 350°F. oven for 15 minutes, or until coconut is golden. Remove from oven and cool. Set aside.
3. Make filling: In medium saucepan, sprinkle gelatin over water. Place over low heat and stir until gelatin dissolves, about 3 minutes. Add ¼ cup sugar and salt and stir until sugar dissolves. Remove from heat.
4. Stir in lemon rind, lemon juice and strawberries. Chill, stirring occasionally, until mixture mounds slightly when dropped from a spoon.
5. Beat egg whites until soft peaks form; beat in remaining ¼ cup sugar and beat until stiff peaks form. Fold into gelatin mixture. Turn into prepared coconut crust. Chill until set, about 3 hours.
6. To serve, garnish with sliced fresh strawberries or a little flaked coconut.

MARILYN'S COCONUT VALENTINE CAKE

MAKES 1 (2-LAYER) CAKE, 8 TO 10 SERVINGS

1 package (18½ ozs.) white or yellow cake mix
1 can (1 lb.) cherry pie filling
1 package (7.2 ozs.) fluffy white frosting mix
1 package (7 ozs.) flaked coconut

1. Preheat oven to 350°F. Grease and flour 2 heart-layer cake pans. Prepare cake mix according to package directions. Divide batter between prepared pans.
2. Bake layers 30 to 40 minutes or until a wooden pick poked in center comes out clean.
3. Cool in pans 10 minutes. Invert, remove pans and completely cool layers on wire rack.
4. Place bottom cake layer on serving plate. Spread with 1½ cups pie filling. Top with second cake layer.
5. Prepare fluffy white frosting mix and frost sides and top of cake. Coat cake completely with coconut. Use remaining ½ cup of pie filling to make heart-shaped design on top of cake.

OLD-FASHIONED VALENTINE SUGAR COOKIES

MAKES 6 LARGE COOKIE HEARTS

4 cups all-purpose flour
1 teaspoon baking powder
½ teaspoon baking soda
½ teaspoon salt
½ teaspoon ground nutmeg
1 cup butter or margarine,
  softened
1½ cups sugar
1 egg
½ cup sour cream

1 teaspoon pure vanilla
  extract
1 egg white
1 tablespoon water

Decorative Toppings:
  Sugar, coarse sugar, red
  sugar
  Colored sprinkles
  Red cinnamon candies
  Silver dragées
  Flaked coconut

1. Sift flour with baking powder, soda, salt and nutmeg; set aside.
2. In large bowl of electric mixer, at medium speed, beat butter, sugar and egg until light and fluffy.
3. At low speed, beat in sour cream and vanilla until smooth.
4. Gradually add to flour mixture, beating until well combined.
5. With rubber scraper, form dough into a ball. Wrap in waxed paper or foil; refrigerate several hours or overnight.
6. Divide dough into 6 equal parts. Refrigerate until ready to roll out.
7. Meanwhile, preheat oven to 375°F. Lightly grease cookie sheets.
8. On well-floured surface, roll dough, one part at a time, ¼ inch thick.
9. Draw a large heart pattern on cardboard 7½ x 8½ inches. Place pattern on rolled-out dough and cut around pattern with sharp knife. Slide cookie sheet under cookie.
10. Beat egg white with 1 tablespoon water. Brush cookies with egg-white mixture.
11. Using cinnamon candies or silver dragées, make mottoes on hearts: "Be Mine," "I Love You," "Yours Forever," "Eat Your Heart Out" and so on. Sprinkle lightly with sugar; edge with sprinkle of coarse sugar, red sugar, colored sprinkles or coconut. Be imaginative!
12. Bake about 12 to 14 minutes or until cookie is golden. Let cool one minute on cookie sheet, then carefully slide off cookie sheet onto rack to cool completely.

RASPBERRY OR STRAWBERRY MOUSSE

MAKES 10 SERVINGS

2 packages (10-oz. size) frozen raspberries or strawberries, thawed
2 envelopes unflavored gelatin
¼ cup sugar
1 teaspoon lemon juice
Dash salt
4 egg whites, room temperature

¼ cup sugar
1½ cups heavy cream
1¼ cups crushed almond or coconut macaroons
2 tablespoons almond, raspberry or peach liqueur
½ cup heavy cream
1 tablespoon sugar
¼ cup crushed almonds or coconut macaroons

1. In electric blender blend raspberries or strawberries until smooth; strain into medium saucepan; discard seeds.
2. Sprinkle gelatin over puréed fruit; cook over low heat, stirring until dissolved.
3. Add ¼ cup sugar, lemon juice and salt. Stir until sugar dissolves; remove from heat.
4. Refrigerate about 20 to 30 minutes or until mixture mounds when dropped from a spoon.
5. In large bowl, with mixer at high speed, beat egg whites until soft peaks form. Beating at high speed; gradually sprinkle in ¼ cup sugar; beat until whites stand in stiff peaks.
6. Gently fold fruit mixture into beaten whites.
7. In small bowl, beat 1½ cups cream until soft peaks form. With rubber spatula, gently fold into fruit mixture.
8. Sprinkle 1¼ cups macaroon crumbs with 2 tablespoons liqueur.
9. Pour half of mousse mixture into 2-qt. serving bowl. Sprinkle with soaked crumbs. Top with remaining mousse mixture; swirl surface prettily. Refrigerate until set—at least 4 hours.
10. At serving time, whip remaining cream in small bowl until soft peaks form; sweeten with 1 tablespoon sugar. Garnish surface of mousse with swirls of whipped cream; finish with a dusting of crumbs.

Savory Slow-Cooking Dishes

NORTHWESTERN BEAN CASSOULET

MAKES 6 TO 8 SERVINGS

3 cups Great Northern beans, rinsed
12 cups water
1 cup chopped celery
1 cup chopped carrots
2 beef bouillon cubes
2 teaspoons salt
   Chicken neck and giblets
1 3-lb. chicken, cut in 8 pieces
1½ teaspoons salt
¼ teaspoon freshly ground black pepper
¼ cup vegetable oil
¾ lb. spicy sausage, thickly sliced
5 slices bacon
1 cup chopped onion
2 cloves garlic, minced
½ teaspoon thyme leaves
1½ cups tomato juice
½ cup dry white wine or water
¼ cup plus 2 tablespoons chopped parsley

1. Soak beans in water overnight in refrigerator. Or for a quick soak, bring them to boil in large kettle. Boil 2 minutes, remove from heat. Cover; let stand 1 hour.

2. Add celery, carrots, bouillon cubes, 2 teaspoons salt, chicken neck and giblets to soaked beans and water. Bring mixture to boiling. Reduce heat and simmer covered 1½ hours, until beans are tender.

3. Meanwhile, sprinkle chicken pieces with 1½ teaspoons salt and pepper. Heat oil in large skillet. Brown chicken and sausage in hot oil, set aside.

4. In skillet fry bacon until crisp; drain and crumble. Sauté onion, garlic and thyme in bacon fat for 5-8 minutes, stirring frequently. Stir in tomato juice, wine and ¼ cup chopped parsley.

5. Drain beans, reserving liquid. Preheat oven to 325°F.

6. To assemble cassoulet: In heavy 4-qt. casserole, arrange alternating layers of beans, crumbled bacon, chicken and sausage. Pour some of the tomato-onion liquid over each layer. Pour 1 cup of reserved bean liquid over casserole.

7. Bake covered for 1 hour, until bubbly, adding a little bean liquid if casserole becomes dry. Sprinkle with chopped parsley just before serving.

Editor's Note: You may make ahead, bake as above, refrigerate. Reheat covered in preheated 350°F. oven for 2 hours. Cassoulet may also be assembled, baked and frozen. When ready to cook, thaw completely in refrigerator and reheat.

POT ROAST DINNER

MAKES 4 TO 6 SERVINGS

---

4 lbs. boneless beef rump, chuck or round roast
1 bottle (18 ozs.) all-purpose barbecue sauce
¼ cup dry red or white wine (or a combination)
2 tablespoons butter or margarine
1 tablespoon vegetable oil
1 cup water
1 cup dry red or white wine (or a combination)

¾ lb. white onions, peeled
1 lb. carrots, peeled, cut in 2-inch chunks
1 lb. white turnips, peeled and halved
1½ lbs. potatoes, peeled and halved
¼ cup water
3 tablespoons all-purpose flour
2 tablespoons finely chopped parsley

1. Place beef rump roast in bowl. Pour barbecue sauce and ¼ cup wine over. Cover with plastic film or foil. Refrigerate overnight, turning once.
2. Next day drain roast well, reserve marinade. In 6-qt. Dutch oven heat butter and oil. Brown meat slowly on all sides. Pour off fat.
3. Pour marinade, 1 cup water and remaining wine over roast. Bring to boil. Cover; reduce heat and simmer, covered, 2 hours.
4. Place prepared vegetables around meat. Return to boiling; reduce heat and let bubble slowly about 30 to 40 minutes, until meat and vegetables are tender.
5. Mix remaining ¼ cup water and flour smoothly. Stir into sauce; heat, stirring, until sauce boils.
6. To serve: Arrange meat on platter, surround with vegetables. Sprinkle with parsley. Pour a little gravy over, serve remaining gravy in heated sauce boat.

BURGOO

MAKES 2
QUARTS, 8 TO
12 SERVINGS

3 lbs. beef shank, bone in, sliced
1 lb. beef or veal soupbone
2½ to 3 lb. chicken, backs and necks
¼ teaspoon crushed red pepper
1 tablespoon salt
Few twists freshly ground black pepper
1 bay leaf
2½ qts. water
2 cups diced potatoes
2 cups chopped onions
2 cups fresh corn kernels or

1 package (10 ozs.) frozen cut corn
2 cups sliced carrots
2 cups cut wax or butter beans or 1 package (10 ozs.) frozen wax beans
2 cups sliced okra or 1 package (10 ozs.) frozen okra, sliced
2 cups chopped green pepper
½ cup finely chopped parsley
1 clove garlic or ½ teaspoon garlic salt
1 can (1 lb. 12 ozs.) tomatoes
Corn bread

1. In large 8-qt. kettle place beef shank, soupbone, chicken, red pepper, salt, pepper, bay leaf and water. Heat to boiling. Reduce heat; cover and simmer 40 minutes, until chicken is fork-tender.

2. Place chicken in large bowl. Cover and refrigerate until cool enough to handle. Cook remaining mixture, covered, 1½ hours longer, or until meat is very tender. Remove the bones and discard.

3. Remove beef and add to chicken. Remove bones and skin from chicken, discard. Cut chicken and beef into large chunks, reserve.

4. Add remaining ingredients (except corn bread) to kettle. Heat to boiling; reduce heat and simmer covered 1 hour.

5. Return beef and chicken to kettle, stir. Heat to boiling. Reduce heat and simmer uncovered 30 minutes to 1 hour, until as thick as desired.

6. Serving suggestion: Place a square of corn bread in bottom of soup plate and ladle the Burgoo onto the bread.

Editor's Note: May be made 1 or 2 days ahead, covered tightly and refrigerated. May also be frozen.

OLD-FASHIONED BROWN BEEF STEW

MAKES 8 SERVINGS

3 lbs. boneless beef chuck, cut in 1½-inch cubes
⅓ cup all-purpose flour
1 tablespoon salt
3 tablespoons pure vegetable oil
1 qt. boiling water
1 onion, studded with 4 cloves
1 small bunch celery leaves
4 sprigs parsley
1 clove garlic, crushed
1 bay leaf
1 teaspoon thyme leaves
2½ tablespoons Worcestershire sauce

1 lb. small white onions, peeled and quartered
1 lb. carrots, peeled and quartered
2 lbs. medium potatoes, peeled and quartered
2 medium white turnips, peeled and quartered
4 celery ribs, cut in 2-inch chunks
¼ cup cold water
1 lb. fresh mushrooms or 2 cans (6 to 8 ozs. each) whole mushrooms
3 tablespoons butter or margarine

1. Pat meat dry with paper towels. Toss beef cubes in flour mixed with salt. Reserve leftover flour mixture.

2. In a large, heavy 6- to 8-qt. Dutch oven heat oil until hot. Brown beef cubes, several at a time, over medium-high heat until well-browned on all sides. Remove pieces as they are done.

3. Add boiling water. Cook and stir to scrape drippings from bottom of pan.

4. Return beef to pan along with clove-studded onion, celery leaves, parsley, garlic, bay leaf, thyme and Worcestershire sauce. Stir to mix. Heat to boiling point. Reduce heat and simmer, covered, for 1½ hours

5. Add onions and carrots; simmer, covered, for 20 minutes. Add potatoes, turnips and celery; simmer, covered, for 20 minutes or until tender.

6. Combine reserved flour with cold water. Slowly stir into stew. Cook and stir for 2 minutes.

7. Rinse, pat dry and halve mushrooms. In large skillet, melt butter. Add mushrooms and sauté for 2 minutes, stirring. Stir into stew. Serve stew steaming hot.

BAVARIAN APPLE POT ROAST

MAKES 6 SERVINGS

4 lbs. chuck blade-bone pot roast
2 tablespoons solid all-vegetable shortening or vegetable oil
1½ teaspoons salt
¾ teaspoon ground ginger
5 whole cloves
1 bay leaf
¼ teaspoon freshly ground black pepper
1 cup apple juice
½ cup dry red wine
4 medium Red or Golden Delicious apples, pared, cored and quartered
1 onion, sliced
2 tablespoons all-purpose flour
¼ cup water

1. In Dutch oven, brown roast on both sides in hot shortening.
2. Add salt, ginger, cloves, bay leaf, pepper, apple juice and wine to meat. Bring to boiling, reduce heat, cover and simmer 2 hours.
3. Add apple and onion slices to meat, cover. Return to simmer and cook ½ hour longer, or until meat is tender.
4. Remove meat to heated platter and surround with apples and onions. Keep warm.
5. Skim off any fat from pan liquid. Stir flour with water smoothly; whisk into sauce, bring to boiling, stirring. Taste, correct seasoning if desired.
6. Spoon a little gravy over meat. Serve rest in a sauceboat.

BEEF BRISKET IN BEER

MAKES 6 TO 8 SERVINGS

1 large onion, thinly sliced and separated into rings
1 clove garlic, sliced
3 or 4 large potatoes, peeled and halved
1 4-lb. fresh beef brisket
½ teaspoon salt
¼ teaspoon freshly ground black pepper
1 can (12 ozs.) beer
¼ cup chili sauce
2 tablespoons dark molasses
½ cup cold water or beer
¼ cup all-purpose flour
Few twists freshly ground black pepper

Slow Cooker

1. Place onion rings, garlic and potatoes in crockery cooker. Trim excess fat from brisket. Cut meat in half if necessary and place on top on onions. Sprinkle with salt and pepper. Pour beer, chili sauce

and molasses over meat. Cover; cook on low-heat setting for 10 to 12 hours.
2. Remove brisket and potatoes from liquid; keep warm. Measure 2 cups liquid; pour into saucepan.
3. Blend ½ cup cold water into flour; stir into liquid. Cook and stir until thickened and bubbly. Taste for seasoning; add a few twists of freshly ground black pepper.
4. Place meat on cutting board and slice across the grain; pass gravy separately.

Dutch Oven

1. Place onion, garlic, potatoes, beef brisket, salt, pepper, beer, chili sauce and dark molasses in Dutch oven. Heat to boiling; reduce heat; cover and boil gently 2 to 2½ hours or until tender.
2. Follow steps 2 to 4 as in slow cooker instructions.

CRANBERRY POT ROAST

MAKES 8 SERVINGS

1 (4 to 5 lb.) boneless rolled chuck roast
1½ teaspoons salt
½ teaspoon freshly ground black pepper
2 tablespoons butter or margarine
2 tablespoons vegetable oil

2 cups chopped onion
2 cups fresh cranberries, rinsed and drained
1 can (10½ ozs.) condensed beef broth, undiluted
Salt and freshly ground black pepper, optional

1. Wipe roast with damp paper towel. Sprinkle roast with salt and pepper. In 6-qt. Dutch oven heat butter and vegetable oil until hot. Brown meat on all sides in hot oil over medium heat.
2. When meat has browned, remove from pan; pour off all pan drippings. Return roast to pan; add onion, cranberries and beef broth. Bring to boiling. Reduce heat, cover and simmer about 2½ hours, turning once or twice, until the meat is tender.
3. Remove meat to a platter, cover with foil and keep warm. Skim excess fat from pan juices with spoon. Pour pan juices into electric blender and blend for 1 minute. Strain juices back into pan. Simmer until bubbly. Taste for seasoning, adding additional salt and pepper if desired.
4. Cut meat into slices and serve with pan-juice gravy.

SLOW-COOKED SHORT RIBS IN WINE

MAKES 6 TO 8 SERVINGS

6 lbs. well-trimmed short ribs
  cut into individual ribs
3 tablespoons liquid gravy
  seasoning
1 lb. fresh or frozen carrot
  chunks
1 lb. fresh or frozen small
  white onions
2 cloves garlic, crushed

2 bay leaves
¼ cup quick-cooking tapioca
½ teaspoon freshly ground
  black pepper
½ teaspoon thyme leaves
2 teaspoons salt
2 envelopes instant bouillon
2 cups red wine
1 cup water

1. Brush short ribs with gravy seasoning and place in bottom of a
5½-qt. crock or slow-cooker. Add carrots, onions, garlic and bay leaves.
2. Combine tapioca, pepper, thyme, salt and instant bouillon. Sprinkle
mixture over short ribs. Pour wine and water over all and cover.
3. Place crock in outer cooking shell. Cook on high setting for 4½ to
5 hours.

CHICKEN A LA PROVENCALE

MAKES 4 TO 6 SERVINGS

6 tablespoons olive oil
4 lbs. chicken parts, rinsed
  and dried
2 cups green pepper strips
  (2 large)
1½ lbs. (4 medium) tomatoes
2 cloves garlic, crushed
1 bay leaf
¼ teaspoon thyme leaves
2 cups sliced onion

¼ lb. spicy sausage, sliced
  (kielbasa, smoky links,
  chorizo or Italian)
2 teaspoons salt
¼ teaspoon freshly ground
  black pepper
2 tablespoons all-purpose
  flour
½ cup water

1. Heat oil in a 5-qt. Dutch oven. Add chicken a few pieces at a time.
Brown slowly on all sides over medium heat. Remove as browned.
2. Sauté green pepper strips in same oil about 5 minutes, stirring. Add
tomatoes, garlic, bay leaf and thyme. Sauté, stirring, for 5 minutes.
3. Return chicken pieces to Dutch oven. Add onion and sausage;
sprinkle with salt and pepper. Heat to boiling. Reduce heat and
simmer covered 30 minutes, until chicken is tender.
4. To thicken sauce, stir flour into water smoothly. Add to Dutch oven.
Heat, stirring, until sauce boils.

Vegetable of the Month: Cabbage

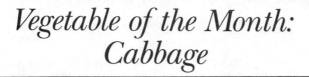

RUSSIAN SAUERKRAUT SOUP

MAKES 4 QUARTS

2 lbs. beef short ribs or beef brisket
2 lbs. beef soupbones, cracked
2 cups chopped carrot
2 cups chopped onion
2 cups chopped celery and tops
8 cups shredded cabbage
3 cloves garlic, crushed
3 qts. water

1 can (28 ozs.) tomatoes
2 bay leaves
3 teaspoons salt
½ teaspoon freshly ground black pepper
1 can (1 lb.) sauerkraut, rinsed and drained
4 tablespoons lemon juice
2 to 3 tablespoons sugar
Sour cream

1. Preheat oven to 450°F. Place short ribs and beef bones in a roasting pan. Bake 20 to 25 minutes, until meat is brown. Turn once.

2. Transfer short ribs and soupbones to an 8-qt. soup kettle. Add carrot, onion, celery, celery tops, cabbage, garlic, water, tomatoes, bay leaves, salt and pepper. Bring to boiling; skim off foam with slotted spoon. Reduce heat; simmer covered 1½ to 2 hours, until meat is tender.

3. Remove soupbones from kettle, discard. Cut meat into chunks and return to soup. Add sauerkraut, lemon juice and sugar to taste. Add more water if necessary.

4. Heat to boiling. Reduce heat and simmer covered 1 hour longer.

5. Serve from heated tureen or ladle directly into soup bowls. Pass sour cream as a garnish.

Editor's Note: This soup may be frozen.

SWEET 'N' SIMPLE COLESLAW

MAKES 2½ QUARTS, 8 SERVINGS

1 large head cabbage,
  shredded, 2½ qts.
2 cups green pepper rings
2 cups Spanish onion rings
¾ cup sugar
1 tablespoon sugar

1 teaspoon ground mustard
1 teaspoon celery seed
1 tablespoon salt
1 cup white vinegar
¾ cup vegetable oil

1. In large 3-qt. bowl layer cabbage, green pepper and onion; sprinkle ¾ cup sugar over all.
2. In saucepan combine 1 tablespoon sugar and remaining ingredients; mix well. Heat to boiling, stirring; pour over slaw. Cover with plastic film or foil and refrigerate at least 4 hours.
3. Just before serving, toss salad thoroughly.

STUFFED CABBAGE ROLLS

MAKES 4 SERVINGS

8 large green cabbage leaves
  Boiling water, salted
1 lb. lean ground beef
¾ cup wheat germ
½ cup finely chopped onion
1 teaspoon salt
⅛ teaspoon freshly ground
  black pepper
1 medium clove garlic,
  minced

½ teaspoon oregano leaves,
  crushed
¼ teaspoon basil leaves,
  crushed
2 eggs
1 can (1 lb.) tomato sauce
¾ cup water
2 tablespoons dark brown
  sugar
2 tablespoons vinegar
1 tablespoon cornstarch

1. Drop cabbage leaves into boiling, salted water in large saucepan. Return to boiling. Boil gently for 4 to 5 minutes. Drain.
2. In medium bowl, mix ground beef, wheat germ, onion, salt, pepper, garlic, oregano, basil and eggs. Blend thoroughly with well-scrubbed hands.
3. Preheat oven to 375°F. Divide beef mixture evenly onto cabbage leaves. Fold sides of leaf over mixture and roll leaf around filling.
4. Place rolls, seamside down, in 2½-qt. baking dish. Blend tomato sauce, water, brown sugar, vinegar and cornstarch smoothly. Pour over rolls. Cover with foil.
5. Bake for 40 to 45 minutes, spooning sauce over rolls once or twice while baking.

March

March winds bring blustery days but there is a glimpse here and
there of spring to come. If we look, the buds seem to be growing
plumper and have a ready air.

When the season changes, our mood changes, too, and the
versatility of the egg appeals to our subtle leaning toward lighter
foods.

It's also time to make things easier on ourselves in the kitchen.
We find the answer in satisfying meal-in-a-bowl soups. Once a
week, at least, they seem easy and warming. What's more, with
a big kettle-full, there's another meal left.

The Vegetable of the Month is the golden, crunchy carrot, en-
joying new popularity in cakes and cookies.

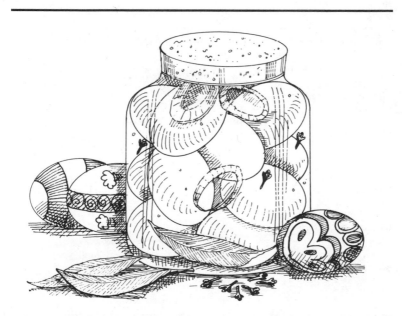

Have It Your Way Omelets

FILLING	ALSO ADD	SEASONING
⅓ to ½ cup	1 or 2 tablespoons	⅛ to ¼ teaspoon
chopped cooked beef	fried onions and avocado	chili powder
chopped cooked ham	sliced, pitted olives	dash cloves
chopped cooked pork	bean sprouts or chopped green pepper	hot sauce
chopped cooked chicken or turkey	chutney and onion rings	curry powder
flaked cooked fish	mayonnaise, chopped pickle	lemon juice
chopped cooked shrimp, crabmeat or lobster	mayonnaise, chopped green pepper	lemon juice, celery salt
chili or taco filling	chopped onion or scallions, avocado slices	coarse ground black pepper
shredded, sliced Cheddar, Swiss, Mozzarella, Gouda, Provolone, Muenster or other firm cheese	chopped parsley	
cottage cheese, Ricotta or cream cheese	drained crushed pineapple, fruit cocktail, mandarin orange sections	dash ground mustard

Easy Souffle Combinations

SOUP	CHEESE	VARIATION	SEASONING
1 can, 10½-10¾ ozs.	1 cup shredded or grated	1 cup	⅛ to ¼ teaspoon
cream of celery, chicken, mushroom, onion or potato	Swiss, Gruyère or Muenster	minced cooked chicken or pork	sage or poultry seasoning
cream of onion, mushroom or potato	Swiss, Gruyère or Muenster	cooked mashed yams	orange peel (½ teaspoon)
cream of mushroom, potato or Cheddar cheese	Swiss, Gruyère	chopped cooked broccoli	basil leaves
Cheddar cheese, onion or mushroom	Cheddar	cooked mashed carrots	dill weed
cream of celery, potato or onion	Swiss	mashed cooked squash or pumpkin	ground cinnamon, ground cloves
cream of celery, chicken or onion	Swiss or Cheddar	cooked kernel corn, finely chopped onion	basil leaves, paprika
cream of celery, chicken or onion	Swiss, Gruyère or Muenster	drained, cooked, chopped spinach	ground nutmeg
cream of celery, chicken or onion	Swiss, Gruyère or Muenster	minced cooked turkey or chicken	curry powder (½ teaspoon)

Basic directions for omelets and souffles can be found on page 46.

Your Own Quiche Combinations

CHEESE

1 cup

Swiss ▪ Cheddar ▪ Muenster

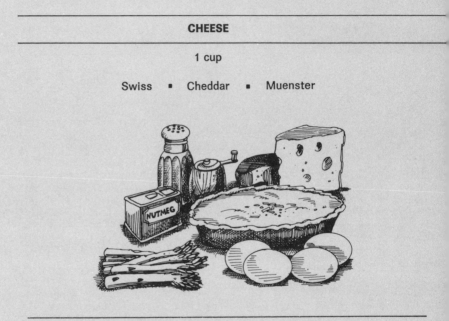

HERE'S HOW TO MAKE THE HAVE IT YOUR OWN WAY OMELETS

Beat 2 eggs with 2 tablespoons water, ¼ teaspoon salt and dash hot pepper sauce. Heat omelet pan with 2 tablespoons butter, until hot enough to sizzle a drop of water. Pour in egg mixture all at once. Shake pan, stirring eggs to cook until set. Add filling, any added ingredients and seasonings. Loosen omelet from edge of pan, slide and fold into plate.

HERE'S HOW TO MAKE OUR EASY SOUFFLE

Heat undiluted soup, cheese, added variation ingredient and seasonings; stir until cheese melts. Beat 6 egg yolks until thick; slowly beat into cheese mixture. Beat 6 egg whites with ¼ teaspoon cream of tartar until stiff. Fold yolk mixture into whites. Pour into greased 2-qt. soufflé dish. Bake at 350°F. 40 minutes.

HERE'S HOW TO MAKE YOUR OWN QUICHE

Beat 6 eggs with 1½ cups half-and-half or milk; add ½ to 1 cup shredded cheese and enough chopped cooked meat, fish, poultry or vegetables to total 2 cups. Season as you like and add any optional flavor variation. Pour into 9-inch unbaked pie shell and bake 30 to 35 minutes at 375°F. Let stand 5 minutes before serving.

LEFTOVERS	SEASONING	OPTIONAL	
1 cup	¼ to ½ teaspoon	2 to 4 tablespoons	
finely chopped corned beef	ground mustard	nuts, onion	**SWISS**
chicken/turkey	poultry seasoning	sliced scallions	
diced cooked potatoes	dill weed	chopped onions	
flaked tuna	tarragon or ground mustard		
cooked cut green beans	basil	slivered toasted almonds	**CHEDDAR**
sliced or chopped cooked carrots	marjoram or nutmeg	chopped walnuts	
cooked crumbled ground beef	hot pepper sauce	diced, drained tomato	
cooked peas	rosemary	chopped onion	
diced cooked ham	ground mustard or caraway seed		
chopped cooked well-drained spinach	onion powder	imitation bacon	**MUENSTER**
chopped cooked broccoli	basil	sliced, pitted ripe olives	
chopped cooked cauliflower	ground mustard		
chopped cooked shrimp	celery salt	sliced scallions	

The Versatile Egg

SAN FRANCISCO QUICHE

MAKES 1 (9- OR 10-INCH) QUICHE,
8 TO 10 SERVINGS

Pastry for 9- or 10-inch
single crust pie
1 package (6 ozs.) frozen crabmeat, thawed and drained
3 tablespoons dry sherry
1 teaspoon brandy
4 large eggs
1 cup light cream
1 cup heavy cream
1 teaspoon salt
1/8 teaspoon ground nutmeg

Good grinding of fresh
black pepper
2 dashes hot pepper sauce
1/2 cup shredded natural
Gruyère cheese
1/2 cup shredded natural Swiss
cheese
1/2 cup diagonally sliced
scallions
2 tablespoons grated
Parmesan cheese

1. Preheat oven to 375°F. Line pie pan with pastry and flute edge. Take a sheet of foil and press lightly into pie pan. Fill with raw rice, raw elbow macaroni or dry beans.

2. Bake pie shell 10 minutes to partially bake. Remove from oven, remove foil and filler. (Filler of course can be used again.)

3. Shred crabmeat coarsely and allow to soak with sherry and brandy.

4. In medium bowl, beat eggs. Stir in light cream, heavy cream, salt, nutmeg, pepper and hot pepper sauce. Add crabmeat, Gruyère cheese, Swiss cheese and scallions. Stir well.

5. Pour filling into prepared crust. Bake 15 minutes, then sprinkle surface with Parmesan cheese. Bake 25 to 30 minutes longer or until well puffed and brown.

6. Let cool 5 minutes. Cut into wedges to serve.

EGGS BENEDICT

MAKES 4 SERVINGS

2 tablespoons butter or margarine
4 packages (8-oz. size) sliced Canadian bacon
Water
2 tablespoons vinegar

8 eggs
4 English muffins, fork-split and lightly toasted
Blender Hollandaise Sauce (recipe below)
4 sprigs parsley

1. Heat butter in electric skillet until melted. Sauté Canadian bacon slices in hot butter until lightly browned on both sides. Place on foil, cover and keep warm.
2. Poach eggs: Pour off fat from electric skillet, wipe clean with paper towel. Pour in water to depth of 1 inch, add 2 tablespoons vinegar to water. (The vinegar helps solidify the egg white.) Heat water to simmer, with bubbles rising and breaking just below surface.
3. Break eggs one at a time into the simmering water. (The fresher the eggs the higher and prettier the whites will be.) Baste eggs gently with simmering water, using large spoon. Cook until whites are firm, yolks soft.
4. Lift eggs gently from water with slotted spoon, draining liquid off eggs and blotting them with paper towel.
5. Meanwhile arrange Canadian bacon slices on toasted English muffins. Place 2 halves on each heated plate. Top each with a poached egg. Spoon a little Blender Hollandaise Sauce over each. Garnish with parsley. Serve at once.

BLENDER HOLLANDAISE SAUCE

MAKES ABOUT 1 CUP

3 egg yolks
2 tablespoons lemon juice
Dash salt

2 drops hot pepper sauce
½ cup (1 stick) butter or margarine

1. Place egg yolks, lemon juice, salt and pepper sauce in warm blender container. Turn motor on and off at medium speed, just to blend.
2. Heat butter in small saucepan until bubbling and very hot.
3. Remove blender cover, turn motor to high speed; drizzle in hot butter slowly until all is added. Turn off blender. Serve warm.

MUSHROOM-GREEN BEAN OMELET

MAKES 1 SERVING

3 tablespoons butter or margarine
½ cup sliced fresh or leftover cooked mushrooms
¼ cup drained cooked green beans
2 eggs
2 tablespoons water

½ teaspoon instant minced onion
¼ teaspoon salt
⅛ teaspoon cayenne pepper or hot pepper sauce
2 tablespoons shredded sharp Cheddar cheese

1. In 8-inch omelet pan or skillet cook mushrooms in 1 tablespoon melted butter until just tender and lightly browned. Add green beans; sauté 1 minute. Remove from pan and set aside.
2. With wire whisk or fork beat eggs, water, onion, salt and pepper until well blended.
3. Heat remaining butter until just hot enough to sizzle a drop of water.
4. Pour in egg mixture all at once. Mixture should set at edge at once.
5. With pancake turner, carefully draw cooked portion at edges toward center so uncooked portions flow to bottom. Tilt pan as necessary so uncooked eggs can flow.
6. Slide pan rapidly back and forth over heat to keep mixture in motion and sliding freely.
7. When eggs are set and surface is moist, increase heat to brown bottom slightly. Quickly turn reserved mushrooms and green beans onto half of omelet.
8. Using pancake turner to loosen omelet if necessary, lift omelet pan allowing omelet to fall onto plate, flipping pan so omelet rolls or folds in half at the same time. Sprinkle with cheese.

LEFTOVER VEGETABLE QUICHE

MAKES 6 SERVINGS

9-inch unbaked pie shell
1 cup (4 ozs.) shredded Cheddar cheese
2 tablespoons grated Parmesan or Romano cheese
1 cup cooked and drained mixed vegetables

6 eggs
1½ cups half and half or milk
1 tablespoon instant minced onion
½ teaspoon oregano leaves, crushed
½ teaspoon salt

1. Preheat oven to 375°F. Sprinkle pie shell with both kinds of cheese, then vegetables.

2. Beat eggs, half and half, onion, oregano and salt together until blended. Pour over cheese and vegetables.

3. Bake 30 to 35 minutes or until knife inserted near center comes out clean. Let stand 5 minutes before serving.

EGGS FLORENTINE

MAKES 4 SERVINGS

2 packages (10 oz. each) frozen spinach
1 teaspoon seasoned salt
Dash ground nutmeg
½ cup (about 2 oz.) shredded Swiss cheese
1 tablespoon butter or margarine
1 tablespoon all-purpose flour
¼ teaspoon garlic salt

⅛ teaspoon freshly ground black pepper
¾ cup milk
1 tablespoon butter or margarine
4 eggs
1 tablespoon butter or margarine, melted
2 tablespoons shredded Swiss cheese
2 tablespoons fine dry bread crumbs

1. Cook spinach according to package directions, adding seasoned salt to the cooking water instead of salt. Drain thoroughly.

2. Put one half the spinach into a greased shallow 5-cup baking dish. Sprinkle lightly with ground nutmeg and then with the ½ cup cheese. Top evenly with the remaining spinach.

3. Set in a 325°F. oven and heat 15 minutes. Remove from oven.

4. Meanwhile, heat 1 tablespoon butter or margarine in a saucepan. Blend in a mixture of the flour, garlic salt, and pepper. Heat until bubbly. Add the milk gradually, stirring until blended. Bring to boiling, stirring constantly, and cook 1 to 2 minutes. Set aside and keep warm.

5. Heat 1 tablespoon butter or margarine in a skillet until hot. Break the eggs, one at a time, into a saucer and slip into skillet. Reduce heat, cover, and cook slowly until eggs are just set, about 4 minutes.

6. Arrange eggs on the hot spinach in a lengthwise row, overlapping the edges slightly. Spoon sauce over eggs. Sprinkle a mixture of the remaining ingredients over sauce. Serve immediately.

IDAHO EGG PIE

MAKES 10 TO 12 SERVINGS

20 slices bacon
 1 package (32 ozs.) frozen
   hashbrowns or 10½ cups
   coarsely shredded Idaho
   potatoes

 1 tablespoon salt
20 large eggs
 1½ teaspoons salt
 ½ cup milk
 ½ cup butter or margarine

1. Preheat oven to 400°F. Place bacon strips on broiler rack. Partially cook bacon 10 minutes. Remove from oven; roll into curls and secure with wooden picks.

2. Return to oven. Continue baking until crisp, about 5 minutes. Turn oven off. Pour off bacon fat and use to fry hashbrowns. Cover bacon with foil and return to oven to keep warm.

3. Blot frozen shredded hashbrowns well with paper towels. If using fresh Idaho potatoes, squeeze shredded potatoes thoroughly in dish towel to absorb excess moisture. Toss potatoes with 1 tablespoon salt.

4. Fry potatoes about 2½ cups at a time in ¼ cup reserved bacon fat, browning on both sides. Press into a 12-inch skillet or shallow baking dish to form a crust. Place in oven with bacon to keep warm.

5. Beat eggs lightly with milk and 1½ teaspoons salt. Heat butter in skillet; when hot, pour in eggs. Cook over medium heat, stirring slowly.

6. When eggs are set but still soft, spoon into hashed-brown-potato crust and top with bacon curls. Cut into wedges, serve on warm plates.

EGG-AND-CHEESE NOODLE CASSEROLE

MAKES 6 SERVINGS

 1 package (8 ozs.) spinach or
   egg noodles, ¼ inch wide
 3 qts. boiling water
 1 tablespoon salt
 ¼ cup butter or margarine
 ¼ cup all-purpose flour
 2 cups milk (whole milk, or
   half whole and half skim
   milk)
 1 teaspoon seasoned salt
 ¾ teaspoon Italian seasoning
   or blended herbs

Few twists freshly ground
  black pepper
 1 tablespoon instant minced
   onion
 1 cup ricotta or cottage cheese
 2 cups (8 ozs.) shredded
   mozzarella or Muenster
   cheese
 5 hard-cooked eggs, sliced
 2 tablespoons grated
   Parmesan or Romano
   cheese

1. Preheat oven to 350°F. Grease a 2-qt. casserole.

2. Cook noodles in 3 qts. boiling water, to which 1 tablespoon of salt has been added, for 6 minutes, or until just tender. Drain, rinse with cold water, drain again.

3. Make sauce: In medium saucepan, heat butter until melted. Stir in flour smoothly. Add milk all at once. Bring to boiling, stirring with wire whisk until bubbly. Season with seasoned salt, Italian seasoning, pepper and instant minced onion.

4. Layer ingredients in prepared casserole as follows: 1/3 of noodles, 1/2 of ricotta, 1/2 of mozzarella, 1/3 of sauce and 1/3 of eggs.

5. Repeat with remaining ingredients, topping casserole with sprinkling of grated Parmesan cheese.

6. Bake for 45 to 50 minutes, or until casserole is bubbly throughout.

PICKLED EGGS

MAKES 12 PICKLED EGGS

1 dozen eggs	1/2 teaspoon salt
1 1/2 cups white vinegar	6 whole cloves
1/2 cup water	1 bay leaf
1 cup sugar	1 onion, sliced

1. Cover eggs with cold water, bring to boil, reduce heat and simmer 15 to 18 minutes.

2. Drain and immediately run cold water over eggs in pan for several minutes.

3. Peel eggs and place in narrow, deep jar.

4. In medium saucepan combine vinegar, water, sugar, salt, cloves and bay leaf. Bring to a boil, reduce heat and simmer 5 minutes.

5. Pour hot vinegar solution over eggs, making sure eggs are completely covered with the liquid.

6. Place onion slices on top of eggs. Cover tightly, place in refrigerator and let stand several days.

7. Eggs may be served whole, halved or sliced, plain or in sandwiches or salads.

Meal-in-a-Bowl Soups

MEDITERRANEAN MINESTRONE

MAKES ABOUT 6 QUARTS

2 lbs. beef soup bones
3 lbs. shin beef, sliced
4 qts. water
1 can (28 ozs.) tomatoes in
purée or juice, undrained
1 can (15 ozs.) tomato sauce
2 medium onions, quartered
¼ cup chopped parsley
2 tablespoons salt
2 teaspoons basil leaves,
crushed
½ teaspoon freshly ground
black pepper
2 cloves garlic, crushed

2 bay leaves
2 cups (1 lb.) sliced carrots
2 cups sliced celery
4 cups (12 ozs.) uncooked
shell macaroni or elbows
2 packages (10 ozs. each)
frozen Italian green beans
1 package (10 ozs.) frozen peas
1 can (1 lb. or 20 ozs.) white
or red kidney beans,
undrained
Parmesan cheese, grated
Italian bread

1. Place soup bones and shin beef in large 8- to 10-qt. soup kettle; add water. Bring to a boil; skim surface of liquid.
2. Add tomatoes, tomato sauce, onions, parsley, salt, basil, pepper, garlic and bay leaves. Bring to a boil again, reduce heat, cover and simmer for 1½ hours.
3. Add carrots and celery; cover and simmer for ½ hour longer or until meat is fork-tender.
4. Remove meat and bones from soup. Discard bones. Trim fat off meat and discard fat. Cut meat into bite-size pieces and return to soup.
5. Heat soup to boiling. Add uncooked macaroni, green beans and peas. Simmer, covered, about 15 to 20 minutes or until macaroni is tender. Stir occasionally.
6. Stir in kidney beans; heat to boiling. Serve in large, deep soup bowls. Pass grated Parmesan cheese and Italian bread.

FRESH VEGETABLE-BEEF SOUP

MAKES ABOUT 7 QUARTS

3 tablespoons butter or margarine
4 lbs. beef shin, bone-in, sliced
2 lbs. beef marrowbones, sliced
4 qts. water
2 cans 10½ ozs. size beef bouillon, undiluted
2 cloves garlic
2 onions, quartered
4 celery tops
2 parsley sprigs
5 large tomatoes, quartered
1 cup sliced carrots
2 bay leaves

1½ teaspoons thyme leaves
6 whole black peppercorns
1 tablespoon plus 2 teaspoons salt
½ teaspoon ground allspice
2 cups chopped onion
2 cups chopped celery
½ cup chopped parsley
2 cups sliced carrots
3 cups chopped cabbage
2 cups green beans, cut into 1-inch pieces
3 cups cubed potatoes
½ teaspoon coarse black pepper
Toasted bread strips

1. In large kettle melt butter and brown shin meat slowly on all sides.
2. Add beef marrowbones, water, beef bouillon, garlic, onion quarters, celery tops, parsley sprigs, tomatoes, 1 cup sliced carrots, bay leaves, thyme leaves, peppercorns, 1 tablespoon salt and allspice. Bring to boiling. Cover, reduce heat slightly and boil gently 2½ hours.
3. Strain stock, discarding vegetables if desired. Lift out meat and marrowbones.
4. Cut meat into small pieces, return to stock. Remove marrow from bones with small spatula, reserve.
5. Add remaining chopped onion, chopped celery, chopped parsley, 2 cups sliced carrots, cabbage, green beans and potatoes to kettle. Season with remaining 2 teaspoons salt and coarse black pepper. Bring to boiling, cover, reduce heat and simmer about 1 hour, until vegetables are very tender.
6. Serve reserved marrow spread on bread strips with soup.

MARILYN'S SPLIT PEA SOUP

MAKES 3 QUARTS

1 lb. split green peas, rinsed
2 qts. water
2 cups chopped carrots
2 cups chopped celery and tops
2 cups chopped onion
½ cup chopped parsley or ¼ cup parsley flakes
1 tablespoon oregano leaves
1 tablespoon salt

½ teaspoon freshly ground black pepper
1 bay leaf
1 meaty smoked ham bone or smoked ham hock
Several twists freshly ground black pepper, optional
Packaged seasoned croutons, optional

1. In 6- to 8-qt. Dutch oven or heavy kettle combine split green peas, water, carrots, celery and tops, onion, parsley, oregano leaves, salt, pepper, bay leaf and ham bone.
2. Heat to boiling, stirring frequently. Reduce heat, and simmer covered 1 hour and 30 minutes, or until peas have cooked down to a thick soup. Stir occasionally to prevent sticking.
3. Remove ham bone from soup. Cut meat from bone, chop coarsely. Return meat to soup, discard bone and fat. Reheat gently, covered.
4. Taste for seasoning, add pepper if desired.
5. Pour into heated tureen or ladle directly into soup bowls. Pass croutons if desired.

DEEP SEA CHOWDER

MAKES 3 QUARTS

1½ cups elbow macaroni or small shell macaroni
1 tablespoon salt
Boiling water
4 strips bacon, chopped, or 4 tablespoons butter or margarine
1 cup chopped onion
1 cup chopped celery
½ cup celery leaves
½ cup chopped parsley
1 clove garlic, minced
2 cans (8 ozs.) minced clams, undrained
Water

1 teaspoon salt
½ teaspoon thyme leaves
¾ teaspoon freshly ground black pepper
1 bay leaf
1 package (1 lb.) frozen fish fillets, thawed and cubed
2 cans (13-oz. size) evaporated milk, diluted
⅓ cup all-purpose flour
⅓ cup cold water
Salt and freshly ground black pepper, optional
Grated Parmesan cheese

1. Gradually add macaroni and 1 tablespoon salt to rapidly boiling water so that water continues to boil.

2. Cook, uncovered, stirring occasionally, until tender. Drain in colander; run cold water through them.

3. In 4- to 6-qt. kettle or Dutch oven, fry bacon until partially cooked. Add onion, celery, celery leaves, parsley and garlic. Cook, stirring occasionally, until vegetables are tender, about 8 to 10 minutes.

4. Drain clams, reserving liquid; add water to make 4 cups. Add liquid to Dutch oven along with one teaspoon salt. Add thyme, pepper and bay leaf. Heat to boiling; cover and simmer 10 minutes.

5. Add drained macaroni, clams, cubed fish and evaporated milk. Heat soup to boiling; reduce heat slightly and boil gently 15 minutes.

6. Smoothly blend flour with cold water. Add to soup, stirring over medium heat until mixture comes to a boil. Taste for seasoning, adding additional salt and pepper if desired.

7. Serve in large, deep soup bowls. Pass grated Parmesan cheese to sprinkle on top.

CANADIAN CHEDDAR CHEESE SOUP

MAKES 6 TO 8 SERVINGS

1 lb. of your favorite medium-sharp Cheddar cheese
2 tablespoons cornstarch
2 cups water
1 teaspoon salt
1/4 teaspoon white pepper
1 teaspoon Worcestershire sauce
Dash garlic powder
8 tablespoons butter

3/4 cup diced cooked cauliflower
1 cup sliced mushrooms
1/2 cup finely chopped carrots
1 cup finely chopped onion
3/4 cup diced Canadian bacon or fully cooked smoked ham
2 cups half-and-half or undiluted evaporated milk

1. Mix cornstarch with shredded cheese. Heat water to boiling in 4- to 6-qt. Dutch oven. Add cheese mixture to boiling water a little at a time, stirring constantly.

2. Continue to cook over medium heat, stirring constantly until cheese is melted and mixture is smooth. Add salt, pepper, Worcestershire, garlic.

3. Sauté each vegetable separately in two tablespoons butter until tender. Add to soup along with ham.

4. Heat, stirring constantly, adding half-and-half until desired thickness is reached.

FAMILY FAVORITE LENTIL SOUP

MAKES 4 QUARTS

1 lb. lentils, rinsed
3 qts. water
2 cups chopped carrots
2 cups chopped celery and tops
2 cups chopped onion
½ cup chopped parsley or ¼ cup parsley flakes
2 teaspoons salt
1½ teaspoons thyme leaves
½ teaspoon freshly ground black pepper

1 bay leaf
4 whole cloves
4 beef bouillon cubes
1 can (1 lb.) tomatoes, undrained
3 lbs. beef neck bones
½ cup dry sherry or Burgundy
Several twists freshly ground black pepper, optional
Chopped parsley, optional

1. In 6- to 8-qt. Dutch oven or heavy kettle, combine lentils, water, carrots, celery and tops, onion, parsley, salt, thyme, pepper, bay leaf, cloves, bouillon cubes, tomatoes and beef bones.
2. Heat to boiling, stirring frequently. Reduce heat and simmer covered 2 hours, until lentils and meat are fork-tender. Stir occasionally to prevent sticking.
3. Remove beef bones from soup. Cut meat from bones, chop coarsely. Return meat to soup, discard bones and fat. Add sherry. Reheat gently, covered.
4. Taste for seasoning, add pepper, if desired.
5. Pour into heated tureen or ladle directly into soup bowls. Sprinkle with parsley if desired.

SHELLFISH GUMBO Z'HERBES

MAKES 8 SERVINGS

1 lb. uncooked shrimp (20 to 24 per lb.), shelled and deveined
2 tablespoons butter or margarine
2 tablespoons butter or margarine
1 lb. okra, sliced
2 onions, finely chopped
1½ tablespoons all-purpose flour
1 cup tomatoes, peeled and

coarsely chopped
Water
12 fresh oysters in liquor (or canned or frozen)
2 teaspoons salt
1 clove garlic, crushed
Pinch cayenne pepper
Few drops hot pepper sauce
Dash Worcestershire sauce
½ lb. crabmeat
2 cups hot cooked white rice

1. In large kettle or Dutch oven, sauté shrimp in 2 tablespoons butter until pink. Set aside in bowl.
2. Heat the second 2 tablespoons butter in kettle, add okra and cook until tender. Add onion and cook until soft.
3. Stir in flour until smooth. Add tomatoes and cook for several minutes.
4. Add enough water to oyster liquor to make 2 quarts and add to okra combination. Add salt, garlic and cayenne.
5. Heat to boiling, reduce heat, cover and simmer for one hour. Add shrimp and simmer for 30 minutes.
6. Just before serving, add oysters and cook until edges curl.
7. Then add hot pepper sauce, Worcestershire sauce and crabmeat. Heat through.
8. Serve in soup plates over a serving of cooked rice.

Passover, Lenten and Easter Favorites

CHICKEN SOUP

MAKES ABOUT 4 QUARTS

4 lb. roasting or stewing
chicken, rinsed
4 qts. water
1 tablespoon salt
1/4 teaspoon freshly ground
black pepper
2 cups chopped celery
2 cups chopped onion

1/2 cup chopped parsley
1 cup diced carrots
1 cup diced parsnip or
cauliflower
1 cup diced potato
Matzo Balls, (recipe below),
optional

1. Place chicken in 6- to 8-qt. soup kettle. Add water, salt and pepper and bring to boil. Reduce heat and simmer covered for 1 hour.
2. Add vegetables, return to boiling; reduce heat and simmer for 1 hour.
3. Taste for seasoning, add more salt if desired.
4. Ladle into deep soup bowls, serving a chunk of chicken and several matzo balls in each bowl.

MATZO BALLS

MAKES ABOUT 20
MATZO BALLS

1/4 cup finely chopped onion
2 tablespoons chicken fat
from top of chicken soup
1 cup boiling chicken broth
1 cup matzo meal
1 egg, slightly beaten

1/2 teaspoon salt
Dash pepper
Dash ground nutmeg
1 teaspoon finely chopped
parsley

60

1. Cook onion in chicken fat 5 minutes, stirring; set aside.
2. Pour boiling chicken broth over matzo meal. Stir until broth is absorbed. Add onion mixture, egg and remaining ingredients. Mix well.
3. Cover and refrigerate until thoroughly chilled.
4. With your own well-scrubbed hands, roll dough into balls the size of a small walnut. If sticky, grease palms of hands or moisten with cold water.
5. Drop matzo balls into boiling chicken soup 15 minutes before serving. Boil gently uncovered.

GLAZED HAM WITH ROSÉ PEARS

MAKES 10 TO 12 SERVINGS

1 5-lb. boneless fully cooked smoked ham
¾ cup Rosé Pear marinade (recipe below)
¾ cup packed dark brown sugar
Rosé Pears (recipe below)
Watercress

1. Preheat oven to 325°F. Place ham on a rack in a shallow foil-lined roasting pan. Heat ham according to directions on label.
2. Meanwhile in small saucepan heat Rosé Pear marinade and brown sugar, bring to boiling; boil uncovered 5 minutes, until syrupy.
3. One half hour before ham is done, turn up oven heat to 425°F. Pour off drippings from pan, score ham fat diamond fashion.
4. Spoon Rosé Pear glaze over ham. Bake 30 minutes longer, basting with glaze 2 or 3 times.
5. To serve, place on large serving platter and surround ham with several Rosé Pears. Garnish with watercress. Serve any remaining Rosé Pears in separate bowl.

ROSÉ PEARS

MAKES ABOUT 16 ROSÉ
PEAR HALVES

2 cans (29-oz. size) Bartlett pear halves

¾ cup rosé wine or cranberry juice

2 tablespoons lemon juice

½ teaspoon mixed pickling spices

5 whole cloves

Few drops red food coloring

1. Drain 1 can of pears, reserve syrup. Drain second can of pears, discarding syrup.

2. In 1-qt. saucepan combine reserved pear syrup, rosé wine or cranberry juice, lemon juice, pickling spices, cloves and red food coloring.

3. Heat to boiling, boil uncovered, 3 minutes.

4. Arrange drained pear halves in a shallow glass baking dish. Strain spiced Rosé Pear marinade over pears, cover with plastic film. Refrigerate overnight.

5. Stir occasionally so pears color evenly.

6. Pour off ¾ cup marinade from pears to use in glaze for ham. Serve remaining Rosé Pears as an accompaniment for Glazed Ham or other meats.

EASTER EGG BREAD

1 COFFEE CAKE

2 packages active dry yeast

½ cup warm water (105°F.-115°F.)

1 cup unsifted all-purpose flour

⅓ cup water

¾ cup butter or margarine

1 tablespoon grated lemon peel

1½ tablespoons lemon juice

¾ cup sugar

1 teaspoon salt

2 eggs (½ cup), well beaten

3¾ to 4¼ cups unsifted all-purpose flour

6 colored eggs (uncooked)

1. Soften yeast in the ½ cup warm water in a bowl. Stir the yeast and mix in the 1 cup flour, then the ⅓ cup water. Beat until smooth.

2. Cover bowl with waxed paper and a towel; let stand in a warm place (about 80°F.) until doubled, about 1 hour.

3. Cream butter or margarine with lemon peel and juice. Mix sugar and salt; add gradually, creaming well. Add beaten eggs in halves, beating thoroughly after each addition.

4. Add yeast mixture and beat until blended. Add about half of the remaining flour and beat thoroughly. Beat in enough flour to make a soft dough. Knead on floured surface until smooth.

5. Put dough into a greased bowl; turn dough to bring greased surface

to top. Cover bowl with waxed paper and a towel; let rise in a warm place until doubled.

6. Punch down dough; divide into thirds. Let rest about 10 min.

7. With hands, roll and stretch each piece into a roll about 26-inches long and ¾-inch thick. Loosely braid rolls together, and on a lightly greased baking sheet or jelly-roll pan shape into a ring, pressing ends together. At even intervals, gently spread dough apart and tuck in a colored egg. Cover and let rise in a warm place until doubled.

8. Bake at 375°F. about 30 min. During baking check bread for browning, and when sufficiently browned, cover loosely with aluminum foil.

9. Transfer coffee cake to a wire rack. If desired, spread a confectioners' sugar frosting over top of warm coffee cake.

EASTER LAMB CAKE

MAKES 8 SERVINGS

½ cup butter or margarine
1 cup sugar
2 eggs
1½ cups unsifted all-purpose flour
2 teaspoons baking powder
½ teaspoon salt
½ cup milk

1 teaspoon pure vanilla extract
Old Fashioned White Frosting (see p. 237)
1 can (3½ ozs.) flaked coconut
Jelly beans, green tinted coconut, 24-inch length ribbon

1. Preheat oven to 375°F. Grease heavily and lightly coat with flour, a 2-part lamb cake mold. The 2 halves of a basic lamb mold will hold 7 cups liquid.

2. In large bowl, with electric mixer at medium speed beat butter until creamy. Gradually add sugar, creaming until fluffy.

3. Add eggs to creamed mixture and beat at high speed until blended.

4. Combine flour, baking powder and salt. Add to the butter mixture, in thirds, alternating with milk. Add vanilla.

5. Place front half of lamb mold on cookie sheet. Fill with cake batter. Top with second half.

6. Bake for 60 to 70 minutes. Remove from oven, allow to cool 5 minutes, remove top half of pan. Cool 5 minutes longer, loosen cake from bottom pan and remove. Cool completely.

7. Place 2 dabs of Old-Fashioned White Frosting on cake platter. Place lamb cake upright on frosting.

8. Continue frosting, covering cake completely. Coat with coconut. Cut a jelly bean in half, for lamb's eyes. Place one whole jelly bean for mouth.

9. Additional jelly beans and green tinted coconut can be placed at base of lamb for garnish. Tie ribbon around lamb neck, making a bow.

HOT CROSS BUNS

MAKES 24 BUNS

1 package active dry yeast
¼ cup very warm water
  (110°-115° F.)
1 cup milk
4 tablespoons butter or
  margarine
⅓ cup sugar
1 teaspoon salt
1 egg, beaten
3½ to 4 cups unsifted all-
  purpose flour

¼ cup wheat germ
1 cup raisins or currants
2 teaspoons grated lemon or
  orange rind
2 teaspoons vegetable oil
2 tablespoons butter, melted
1 egg yolk
2 tablespoons water
1¼ cups confectioners' sugar
2 tablespoons water

1. In large warm bowl, dissolve yeast in very warm water.

2. In 1-qt. saucepan heat milk until a rim of tiny bubbles forms around side of pan. Stir in 4 tablespoons butter, sugar and salt; cool to lukewarm.

3. Pour lukewarm milk mixture into dissolved yeast along with egg. Gradually add half the flour, beating hard with a wooden spoon or electric mixer at medium speed for 3 to 5 minutes.

4. Add wheat germ, raisins, lemon rind and remaining flour a little at a time, to make a moderately stiff dough. Scrape down side of bowl. Sprinkle surface of dough with oil. Cover and let rise in warm place (75° to 80°F.) for about 1½ hours, until light and double in size.

5. Punch down dough. Turn out onto lightly floured board and divide into 24 equal pieces. Shape dough into rounds and place about 1 inch apart in 3 greased, 8-inch round baking pans.

6. Brush with melted butter and let rise in warm place about 35 to 40 minutes, or until double in size. (One hour for refrigerated dough.)

7. Beat egg yolk with 2 tablespoons water and brush surface of buns with it. Bake buns in preheated 400°F. oven about 20 minutes, or until golden brown.

8. Remove from oven and cool. Combine confectioners' sugar with 2 tablespoons water smoothly and decorate each with sugar-icing cross while buns are still warm.

Vegetable of the Month: Carrots

GLAZED CARROTS FINE HERBES

MAKES 6 SERVINGS

3 dozen young carrots, whole
  or sliced
Salted water
2 tablespoons butter or
  margarine
2 tablespoons dark brown

sugar or honey
Chopped chives, chervil,
  tarragon and basil leaves
Salt
Freshly ground black pepper

1. Cook carrots in small amount of salted water until tender and water has boiled away, about 10 minutes.
2. Add butter and sugar and cook, turning often, until carrots are evenly cooked and well glazed.
3. Sprinkle carrots lightly with chopped chives, chervil, tarragon, basil, salt and pepper.

GINNY'S CARROT MOLD

MAKES 6 SERVINGS

1½ cups grated carrots
  1 cup dark brown sugar
 ½ cup soft butter or
  margarine
  1 cup all-purpose flour
 ½ teaspoon baking powder

½ teaspoon salt
⅛ teaspoon freshly ground
  black pepper
  Dash ground nutmeg
1 egg, beaten

1. Combine all ingredients; mix well. Place in greased 5½-cup ring mold. Bake in preheated 350°F. oven about 45 minutes. Unmold. Serve on platter with cooked green peas in the center.

GLAZED CARROTS AND BANANAS

MAKES 4 SERVINGS

2½ cups diagonally sliced
    peeled carrots
½ cup water
2 tablespoons butter or
    margarine

3 tablespoons sugar, corn
    syrup or honey
1 tablespoon lemon juice
½ teaspoon salt
¼ cup chopped parsley
2 bananas

1. Put carrots and water in large skillet. Bring to boiling. Cover; reduce heat and boil gently 15 minutes, or until tender. Drain carrots and put in bowl.
2. Melt butter in skillet. Add sugar, lemon juice and salt; stir until sugar dissolves. Add carrots and parsley. Cook, stirring occasionally, until carrots are glazed.
3. Peel bananas, cut into diagonal slices and add to skillet. Heat.

BAKED CARROTS JULIENNE

MAKES 4 SERVINGS

¼ cup margarine
1 tablespoon lemon juice
½ teaspoon salt

6 medium carrots, peeled and
    cut julienne style
¼ cup water
1 tablespoon chopped parsley

1. Melt margarine; stir in lemon juice and salt.
2. Arrange carrots in layers in small baking dish, pouring some margarine mixture over each layer and all remaining mixture over top. Add water. Cover. Bake in 350°F. oven until carrots are tender, 50 to 60 minutes. Sprinkle with parsley.

    Baked Carrots and Onion Rings: Follow recipe for Baked Carrots Julienne, arranging thin onion rings (1 medium onion) in layers with carrots and adding ½ teaspoon sugar to margarine mixture.

GOLDEN CARROT NUT CAKE

MAKES 1 (10-INCH) CAKE,
16 SERVINGS

1 cup soft butter or margarine	2 cups finely grated peeled carrots
1½ cups sugar	½ cup finely chopped walnuts
½ cup packed dark brown sugar	3 cups unsifted all-purpose flour
1 teaspoon ground cinnamon	1 tablespoon baking powder
½ teaspoon ground nutmeg	½ teaspoon salt
1 tablespoon grated lemon rind	½ cup orange juice
4 eggs	Orange Glaze (recipe below)
1 teaspoon pure vanilla extract	

1. In large bowl of electric mixer cream butter and sugars until light. Add cinnamon, nutmeg and lemon rind.

2. Beat in eggs, one at a time. Stir in vanilla, carrots and walnuts.

3. Sift together flour, baking powder and salt; add alternately with orange juice. Turn into a greased and floured 10-inch tube pan.

4. Bake in a preheated 350°F. oven 60 to 70 minutes, until cake tester inserted in center comes out clean.

5. Cool in pan 5 minutes, turn out of pan and cool completely on wire rack. Spoon Orange Glaze over top letting it run down sides of cake and decorate with freshly grated carrot.

ORANGE GLAZE

MAKES 1 CUP GLAZE

1½ cups unsifted confectioners' sugar	2 to 3 tablespoons fresh orange juice
1 tablespoon soft butter or margarine	

1. In small bowl, beat confectioners' sugar with butter and vanilla. Beat in enough orange juice to make a slightly runny glaze.

CRUNCHY BUMPY
MUNCHY COOKIES

MAKES 18 COOKIES

¾ cup solid all-vegetable shortening

¾ cup granulated brown sugar, or ¾ cup light brown sugar, packed

1 egg

½ cup cider or apple juice

1 teaspoon pure vanilla extract

1 cup unsifted all-purpose flour

1 teaspoon salt

½ teaspoon baking soda

1 cup coarsely grated carrot

1 package (5¾ ozs.) milk-chocolate morsels

2 cups quick or old-fashioned oats, uncooked

1½ cups ready-to-eat flaked cereal or crisp rice cereal

½ cup raisins

1 cup confectioners' sugar

1½ to 2 tablespoons water

1. Preheat oven to 375°F. Grease cookie sheets.

2. In large bowl beat shortening and brown sugar together with electric mixer.

3. Add egg, cider and vanilla and beat until smooth.

4. Sift flour, salt and baking soda together. Gradually add to brown-sugar mixture, beating at low speed. Scrape sides of bowl with scraper.

5. With large cooking spoon stir in remaining ingredients, except confectioners' sugar and water.

6. Spoon 2 heaping tablespoons dough for each cookie onto greased cookie sheet. With back of spoon flatten to a 3½-inch circle. Allow 2 inches between cookies for spreading.

7. Bake for 15 minutes. Remove from oven, place on rack; let cool one minute before removing from cookie sheet.

8. Continue spooning and baking cookies until all are baked. Grease cookie sheet after each baking.

9. Frost if desired when cool. In small bowl combine 1 cup confectioners' sugar and 1½ to 2 tablespoons water smoothly. Drizzle on cookies in spiral fashion.

April

The air has a certain lightness now, and the sun, though still timid, is more friendly. A sudden shower freshens the ground and the air and the buds unfold daily while the grass grows greener.

The arrival of seasonal foods—spring lamb and tender, green asparagus—is a welcome change. The light taste of fish and seafood pleases the palate, too.

Taking meat loaves a step beyond, we explore the world of pates and terrines.

Looking out of doors, we know it is time to plan our vegetable garden. Remembering what did well last year, what were family favorites and what we have room for will all influence our scheme. Our feature, Plan Your Summer Vegetable Garden, is a helpful aid.

The Vegetable of the Month is elegant asparagus. Great served by itself, it always lends a special touch to other foods.

Plan Your Summer Vegetable Garden

VARIETY	OUTDOOR PLANTING DATE	WHERE	NUMBER OF PLANTS
Sweet Corn	Late May, 2 to 3 week intervals to July 1st.	Open Sunny Site Light, Sandy, Fertile	12 plants
Cabbage *spring *summer & red *winter & savory	Late Summer Very Early Spring Late Spring, Early Summer	medium light soil	6 plants
Carrots	Mid Spring to Mid Summer	Full sun deep, light loam	14 plants
Celery	Late Spring, Early Summer	Sunny, Open	6 plants
Cucumbers	Late Spring, Early Summer	Sunny, Open	3 plants
Eggplant	Late Spring	Sunny site, drained rich soil	4 plants

DISTANCE BETWEEN ROWS	SOWING TO HARVEST	COOKING	PRESERVES
9 to 12 inches	9 to 14 weeks	on cob, roast in husk, steamed, corn fritters, corn pudding, soups	corn relish, frozen corn, canned corn
9 to 12 inches	11 to 13 weeks	slaw, stir-fry, boiled, steamed, cabbage rolls, soups	relish, sauerkraut, frozen
9 to 12 inches	14 to 18 weeks	raw, glazed, steamed, baked, soups, stews, cakes	freeze, can, pickle
12 inches	6 to 8 months	raw, steamed, soups, stews, stir-fry	pickles, relish
3 feet	10 to 14 weeks	raw, salads, sauteed, soups	pickles
3 feet	8 to 11 weeks	casseroles, fried, stews, salads	pickles

VARIETY	OUTDOOR PLANTING DATE	WHERE	NUMBER OF PLANTS
Green beans	Late Spring	Sunny site, rich, light soil	10 plants
Peppers	Late Spring	Sunny site, rich, well-drained	4 plants
Leeks	Early Spring	Light, moist soil	10 plants
Lettuce	Early Spring	Sunny, moist, well drained soil	10 heads
Onions	Early Spring	Sunny site, fertile light soil	12 plants
Potatoes	Middle Spring	Generally good soil	12 plants
Pumpkin	Late Spring	Rich, fertile soil	2 plants
Spinach	Spring	Light, rich soil	8 plants
Zucchini	Late Spring	Full sun, rich heavy soil	6 plants

DISTANCE BETWEEN ROWS	SOWING TO HARVEST	COOKING	PRESERVES
6 inches	6 to 7 weeks	raw, steamed, sauteed, soups	pickles
24 inches	8 to 11 weeks	raw, sauteed casseroles, soups	freezing, relishes
2 feet	23 weeks	steamed, marinated, soups	frozen
12 to 15 inches	8 to 14 weeks	salads, garnishes	———
1 foot	14 to 23 weeks	salads, soups, stews, casseroles	pickles, relishes
1 foot	13 to 17 weeks	salads, soups, stews, casseroles, baked goods	———
3 feet	11 to 17 weeks	steamed, soup, baked goods, pies	———
1 foot	6 to 8 weeks	steamed, salads, casseroles	———
2 feet	7 weeks	steamed, sauteed stews, casseroles	pickles, relishes

Spring Lamb

ROAST SPRING LAMB WITH HERBS

MAKES 6 TO 8 SERVINGS

2 tablespoons fresh, frozen or dried chopped chives
1 clove garlic, crushed
1 bay leaf
Salt
½ teaspoon basil leaves
½ teaspoon rosemary leaves
½ teaspoon tarragon leaves
Freshly ground black pepper
1 cup dry white wine or chicken broth
2 tablespoons lemon juice

¼ cup olive oil or vegetable oil
1 6-lb. oven-ready leg of lamb
Water
3 tablespoons all-purpose flour
½ teaspoon liquid gravy seasoning
Few twists freshly ground black pepper
½ teaspoon salt, optional
½ lb. white onions, cooked
8 potatoes, cooked

1. In small bowl combine chives, garlic, bay leaf, ½ teaspoon salt, basil, rosemary, tarragon, ⅛ teaspoon pepper, white wine, lemon juice and oil.

2. Wipe meat with damp paper towels, place in large heavy-duty plastic bag. Pour marinade over meat. Seal bag with twister. Refrigerate lamb overnight, turning once to marinate evenly.

3. Preheat oven to 325°F. Remove lamb from marinade, place on rack in a shallow roasting pan. Insert a meat thermometer in thickest part, away from bone.

4. Roast, basting several times with reserved marinade: about 20 to 25 minutes per pound for pink lamb (internal temperature: 150-155), and about 30 to 35 minutes per pound for well-done lamb (internal temperature: 175-180).

5. Remove lamb to heated serving platter, cover with foil, keep warm.

6. Make gravy: Pour off all drippings from roasting pan into a 2-cup measuring cup. Skim off fat, discard. Pour ¼ cup drippings into 1-qt. saucepan, add water to remaining drippings to make 2 cups liquid.

7. Blend flour into ¼ cup drippings smoothly. Gradually stir in reserved 2 cups liquid. Bring to boiling, stirring. Add liquid gravy seasoning, a few twists of pepper from pepper mill, stir. Taste, add ½ teaspoon salt if necessary. Pour into hot gravy boat, serve with lamb.

GRILLED MINTED LEG OF LAMB

MAKES 8 SERVINGS

1 cup dry white wine
¼ cup finely chopped fresh
   mint leaves or 2 teaspoons
   dried mint leaves
2 cloves garlic, crushed

1 teaspoon salt
½ teaspoon coarsely ground
   black pepper
Butterflied leg of lamb

1. Combine marinade ingredients in large shallow glass or ceramic container.

2. Place lamb in marinade, turning to coat both sides. Cover with plastic film; marinate in refrigerator for about 3 to 4 hours. Turn lamb once during marinating time.

3. Remove lamb from marinade. Grill about 4 inches from medium-hot coals for about 15 minutes per side for medium doneness.

4. Brush occasionally with marinade during grilling. To check for doneness, make a small cut in thickest part of meat.

5. Place grilled lamb on cutting board. Slice crosswise in ¼-inch-thick slices.

Editor's Note: To butterfly, select a 7- to 8-lb. leg of lamb. Have your butcher remove the bone and flatten the leg so that it's roughly the same thickness throughout and resembles a steak.

GREEK-STYLE LEG OF LAMB

MAKES 8 SERVINGS

2 cloves garlic, crushed
¼ cup lemon juice
¼ teaspoon coarse ground
black pepper
¼ teaspoon ground or crushed
anise seed

1 cup (½ pt.) plain yogurt
1 leg of lamb (6 to 7 lbs.)
boned, trimmed and
butterflied

1. Combine all marinade ingredients in large, shallow, glass baking pan. Dip lamb in marinade, coating both sides. Marinate, covered, in refrigerator several hours or overnight.
2. Preheat oven to 500°F.
3. Place lamb in shallow baking pan. Roast for 30 minutes. Baste with marinade. Turn and roast 15 minutes longer. Outer thin parts of lamb will be well done. Thick portions will be slightly pink.
4. Slice thinly on diagonal.

LAMB STEW PICASSO

MAKES 6 SERVINGS

2 lbs. lamb stew meat, cut in
2-inch pieces
¼ cup all-purpose flour
1 teaspoon salt
¼ teaspoon freshly ground
black pepper
¼ cup olive oil
1 cup beef broth
2 medium green peppers,
chopped
½ teaspoon marjoram leaves

3 cloves garlic, crushed in a
garlic press or minced
1 lb. potatoes, pared and
sliced
2 medium onions, sliced
1 cup chopped celery
2 medium tomatoes, cut in
wedges
1 cup pimiento-stuffed olives
Seasoned all-purpose flour,
optional
Water, optional

1. Coat lamb pieces with a mixture of the next three ingredients.
2. Heat olive oil in a large skillet; add lamb and brown evenly on all sides. Add beef broth slowly, then stir in the green pepper, marjoram, and garlic. Cover and cook over low heat 30 minutes.
3. Add potatoes, onions, and celery; cook, covered, about 10 minutes, or until potatoes are tender. Mix in the tomatoes and olives; heat thoroughly.
4. If a thicker stew is desired, blend in a mixture of seasoned flour and water, bring to boiling, and cook 1 to 2 minutes longer.

SHISH KEBAB

MAKES 10 TO 12 SERVINGS

4 to 4½ lbs. boneless lamb cubes
Rind from 1 lemon, cut in large pieces
¼ cup lemon juice
½ cup olive oil or vegetable oil
2 tablespoons finely chopped parsley
4 cloves garlic, crushed
1 tablespoon salt
1 tablespoon coriander seeds, crushed, or 1½ teaspoons ground coriander

1 teaspoon whole black peppercorns, crushed
¼ teaspoon crushed red pepper
4 large hard-ripe tomatoes, quartered
4 green peppers, quartered, seeded and deribbed
4 medium onions, quartered
Olive oil or vegetable oil
Salt
Freshly ground black pepper
10 to 12 lemon wedges

1. Place lamb cubes in shallow glass pan. Sprinkle lamb with lemon rind, lemon juice, ½ cup olive oil, parsley, garlic, salt, coriander, black pepper and red pepper. Turn lamb cubes in marinade ingredients to coat evenly. Cover with plastic wrap, refrigerate all day or overnight.

2. Thread lamb cubes on 10 to 12 skewers, about 5 per skewer. Drizzle remaining marinade on cubes.

3. Thread tomatoes, peppers and onions alternately on separate skewers. Sprinkle with oil, salt, pepper.

4. Broil skewered lamb and vegetables on broiler rack or on grill about 4 inches from source of heat 8 minutes; turn and grill 3 to 5 minutes on second side for medium-well-done lamb. Watch carefully. Vegetables will cook faster than lamb, remove when done.

5. Arrange skewers on heated platter garnished with lemon. Serve with bulgur pilaf or rice.

Fish and Seafood

BAKED STUFFED CLAMS

¾ cup butter or margarine
½ cup chopped celery
½ cup chopped onion
½ cup chopped parsley
1 cup chopped boiled ham
1 can (10½ ozs.) minced clams, undrained
1 package (8 ozs.) herb-seasoned stuffing mix
½ teaspoon seasoned salt
¼ teaspoon thyme leaves
¼ teaspoon freshly ground black pepper
Dash celery seed
½ cup grated Parmesan cheese
1 can (10¾ ozs.) cream of mushroom soup

1. Preheat oven to 350°F.
2. In large skillet, melt butter. Stir in celery, onion and parsley; cook for 5 minutes.
3. In large bowl, mix butter-celery mixture, boiled ham, clams, stuffing mix, seasoned salt, thyme, pepper, celery seed, Parmesan cheese and mushroom soup.
4. Spoon into 24 scrubbed clam shells. (Or shape 24 pieces of heavy-duty foil into 2½- x 2½-inch shell shapes and fill.) Bake for 15 minutes.

PACIFIC COAST KING CRAB

MAKES 8 SERVINGS

1 lb. frozen Alaska King Crab or 2 cans (7½-oz. size) Alaska King Crab
2 cucumbers
1 teaspoon salt
Crisp salad greens
Green Goddess Dressing (recipe below)

1. Defrost and drain frozen crab or drain canned crab. Cut whole-leg pieces of crab into chunks and coarsely slice remaining crab. Chill.

2. Thinly slice cucumbers and place in shallow bowl. Sprinkle with salt and refrigerate one hour.

3. To serve: Line stemmed glasses with salad greens. Arrange cucumber slices and crab in center. Serve with Green Goddess Dressing.

GREEN GODDESS DRESSING

MAKES 1½ CUPS

1 cup mayonnaise
2 anchovy fillets, minced
1 green onion, finely chopped
1 tablespoon chopped chives

2 tablespoons chopped parsley
1 teaspoon tarragon leaves, crumbled
2 tablespoons tarragon vinegar

1. Combine all ingredients in small bowl. Refrigerate covered at least 1 hour, to blend flavors.

SHRIMP CREOLE

MAKES 8 SERVINGS

2 lbs. medium, cleaned shrimp
6 cups water
1 teaspoon salt
½ teaspoon hot pepper sauce
2 ribs celery with leaves, broken
⅓ cup butter or margarine
3 cups cooked, diced ham
1 cup chopped onion
1 cup chopped green pepper

1 clove garlic, minced
1 bay leaf
¼ teaspoon thyme leaves
2 cans (1-lb. size) tomatoes
1 can (14 ozs.) chicken bouillon
1 teaspoon salt
½ teaspoon hot pepper sauce
Hot cooked rice
1 cup chopped scallions

1. First cook shrimp: Combine water, 1 teaspoon salt, ½ teaspoon hot pepper sauce and celery in a large saucepan. Bring to a boil. Add shrimp, return to a boil and cook 3 to 5 minutes, uncovered. Drain, set aside.

2. Make Creole sauce: In same saucepan, melt butter, add ham and brown lightly, stirring. Add onion, green pepper, garlic, bay leaf and thyme. Cook, stirring occasionally, 5 minutes.

3. Stir in tomatoes, bouillon, remaining 1 teaspoon salt and ½ teaspoon hot pepper sauce. Quickly bring mixture to a boil. Reduce heat, cover and simmer 20 minutes.

4. Add shrimp; cover and cook 10 minutes longer.

5. To serve: Keep Creole sauce warm in chafing dish.

6. Serve over hot cooked rice; sprinkle with chopped scallions.

BAKED WHOLE STUFFED FISH

MAKES 4 TO 6 SERVINGS

⅓ cup oil
⅓ cup finely chopped onion
3 cups (¼ inch) stale bread cubes, about 5 slices
1 cup chopped celery, ribs and leaves
¼ cup finely chopped parsley
1 tablespoon lemon juice
2 tablespoons hot water
½ teaspoon salt
¼ teaspoon freshly ground black pepper
1 (3 to 5 lbs.) whole fish (striped bass, bluefish, red snapper, carp, lake trout), rinsed and cleaned
2 teaspoons oil
Parsley sprigs
Lemon wedges
Carrot slice

1. Heat ⅓ cup oil in medium skillet. Add onion and cook, stirring, about 5 minutes.

2. Add bread cubes and stir until coated with oil. Remove from heat. Add celery, parsley, lemon juice, water, salt and pepper; mix well.

3. Preheat oven to 500°F. Line 15- x 10- x 1-inch baking pan with foil and oil lightly.

4. Place fish in pan. Stuff body cavity with dressing. Close with wooden toothpicks. Brush fish lightly with 2 teaspoons oil.

5. Bake 5 minutes on rack in middle of oven. Reduce heat to 400°F. and continue baking 40 to 65 minutes (allowing 12 minutes per pound), until fish flakes easily with fork.

6. With two large spatulas, remove from baking pan to heated serving platter or wooden plank. Garnish with parsley sprigs and lemon. Cover fish eye with carrot slice. Serve immediately.

FLOUNDER ROLLS FLORENTINE

MAKES 6 SERVINGS

2 tablespoons butter or margarine
2 tablespoons chopped onion
1 package (10 ozs.) frozen chopped spinach, thawed
2 tablespoons all-purpose flour
2 tablespoons fine dry bread crumbs or wheat germ
½ cup (2 ozs.) shredded Swiss cheese
1 teaspoon salt

⅛ teaspoon hot pepper sauce
6 flounder fillets (2 lbs.), fresh or frozen, thawed
1 can (10¾ ozs.) condensed cream of mushroom soup
⅛ teaspoon hot pepper sauce
2 tablespoons butter
2 tablespoons fine dry bread crumbs or wheat germ
Parsley sprigs
Lemon wedges

1. Preheat oven to 375°F. Lightly grease a shallow 2-qt. baking dish.
2. Melt 2 tablespoons butter in medium saucepan. Add onion and spinach; cover and cook 5 minutes. Remove from heat, blend in flour and 2 tablespoons bread crumbs.
3. Cook, stirring, until mixture boils. Remove from heat; stir in cheese, salt and ⅛ teaspoon Tabasco.
4. Place ¼ to ⅓ cup spinach filling in center of each fish fillet and roll up. Place flounder rolls seam side down in baking dish.
5. Mix soup with ⅛ teaspoon hot pepper sauce and spoon over fish, coating well. Melt 2 tablespoons butter, stir in 2 tablespoons bread crumbs. Sprinkle over fish rolls.
6. Bake 25 to 35 minutes, or until fish flakes easily when tested with a fork. Serve garnished with parsley sprigs and lemon wedges.

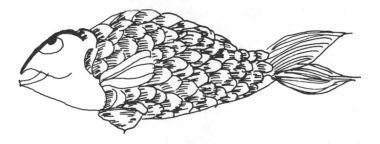

Meat Loaves, Patés and Terrines

MEAT LOAF WELLINGTON

MAKES 8 SERVINGS

1½ lbs. ground chuck
¾ cup fine dry bread crumbs
⅓ cup chopped onion
2 tablespoons ketchup
1 egg, slightly beaten
2 tablespoons milk
1 teaspoon rosemary leaves, crumbled
1 teaspoon Worcestershire sauce
1¼ teaspoons salt
¼ teaspoon freshly ground black pepper

1 can (4¾ ozs.) liverwurst spread
1 can (3 ozs.) chopped mushrooms, undrained
2 tablespoons fine dry bread crumbs
1 package (10 ozs.) pie-crust mix
Cold water
1 egg yolk
1 tablespoon cold water

1. Preheat oven to 350°F. In large mixing bowl, combine ground chuck, ¾ cup bread crumbs, onion, ketchup, egg, milk, rosemary, Worcestershire, salt and pepper; blend well.

2. On sheet of waxed paper, shape meat into a 7- x 4-inch rectangle. Place loaf on a baking sheet; bake for 40 minutes. Cool for 25 minutes, until just warm.

3. Meanwhile in a small bowl, combine liverwurst spread with drained chopped mushrooms (save liquid for Sauce) and 2 tablespoons bread crumbs; set aside.

4. Prepare pie-crust mix according to package directions and divide into two parts, one slightly larger.

5. Roll smaller piece of dough into a rectangle 2 inches wider and longer than cooled meat loaf. Place on foil-lined baking sheet.

6. Place meat loaf on bottom crust. Spread surface of meat loaf with liverwurst mixture. Set oven at 400°F.

7. Roll out remaining dough into a rectangle large enough to cover top and sides of meat loaf. Cover meat loaf with top crust. Seal edges together smoothly with cold water. Trim edges of crust as necessary. Prick surface and decorate as desired with pastry flowers.
8. Combine egg yolk with 1 tablespoon cold water and brush entire crust with glaze.
9. Bake for about 20 to 25 minutes, or until crust is golden brown.

SAUCE FOR MEAT LOAF WELLINGTON
MAKES ABOUT 2 CUPS

2 envelopes (¾-oz. size) brown gravy mix	¾ cup dry red wine
Liquid from mushrooms	¼ teaspoon rosemary leaves, crushed
1¼ cup water	

1. Make up brown gravy mix as package label directs except use mushroom liquid, water, wine and rosemary in quantities given above.
2. Bring to boiling, stirring. Add additional wine or water if too thick. Season to taste.

MEAT LOAF MAGNIFIQUE
MAKES 8 SERVINGS

1½ lbs. ground beef	2 tablespoons butter or margarine
1 lb. bulk pork sausage	1 cup sliced mushrooms
2 cups raisin or white bread crumbs	1 can (10½ ozs.) condensed cream of mushroom soup, undiluted
½ cup chopped mushrooms	
¼ cup chopped parsley	⅓ cup white wine
½ cup sour cream	2 lbs. new potatoes, cooked
1 egg, slightly beaten	Chopped parsley, for garnish
⅓ cup white wine	
½ cup sliced mushrooms	

1. In large bowl, combine beef, sausage, crumbs, chopped mushrooms, parsley, sour cream, egg and ⅓ cup of the wine; blend thoroughly.
2. Place ½ cup of the sliced mushrooms in bottom of greased 8-cup ring mold. Spoon meat mixture over mushrooms. Bake in 350°F. oven for 1 hour.
3. About 10 minutes before meat loaf is done, melt butter in saucepan and add 1 cup sliced mushrooms. Cook, stirring until lightly browned.
4. Blend in soup and ⅓ cup wine smoothly and heat, stirring occasionally, until hot. Serve with meat loaf and potatoes. Garnish with a little sprinkle of parsley.

COPPERMINE COUNTRY PATE

MAKES 6 SERVINGS

1 qt. chicken stock
1 rib celery, diced
2 sprigs parsley, minced
6 whole peppercorns
12 ozs. duck or chicken livers, diced
½ medium onion, minced
2 cloves garlic, minced
½ teaspoon ground nutmeg
Pinch cayenne
2 teaspoons ground mustard
¼ teaspoon ground cloves
1 tablespoon cognac
1 lb. sweet butter, softened
Lettuce leaves
Small gherkins

1. Heat chicken stock to boiling. Add celery, parsley and peppercorns; simmer for 7 minutes.
2. Add duck livers, onion and garlic; simmer 5 minutes. Strain; reserve stock.
3. Blend vegetables and livers in food processor or blender until mixture is like a paste. Add nutmeg, cayenne, mustard, cloves and cognac. Mix well. Add a little reserved stock if necessary.
4. Blend softened butter with the liver paste blended above; when all the butter is absorbed, place in buttered mold and chill. Serve in slices on a lettuce leaf with small gherkins.

QUICK LIVER PATE

MAKES 2 CUPS

1 package (8 ozs.) cream cheese, room temperature
1 package (8 ozs.) liverwurst sausage, chopped
2 tablespoons dry sherry
1 teaspoon prepared mustard, preferably Dijon
1 tablespoon parsley, finely chopped
¼ teaspoon basil leaves, finely crumbled
Paraffin

1. In large bowl, with electric mixer, blend cream cheese with liverwurst until smooth.
2. Add sherry, mustard, parsley and basil. Beat until very smooth.
3. Pack into attractive crock. Seal surface with melted paraffin. Allow to cool, then refrigerate.

COUNTRY PATE IN TERRINE

MAKES 12 TO 15 SERVINGS

1 lb. pork liver
1 lb. salt pork
¼ lb. boneless veal or
  chicken
3 large eggs
2 tablespoons butter or
  margarine
1 cup finely chopped onion
1 teaspoon freshly ground
  black pepper
½ teaspoon sage leaves
½ teaspoon thyme leaves

¼ teaspoon ground cloves
⅓ cup all-purpose flour
1¼ cups milk
2 tablespoons brandy or
  sherry
4 strips bacon
  Water
  Parsley sprigs, small
  gherkins
  Thin strips of toast, or
  melba toast

1. Preheat oven to 350°F. Grease 2-qt. casserole or terrine with lid.

2. With sharp knife cut liver into strips. Gradually add liver to food processor with metal chopping blade and grind until a puree.

3. Cut salt pork into strips and add to processor and grind to a puree. Repeat with veal.

4. Add eggs, process until blended.

5. Melt butter in saucepan, add onion and cook stirring until tender, 5 to 8 minutes.

6. Stir pepper, sage, thyme and cloves into onion mixture. Add flour, stir until blended. Add milk and cook, stirring constantly until mixture comes to boiling.

7. Gradually add onion-milk mixture to liver mixture in processor, process until smoothly blended. Add brandy, blend.

8. Pour pate into prepared terrine.

9. Blanch bacon: Heat 2 qts. water in large skillet to boiling, add bacon strips, return to boiling. Remove bacon, drain on paper towels.

10. Place bacon strips on top of pate mixture, covering surface completely. Cover with terrine lid or tightly with foil.

11. Place casserole in large pan, add hot water halfway up sides of casserole. Bake for 1 hour and 45 minutes to 2 hours, or until pate mixture comes away from side of pan.

12. Remove from water bath, remove cover and bacon strips. Place sheet of foil with heavy plate on top to weight down pate.

13. Refrigerate to chill completely, preferably overnight.

14. To serve, turn out of terrine onto serving plate or serve directly from terrine. Garnish with parsley. Serve with gherkins and toast.

WALNUT-GHERKIN TERRINE

MAKES 12 SERVINGS

2 eggs
1 large onion, coarsely
chopped
¾ cup coarsely chopped sweet
gherkins
1 teaspoon salt
⅛ teaspoon freshly ground
black pepper

2 lbs. lean ground beef
1 lb. bulk pork sausage
1 cup coarsely chopped
walnuts
½ cup dry bread crumbs
Whole sweet gherkins
Crisp salad greens, radish
roses

1. Combine eggs, onion, gherkins, salt and pepper in electric blender
or food processor; process until onions and gherkins are finely chopped.
2. Combine with beef, sausage, walnuts and crumbs; mix well.
3. Pack half of mixture in 9- x 5-inch loaf pan. Arrange whole gherkins
down length of pan, pressing them firmly into meat mixture. Top
with remaining meat mixture; press down to pack well.
4. Bake in preheated 350°F. oven 1 hour and 15 minutes. Let stand
15 minutes. Carefully pour out fat. Cover and refrigerate overnight.
5. Turn out onto serving platter, garnish with salad greens, additional
gherkins and radish roses. Cut in slices to serve.

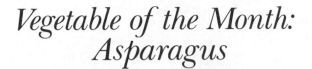

Vegetable of the Month: Asparagus

ASPARAGUS-BUTTERMILK SOUP

MAKES 5½ CUPS

3 cups buttermilk
1 lb. cooked fresh asparagus, undrained, or 1 can (15 or 16 ozs.) asparagus, undrained, or 1 package (10½ ozs.) frozen asparagus, cooked, undrained

½ teaspoon salt
1 tablespoon snipped fresh dillweed or 1½ teaspoons dry dillweed
2 dill pickles, cut in chunks
¼ cup dill-pickle juice
Ice cubes

1. Combine all ingredients, except ice cubes, in large bowl.
2. Blend covered, about 3 cups at a time, in electric blender, 20 to 30 seconds, until smooth.
3. Refrigerate, covered, until serving time. Just before serving, blend again or beat with wire whisk.
4. Pour over ice cubes in soup bowls or glasses.

LEMON-BUTTER ASPARAGUS

MAKES 8 TO 10 SERVINGS

4 packages (10-oz. size) frozen asparagus spears
3 tablespoons butter or margarine

3 tablespoons lemon juice
1 tablespoon butter

1. Cook asparagus according to package directions, drain. Arrange asparagus in serving dish, cover with foil, keep warm.
2. In small skillet heat 3 tablespoons butter until melted, stir in lemon juice, heat to boiling.
3. Pour lemon butter over asparagus. Top with 1 tablespoon butter.

SPRING VEGETABLE POT

MAKES 6 SERVINGS

2 lbs. new potatoes, scrubbed
2 cups water
1 teaspoon salt
¼ teaspoon freshly ground
black pepper
1 lb. asparagus, cleaned

1 lb. mushrooms, rinsed
1 bunch scallions, rinsed
2 tablespoons snipped chives
½ cup butter or margarine,
melted

1. Put potatoes, water, salt and pepper in large saucepan or Dutch oven. Heat to boiling. Cover; reduce heat and simmer 15 minutes.
2. Cut asparagus in thirds, mushrooms in half and scallions in thirds. Add to potatoes. Return to boiling; reduce heat and simmer 10 to 15 minutes longer, until just tender. Do not drain.
3. Add chives to melted butter. Serve Vegetable Pot in bowls with a little butter-and-chive mixture poured over each serving.

BAKED ASPARAGUS
AND FLOUNDER

MAKES 4 SERVINGS

2 lbs. fresh asparagus
½ cup water
¼ teaspoon salt
1½ lbs. fresh or frozen thawed
flounder fillets
2 tablespoons butter or
margarine
¼ cup chopped onions
2 tablespoons all-purpose
flour
1¾ cups milk

¼ cup dry white wine
2 teaspoons fresh lemon
juice
½ teaspoon salt
¼ teaspoon dried dill weed
⅛ teaspoon freshly ground
black pepper
2 tablespoons chopped
parsley
2 tablespoons shredded
Swiss cheese

1. Wash asparagus; shear off large scales with vegetable peeler or paring knife. Cut off woody ends; rinse again.
2. Place asparagus in large skillet; add water and ¼ teaspoon salt. Bring to boiling; reduce heat and simmer, covered, just until tender— about 2 minutes for thin asparagus spears, 3 minutes for medium and 5 minutes for thick. Drain.
3. Divide asparagus into 4 portions, about 8 spears each.
4. Wrap 1 fish fillet around each bundle. Arrange in shallow baking dish.

5. Melt butter in small saucepan. Add onion and cook over medium heat until tender. Blend in flour smoothly. Add milk all at once; heat, stirring constantly, until mixture thickens, then bring to a boil.
6. Remove from heat; stir in wine, lemon juice, ½ teaspoon salt, dill, pepper and parsley. Spoon sauce over fish. Sprinkle with cheese.
7. Cover and bake in preheated 350°F. oven, about 30 to 35 minutes or until fish flakes when tested with a fork.

FLUFFY OMELET A LA SWISS

MAKES 4 SERVINGS

2 tablespoons quick-cooking tapioca
¾ teaspoon salt
⅛ teaspoon freshly ground black pepper
¾ cup milk
1 tablespoon butter or margarine

4 eggs, separated
1 tablespoon butter
1 package (10 ozs.) frozen asparagus spears, cooked and drained
Swiss Sauce, recipe below

1. Preheat oven to 350°F. In small saucepan combine tapioca, salt, pepper and milk. Cook, stirring, over medium heat until mixture boils.
2. Remove from heat, add 1 tablespoon butter. Allow to cool slightly.
3. In medium bowl, beat egg yolks until thick and lemon colored. Stir in milk mixture.
4. In large bowl, with clean beaters, beat egg whites until they hold stiff peaks. Lightly fold egg-yolk mixture into beaten whites.
5. Melt 1 tablespoon butter in 10-inch oven-proof skillet. Add omelet mixture. Cook 3 minutes over low heat.
6. Continue cooking in oven about 15 minutes until well puffed. Omelet is done when a knife inserted in center comes out clean.
7. Cut across omelet at right angles to pan handle, but don't cut through. Slide onto serving plate. Top one half with asparagus, fold other half over. Pour some sauce over top. Pass remaining sauce in separate bowl.

SWISS SAUCE

MAKES 2 CUPS SAUCE

1 can (10¾ ozs.) cream of mushroom soup
⅓ cup milk

1 cup cubed leftover turkey, chicken or ham
¼ cup shredded Swiss cheese

1. Blend all ingredients in a saucepan.
2. Heat, stirring, until cheese melts.

ASPARAGUS QUICHE

MAKES 1 (9-INCH) QUICHE,
6 TO 8 SERVINGS

12 to 15 asparagus spears,
   trimmed
   Boiling water
¼ teaspoon salt
½ cup grated process Gruyère
   cheese
  1 cup grated Swiss cheese

4 eggs
2 cups light cream
1 teaspoon salt
⅛ teaspoon ground nutmeg
¼ teaspoon freshly ground
   black pepper

1. Preheat oven to 425°F. Line a 9-inch pie pan with pastry and flute edges.

2. Cook asparagus in ½ inch of boiling water with ¼ teaspoon salt for 5 minutes until just tender. Drain well.

3. Spread cheeses evenly in pastry crust. Place asparagus in pie pan like the spokes of a wheel, tips at perimeter.

4. Beat together eggs, light cream, 1 teaspoon salt, nutmeg and pepper. Pour over cheese and asparagus.

5. Bake about 40 minutes until puffed and golden. Cool 5 minutes before cutting into wedges.

May

The soft warm days of May burst forth, surrounding us with an array of flowers: tulips, lilacs, azaleas, dogwood and more.

We feel more alive and want our whole body to reflect that aliveness. It's time to trim calories to get in shape for summer sunning. Our Feature of the Month is a diet menu planner with fresh ideas to lighten our calorie intake at everyday meals.

Look further and you'll find just what you've been looking for: slim line main dishes, salads and desserts, all calorie-trimmed and appetizing recipes.

The Vegetable of the Month is crisp, low-calorie celery, destined to be used in many ways.

Slimming Meals for Summer Sunning

BREAKFAST	LUNCH
COTTAGE CHEESE AMBROSIA MELBA TOAST COFFEE TEA	TOMATO JUICE CRISP 'N' CRUNCHY TUNA SALAD SLICE WHOLE WHEAT BREAD ICED TEA
¼ CANTALOUPE 1 POACHED EGG 1 SLICE TOAST 1 TEASPOON BUTTER OR MARGARINE COFFEE TEA	MEDITERRANEAN GARDEN SALAD 1 SLICE PROTEIN BREAD FROZEN ORANGE GELATO
GRAPEFRUIT JUICE OPEN GRILLED SWISS CHEESE ON ONE SLICE BREAD COFFEE TEA	TUNA SALAD NICOISE PEPPER BREAD STICKS FRUIT CUP ICED TEA
TOMATO JUICE PLAIN YOGURT WITH SLICED BANANA AND BRAN 1 TABLESPOON HONEY COFFEE TEA	SALMON ROLL-UPS WITH CUCUMBER SAUCE 1 MEDIUM ORANGE SLICED ICED TEA OR RED WINE SPRITZER
ORANGE JUICE MEDIUM BRAN MUFFIN 1 SLICE CHEDDAR CHEESE COFFEE TEA	COTTAGE CHEESE VEGETABLE SALAD BLUSHING YOGURT DRESSING ¼ CANTALOUPE COFFEE TEA

DINNER	SNACKS
BROILED LEAN GROUND BEEF PATTY BRAISED CELERY WEDGES SMALL BOILED POTATO COFFEE TEA	1 MEDIUM APPLE
SPICED BEEF MACE SQUASH CUBES MASHED CAULIFLOWER LETTUCE AND TOMATO SALAD	GLASS BUTTERMILK OR SKIM MILK
QUICK LEMONY SAUTEED LIVER WATERCRESS STEAMED ZUCCHINI LIGHT 'N' LEMONY CHEESECAKE	RIBS OF CELERY
MARINATED FLANK STEAK PLAIN BOILED RICE (½ cup) GRAPEFRUIT AND AVOCADO SALAD COFFEE TEA	¼ CUP SEEDLESS GRAPES
TARRAGON 'N' THYME CHICKEN PLAIN NOODLES (½ cup) STEAMED ASPARAGUS LEMON VANILLA YOGURT BAVARIAN	3 PITTED READY-TO-EAT PRUNES

Diet and Nutrition Chart

KNOW YOUR "BASIC FOUR" FOOD PLAN

(It's the Easy Way to a Balanced Menu!)

1. MEATS

Importance: Basic source of protein.

Amounts recommended: Two or more servings per day of 2-3 ozs. of lean cooked meat, poultry, fish, shellfish and eggs. Alternate with 1 cup cooked dry beans, dry peas or lentils, or 4 tablespoons peanut butter. One egg may replace one-half serving of meat.

2. FRUITS AND VEGETABLES

Importance: Basic source of **vitamin C** (citrus; fresh strawberries; broccoli; brussels sprouts; peppers) and **vitamin A** (dark-green, orange and deep-yellow vegetables).

Amounts recommended: Four or more servings every day, including one serving of a good source of vitamin A. The remaining servings may be of any other vegetable or fruit.

3. DAIRY PRODUCTS

Importance: Source of bone-building calcium; vitamin A and vitamin D.

Amounts recommended: Children under 9: 2-3 glasses milk; children 9-12: 3 or more glasses; teenagers: 4 or more glasses; adults: 2 or more glasses.

Milk products such as cheese, ice cream or yogurt may replace part of the milk directly or in cooking. One cup of whole fluid milk equals 1 cup plain yogurt or 1½ cups cottage cheese or three scoops of ice cream, or 2 1-inch cubes of hard cheese (Cheddar, etc.) are interchangeable.

4. BREADS AND CEREALS

Importance: Carbohydrates (for energy); B vitamins; calcium.

Amounts recommended: Four servings or more daily. Count as one serving: 1 slice of whole grain or enriched bread; 1 oz. ready-to-eat cereal; ½-¾ cup cooked cereal, cornmeal, grits, barley, macaroni, etc.

OTHER FOODS:

To fill out meals and to get needed energy, almost everyone will use some foods not specified in the four food groups. Such foods include unenriched, refined breads, cereals, flours, sugars, butter, margarine or other fats. These are often ingredients in a recipe or added to other foods during preparation or at the table. Try to include some vegetable oil among the fats used. Also, a quart of liquid a day is a minimum, to be taken in the form of water, coffee, tea, soft drinks, fruit juices and so forth.

HOW MANY CALORIES DO YOU BURN UP?

SEDENTARY ACTIVITIES	CALORIES PER HOUR
Reading; sewing; watching television	80 to 100
LIGHT ACTIVITIES	
Preparing food; doing dishes; ironing; office work	110 to 160
MODERATE ACTIVITIES	
Making beds; mopping and scrubbing; light carpentry work; walking moderately fast	170 to 240
VIGOROUS ACTIVITIES	
Heavy scrubbing and waxing; walking fast; bowling; golfing and gardening	250 to 350
STRENUOUS ACTIVITIES	
Swimming; tennis; running; bicycling; playing football	350 and more

WHAT SHOULD YOU WEIGH?

An approximate guide to what an adult should weigh is his weight at age 25 if he was in good physical shape.

The United States Department of Agriculture says a person who leads a moderately active life needs 15 calories per pound every day. So look at a height-weight chart and find out how much you should weigh for your sex, body-build and age. Multiply by 18 for a man, by 16 for a woman, and the answer is the number of calories you need to keep that weight.

If you want to lose weight, figure how many pounds you want to lose in a week. (Two pounds a week is the USDA suggested limit for a safe rate of loss.) There are 3,500 calories in a pound of fat. So if you want to lose two pounds a week, you have to cut back 7,000 calories, or 1,000 calories a day.

Slim Line Salads

MEDITERRANEAN GARDEN TRAY

MAKES 8 SERVINGS

1 large head lettuce
1 bottle (8 oz.) low-calorie
  Italian Dressing
1½ cups cooked shrimp
1½ cups sliced fresh
  mushrooms
1½ lbs. fresh asparagus, cooked
1 can (1 lb.) garbanzos,
  drained
½ cup each ripe and

pimiento-stuffed green
  olives
1 package (9 ozs.) frozen
  artichoke hearts, cooked
Thin onion rings
½ small cucumber, sliced
1 cup cherry tomatoes
Radish roses
Carrot curls
Yogurt Vegetable Dressing
(recipe below)

1. Core, rinse and thoroughly drain lettuce; chill in disposable plastic bag or plastic crisper.
2. Add about 3 to 4 tablespoons Italian Dressing to each of the following and let chill about 1 hour; shrimp, mushrooms, asparagus, garbanzos, olives and artichoke hearts combined with onion rings.
3. Shortly before serving, remove outer leaves of lettuce and line tray.
4. Cut remaining head lengthwise into halves. Place cut sides down; cut each half into thirds or quarters for 6 or 8 thin wedges and arrange on separate tray or in bowl. Cover with plastic wrap and refrigerate until serving time.
5. Drain shrimp and vegetables, saving marinade. Arrange marinated shrimp and vegetables on tray, along with cucumber slices, cherry tomatoes, radishes and carrot curls. Serve with Yogurt Vegetable Dressing.

Approximate calorie count: 1,304 total; 163 per serving.

YOGURT VEGETABLE DRESSING

MAKES ABOUT 1½ CUPS

Low-calorie Italian dressing drained from vegetables
1 cup plain low-fat yogurt
¼ cup each chopped green pepper and pimiento

1 tablespoon each chopped green onion and parsley
1 teaspoon sugar
½ teaspoon seasoned salt
¼ teaspoon seasoned pepper

1. Gradually beat the dressing into the yogurt.
2. Add green pepper, pimiento, onion and parsley, and mix well.

COTTAGE CHEESE VEGETABLE SALAD

MAKES 6 SERVINGS

6 crisp lettuce leaves or cups
2 cups cottage cheese
1 medium cucumber, peeled and thinly sliced
¼ lb. fresh mushrooms, sliced

1 medium zucchini, cut in strips
2 medium tomatoes, cut in 12 wedges
Blushing Yogurt Dressing (recipe below)

1. Arrange lettuce leaves on serving platter, leaving space in center.
2. Divide cottage cheese and place a small mound in center of each lettuce leaf. Arrange cucumber, mushrooms, zucchini and tomatoes around cottage cheese.
3. Place small bowl of Blushing Yogurt Dressing in center.

Approximate calorie count: 101 per serving without dressing.

BLUSHING YOGURT DRESSING

MAKES ABOUT 1¼ CUPS

½ cup plain yogurt
½ cup corn oil
3 tablespoons ketchup
1 teaspoon salt

¼ teaspoon paprika
½ teaspoon dry or liquid low-calorie sweetener

1. Combine all ingredients in blender, cover. Blend 20 to 30 seconds, until smooth. Or combine ingredients in jar, cover tightly and shake well.

Approximate calorie count: 46 calories per tablespoon.

CRISP AND CRUNCHY TUNA SALAD

MAKES 4 SERVINGS

1 envelope unflavored gelatin
1 can (10½ ozs.) condensed beef consommé or beef bouillon, undiluted
2 large nicely shaped green peppers
½ cup coarsely chopped onion
1 can (7 ozs.) solid white tuna, packed in water, drained and flaked
¾ cup seeded coarsely chopped tomato
1 cup finely shredded, coarsely chopped iceberg lettuce
½ teaspoon grated lemon rind
4 teaspoons lemon juice
½ teaspoon seasoned salt
Freshly ground black pepper
4 crisp lettuce leaves
4 teaspoons sour cream
4 lemon wedges

1. In 2-qt. saucepan, sprinkle gelatin over consommé; let stand 5 minutes to soften.

2. Cut peppers in half crosswise, to form shells; carefully remove core and seeds. Bring consommé to boiling; add pepper shells, cut-side up. Cover and boil 3 minutes; peppers will be bright green but still crisp.

3. Remove shells; turn upside down a moment to drain; then refrigerate.

4. Bring consommé back to boiling, add onion and boil for 30 seconds only. Pour into a bowl set over ice and water to chill until thick but not set. Takes about 30 to 35 minutes.

5. Add tuna, tomato, iceberg lettuce, lemon rind, lemon juice, seasoned salt and few twists of pepper from pepper mill to thickened consommé; toss lightly to mix well.

6. Fill each pepper shell with mixture, piling high. (Mixture will hold its shape if consommé is thickened enough.) Chill.

7. To serve, place peppers on crisp lettuce leaves, garnish with 1 teaspoon sour cream and lemon wedge each. Serve with crisp rye wafers.

Approximate calorie count: total calories 460; 115 calories for 1 serving.

MARINATED VEGETABLE SALAD

MAKES ABOUT 7 CUPS

1 can (10½ oz.) condensed chicken broth
1½ cups sliced carrots
2 cups cauliflowerets
2 cups diagonally sliced zucchini

1 cup sliced mushrooms
¼ cup wine vinegar
1 envelope (about 6 ozs.) Italian salad-dressing mix

1. In qt. saucepan bring chicken broth to boiling. Add carrots, return to boiling, reduce heat and simmer covered, 2 minutes. Pour into bowl, cool to room temperature.

2. Stir in remaining ingredients, toss to mix well. Cover with plastic wrap or foil. Refrigerate 3 to 4 hours.

3. To serve: Place in attractive serving bowl, serve with wooden picks. Or arrange ½ cup drained vegetables on lettuce leaf and serve as an individual salad.

Approximate calorie count: 346.75.

TUNA SALAD NICOISE

MAKES 4 SERVINGS

1 head lettuce, washed and chilled
2 cans (6½- or 7-oz. size) tuna in water, drained
2 medium potatoes, peeled and sliced
1 tablespoon bottled diet French or Italian dressing
½ lb. whole, cooked green beans

2 hard-cooked eggs, quartered
2 tomatoes, quartered
8 ripe olives
½ can (2 ozs.) rolled anchovies, drained
1 red onion, sliced or chopped
Pimiento strips
Bottled diet French or Italian dressing

1. Line a large platter with lettuce leaves. Break tuna into large chunks and pile in center. Toss potatoes with 1 tablespoon dressing. Arrange potatoes, green beans, eggs, tomatoes and olives around tuna.

2. Decorate with anchovies, red onion and pimiento strips. Cover and refrigerate until serving time. Serve with bottled diet French or Italian dressing to which you have added ½ teaspoon tarragon leaves and 1 teaspoon drained capers for each ½ cup of dressing.

Approximate calorie count: 287 per serving.

GRAPEFRUIT AND AVOCADO SALAD

MAKES 6 SERVINGS

2 avocados, peeled, pitted and sliced
2 tablespoons lemon juice
1 medium head curly chicory, washed and torn
3 endives, washed and separated into leaves

2 medium grapefruit, peeled and sectioned
2 small tomatoes, cut in wedges
12 pitted black olives
Vinaigrette Dressing (recipe below)

1. Sprinkle avocado slices with lemon juice.
2. Arrange greens in salad bowl and top with avocado slices, grapefruit sections, tomato wedges and olives.
3. Just before serving, toss gently with a little Vinaigrette Dressing.
Approximate calorie count: 286 per serving.

VINAIGRETTE DRESSING

MAKES ¾ CUP

4 tablespoons tarragon vinegar
1 tablespoon finely chopped onion
½ teaspoon thyme leaves, crushed
½ teaspoon savory leaves, crushed

½ teaspoon ground mustard
1 teaspoon salt
Freshly ground black pepper
½ cup plus 2 tablespoons olive oil

1. Combine vinegar, onion, thyme, savory, dry mustard, salt and pepper in small bowl.
2. Using a wire whisk, add oil slowly, beating constantly until dressing is smooth and thick.

Slim Line Main Dishes

CURRIED CHICKEN SOUFFLÉ

MAKES 6 SERVINGS

1 tablespoon fine dry bread crumbs
¼ cup margarine
2 tablespoons finely chopped onion
½ teaspoon curry powder
⅓ cup flour
1 can (10½ ozs.) chicken broth, undiluted
¼ teaspoon salt
Dash freshly ground black pepper

¼ cup finely chopped green pepper or 2 tablespoons snipped chives
1½ cups chopped cooked chicken or 2 cans (5-oz. size) boned chicken, drained and chopped
1 cup frozen cholesterol-free egg substitute, thawed
3 egg whites, room temperature

1. Preheat oven to 375°F. Oil a 2-qt. soufflé dish and sprinkle with bread crumbs.
2. Heat margarine in 1-qt. saucepan until melted. Add onion and curry powder. Sauté, stirring frequently, 5 minutes.
3. Remove from heat, stir in flour smoothly. Gradually add broth. Heat to boiling, stirring constantly with wire whisk.
4. Stir in salt, pepper, green pepper and chicken; cool 5 minutes. Blend in egg substitute.
5. Beat whites until stiff, but not dry. Fold lightly into mixture. Pour into soufflé dish.
6. Bake 50 to 55 minutes, until well-puffed and golden brown.

Approximate calorie count: 245 per serving.

TARRAGON 'N' THYME CHICKEN

MAKES 8 SERVINGS

2 (2½- to 3-lb. size) broiler-
   fryer chickens, quartered
2 teaspoons salt
¼ teaspoon freshly ground
   black pepper
2 teaspoons tarragon leaves
½ teaspoon ground thyme

3 tablespoons lemon juice
2 tablespoons tarragon
   vinegar
2 tablespoons chopped
   parsley
Thin slices lemon
Parsley sprigs

1. Preheat oven to 375°F. Rinse chicken in cold water, pat dry with paper towels.
2. Place chicken, skin-side up, in shallow foil-lined baking pan. Sprinkle with salt, pepper, tarragon, thyme, lemon juice and tarragon vinegar.
3. Cover tightly with foil. Bake 40 minutes. Remove foil and bake 20 to 25 minutes longer, until fork-tender.
4. To serve: Remove chicken to heated platter. Pour pan juices over chicken. Sprinkle with chopped parsley. Garnish with lemon slices and parsley sprigs.

Approximate calorie count: total calories, 1,359; calories per serving, 169.8.

SPICED ROAST OF BEEF

MAKES 10 SERVINGS

1¾ cups wine vinegar
1 cup vegetable oil
1 can (8 ozs.) tomato sauce
4½ teaspoons salt
2 teaspoons ground mustard
1½ teaspoons celery seed
¾ teaspoon thyme leaves
1 teaspoon freshly ground
   black pepper
¾ teaspoon ground cloves
¾ teaspoon garlic powder

5 lbs. bottom round or top
   round of beef
¾ cup mixed vegetable flakes
½ cup instant minced onion
2 bay leaves
¾ teaspoon thyme leaves
1 cup water
¼ cup water, optional
   Mushroom Gravy (recipe
   below)

1. In medium bowl combine vinegar, vegetable oil, tomato sauce, salt, powdered mustard, celery seed, ¾ teaspoon thyme, pepper, cloves and garlic powder; mix well.
2. Wipe meat with damp paper towels, place in heavy-duty plastic bag. Pour marinade over meat, seal with twister, refrigerate 16 hours or

longer. (For safety's sake, place bag in large pan in case plastic tears.) Turn meat once or twice to marinate evenly.

3. Approximately 3 hours before serving, remove meat from refrigerator. Let stand 1 hour at room temperature.

4. Preheat oven to 300°F. Scatter vegetable flakes, onion, bay leaves and ¾ teaspoon thyme in bottom of roasting pan. Pour 1 cup water over vegetables.

5. Remove meat from marinade. Place on top of vegetables. Pour ¾ cup marinade over meat, discard rest. Insert meat thermometer into thickest part of beef.

6. Roast uncovered for approximately 2 hours, or until temperature of meat registers 140°F. for rare or 160°F. for medium. Add ¼ cup more water to vegetables if they dry out.

7. Remove meat to heated serving platter. Cover with foil and keep warm. Prepare Mushroom Gravy from pan drippings. Serve approximately ¼ cup gravy per portion.

Approximate calorie count: total calories, 3,260; 326 per portion without gravy; 377 calories per portion with gravy.

MUSHROOM GRAVY
MAKES 2½ CUPS GRAVY

Pan drippings from Spiced
Roast of Beef
Water
½ lb. fresh mushrooms, rinsed
and sliced, or 1 can (6 to 8
ozs.) sliced mushrooms

1 tablespoon margarine or
butter
1 tablespoon all-purpose flour
Salt, optional

1. Scrape pan drippings, including vegetables, into a 1-qt. measure. Add water, or canned mushroom liquid plus sufficient water, to make 2½ cups.

2. Pour into 1-qt. saucepan and bring just to boiling. Strain. Skim off fat and measure 2 cups of liquid. Discard fat and vegetables.

3. In same saucepan heat margarine until melted, remove from heat. Stir in flour until smooth. Gradually add reserved liquid, stirring. Bring to boiling, stirring constantly. Add mushrooms and boil slowly, uncovered, 10 minutes, stirring occasionally.

4. Taste for seasoning, add salt if necessary. Pour gravy into heated gravy boat, serve with meat.

Approximate calorie count: total calories, 510; 51 calories per ¼ cup.

MARINATED FLANK STEAK

MAKES 6 SERVINGS

1½ to 2 lbs. flank steak
¼ cup sesame seed
¼ cup corn oil
¼ cup soy sauce
¼ cup dark corn syrup
2 tablespoons dry sherry

1 small onion, sliced
1 clove garlic, crushed, or ⅛ teaspoon garlic powder
¼ teaspoon freshly ground black pepper
¼ teaspoon ground ginger

1. Trim steak of excess fat. Cut steak diagonally ⅛-inch deep to score. Snip narrow end of meat to prevent curling.
2. Stir remaining ingredients together.
3. Place steak in marinade, turning to coat both sides. Cover with foil or plastic wrap and refrigerate several hours or overnight. (You may also use a heavy-duty plastic bag to marinate steak. Fill bag with marinade, add steak. Close securely. Place bag in pan to prevent any spills, refrigerate as above.)
4. Preheat broiler if necessary. Place steak on broiler rack and broil 6 inches from source of heat, turning once. Broil about 5 minutes first side and 3 minutes second side, a total of 8 minutes for medium rare.
5. Place steak on serving platter or board and slice thinly on the diagonal, across grain of meat.

Approximate calorie count: 200 to 225 calories per serving.

QUICK LEMONY SAUTÉED LIVER

MAKES 6 SERVINGS

¼ cup corn oil
½ cup sliced onion
1½ lbs. beef liver, sliced (½ inch thick), cut into 2- x ½-inch strips

½ teaspoon salt
Few twists freshly ground black pepper
2 tablespoons lemon juice
¼ cup finely chopped parsley

1. Heat oil in large skillet. Add onion and sauté until golden, about 5 to 8 minutes. Remove to paper towel, cover.
2. Add liver to skillet and sauté quickly over medium-high heat, stirring frequently, until browned on both sides. (Takes about 5 minutes.) Season with salt and pepper.
3. Sprinkle with lemon juice and parsley, toss. Arrange on serving platter, top with onions.

Approximate calorie count: 260 per serving.

SALMON ROLL-UPS WITH CUCUMBER SAUCE

MAKES 4 SERVINGS

4 thin fillets of flounder or sole (2¾-ozs. each, approximately 9-inches long)
½ teaspoon salt
½ teaspoon paprika
2 teaspoons capers, drained
1 tablespoon chopped pimiento
½ teaspoon salt

1 tablespoon finely chopped onion or 1½ teaspoons instant minced onion, rehydrated
½ teaspoon grated lemon rind
1 tablespoon plus 1 teaspoon lemon juice
1 can (7¾ ozs.) salmon, drained and flaked
Cucumber Sauce (recipe below)

1. Preheat oven to 400°F. Season fillets on both sides with ½ teaspoon salt and paprika.
2. Turn fillets dark side up; sprinkle with capers and pimiento. Combine ½ teaspoon salt, onion, lemon rind, lemon juice and flaked salmon. Mound 3 tablespoons of the mixture on each fillet.
3. Roll up, jelly-roll style; place in shallow baking dish. Cover with lid or aluminum foil. Bake at 400°F. for 10 minutes; uncover and bake 15 minutes longer. Top each serving with 1 or 1½ tablespoons Cucumber Sauce.

CUCUMBER SAUCE

MAKES ⅔ CUP, ABOUT 4 SERVINGS

⅓ cup peeled, seeded, coarsely grated cucumber
¼ cup imitation sour cream or sour cream
1 tablespoon finely chopped onion or 1½ teaspoons instant minced onion, rehydrated

½ teaspoon salt
½ teaspoon grated lemon rind
1½ teaspoons lemon juice
3 tablespoons finely chopped parsley

1. In small bowl, combine all ingredients. Refrigerate; serve cold.

Approximate calorie count for Roll-ups with Sauce: total calories, 720; 180 calories per serving.

Slim Line Desserts

FRUIT CUP

MAKES 2 SERVINGS

1 cup grapefruit sections
½ cup melon balls
¼ cup sliced strawberries

¼ cup halved green grapes or
blueberries
¼ teaspoon ground ginger
1 tablespoon sugar

1. In medium bowl, combine all ingredients. Cover and refrigerate.

Approximate calorie count: 75 per serving.

VANILLA-YOGURT BAVARIAN

MAKES 6 SERVINGS

1 envelope unflavored gelatin
½ cup skim milk
1 cup (½ pt.) vanilla yogurt
2 teaspoons pure vanilla
extract

2 egg whites, room
temperature
2 tablespoons sugar
Vanilla Poached Pears with
Strawberries (recipe below)

1. In a small saucepan combine gelatin and milk. Cook over low heat, stirring constantly until gelatin is dissolved.
2. Remove from heat; stir in yogurt and vanilla extract. Pour into bowl, cover. Refrigerate until slightly thickened.
3. In small bowl, beat egg whites until soft peaks form. Add sugar gradually, beating until stiff. Fold whites into gelatin mixture.
4. Pour mixture into a 4-cup mold, cover with plastic wrap or foil, refrigerate until firm.
5. Unmold on chilled plate and serve with Vanilla Poached Pears with Strawberries. Garnish with sliced strawberries if desired.

Approximate calorie count: total calories, 405; 67.5 calories for 1/6 of Vanilla-Yogurt Bavarian.

106

VANILLA POACHED PEARS
WITH STRAWBERRIES

MAKES 6 SERVINGS

2 cups water
1 tablespoon lemon juice
1 tablespoon no-calorie liquid
food sweetener

4 pears, hard-ripe, peeled,
cored and quartered
1 tablespoon pure vanilla
extract
1 cup sliced fresh strawberries

1. In a 3-qt. saucepan, combine water, lemon juice and sweetener. Bring to boiling point.
2. Add pears; cover and simmer about 10 to 12 minutes, or until pears are tender. Add the vanilla extract.
3. Pour into bowl, cover with plastic wrap or foil, refrigerate.
4. Just before serving, stir in strawberries.

Approximate calorie count: total calories, 317; 52.8 calories per serving.

FROZEN ORANGE GELATO

MAKES 10 SERVINGS, ½ CUP EACH

1 envelope unflavored gelatin
½ cup sugar
½ cup instant nonfat dry-milk
solids
2 cups skim milk
1 tablespoon grated orange
rind

6 tablespoons frozen orange-
juice concentrate, thawed,
undiluted
2 egg whites
Mint sprigs, optional

1. Combine gelatin, sugar and dry-milk solids in 1-qt. saucepan. Stir in milk.
2. Place over low heat; stir constantly until gelatin dissolves, 5 to 8 minutes; remove from heat. Pour into freezer tray or shallow pan and freeze until firm.
3. Break up with fork and turn into chilled bowl. Add orange rind, undiluted orange-juice concentrate, and egg whites.
4. Beat at high speed with electric mixer until mixture is smooth. Return to freezer tray and freeze until firm.
5. Allow to stand at room temperature about 5 to 7 minutes before serving. Garnish with mint sprigs if desired.

Approximate calorie count: total calories, 900; 90 calories per ½ cup serving.

ORANGE PARADISE

MAKES 12 SERVINGS,
½ CUP EACH

1 envelope unflavored gelatin
½ cup cold water
1 can (6 ozs.) frozen orange-juice concentrate, thawed, undiluted
1 tablespoon no-calorie liquid food sweetener

2 egg whites, room temperature
¼ cup sugar
½ cup instant nonfat dry-milk solids
½ cup ice water
Mint sprigs, optional
Orange sections, optional

1. Sprinkle gelatin over water in small saucepan. Place over low heat; stir constantly until gelatin dissolves, 2 to 3 minutes; remove from heat.

2. Reserve 1 tablespoon undiluted orange-juice concentrate for beating with whipped milk; add the rest with liquid sweetener to dissolved gelatin and stir until melted. Pour into bowl, cover. Refrigerate, stirring occasionally until mixture thickens and mounds slightly.

3. Beat egg whites until soft peaks form; gradually add sugar and beat until stiff. Fold into orange mixture. In same mixing bowl combine dry-milk solids and ice water. Using the same beater, beat until soft peaks form, 3 to 4 minutes. Add reserved 1 tablespoon undiluted orange-juice concentrate.

4. Continue beating until firm peaks form, 3 to 4 minutes longer. Fold into orange mixture. Spoon into small dessert dishes or demitasse cups, piling the mixture high. Refrigerate until set.

5. Serve garnished, if desired, with mint sprigs and orange sections.

Approximate calorie count (without garnish): total calories, 684; 57 calories per ½ cup serving.

LIGHT 'N' LEMONY CHEESECAKE

MAKES 1 (8-INCH) CAKE,
8 TO 12 SERVINGS

2 envelopes unflavored gelatin
½ cup cold skim milk
1 cup skim milk, heated to boiling
2 teaspoons grated lemon rind
3 tablespoons lemon juice
2 tablespoons no-calorie liquid food sweetener

1 teaspoon pure vanilla extract
2 eggs, separated
¼ teaspoon salt
3 cups (24 ozs.) partially creamed cottage cheese
¼ cup sugar
⅓ cup graham cracker crumbs
¼ teaspoon ground cinnamon
⅛ teaspoon ground nutmeg

1. Sprinkle gelatin over cold milk in blender container, allow to soften.
2. Add boiling milk; cover and process 35 to 60 seconds, until gelatin dissolves.
3. Add lemon rind, lemon juice, liquid sweetener, vanilla, egg yolks and salt; cover and blend at high speed 1 minute.
4. Add cottage cheese, one cup at a time, blending (covered) after each addition until smooth. Pour into large bowl; cover and refrigerate about 30 minutes, stirring occasionally, until mixture mounds slightly when dropped from a spoon.
5. Beat egg whites until stiff but not dry; gradually add sugar and beat until very stiff. Fold into gelatin mixture.
6. Combine graham cracker crumbs with spices; sprinkle 3 tablespoons of mixture over bottom of 8-inch springform pan. Slowly pour gelatin mixture into pan. Sprinkle remaining crumbs over top. Chill until firm. Refrigerate after serving.

Approximate calorie count: total calories, 1,141; 95 calories for 1/12 of cake and 71.3 calories for 1/16 of cheesecake.

Vegetable of the Month: Celery

CELERY ANTIPASTO

MAKES 8 SERVINGS

2 stalks celery
1 chicken bouillon cube
¾ cup boiling water
⅓ cup olive oil
2 garlic cloves, crushed
2 cans (2-oz. size) anchovy
  fillets, drained and chopped
1 can (4 ozs.) pimientos,
  drained, and cut into strips

¼ cup finely chopped parsley
2 tablespoons wine vinegar
⅛ teaspoon freshly ground
  black pepper
Lemon wedges
Black olives
Carrot slices

1. Remove celery leaves and trim stem ends from each stalk, keeping base intact.
2. Cut stalks into 6-inch lengths. (Reserve tops for soups, stews, garnishing.) Cut each stalk into quarters lengthwise.
3. Place celery in large skillet. Dissolve bouillon cube in water; pour over celery.
4. Cover and simmer 10 minutes or until celery is just crisp-tender. Drain and arrange on platter.
5. Meanwhile, in small skillet heat oil; add garlic and gently sauté, stirring, 5 minutes. Do not brown.
6. Stir in anchovies, pimientos, parsley, vinegar and pepper. Heat thoroughly; pour over celery.
7. Garnish with lemon wedges, black olives and carrot slices.

110

BRAISED FRUITED CELERY

MAKES 6 SERVINGS

2 tablespoons butter or margarine
3 cups diagonally sliced celery
⅓ cup chopped onion
1 large apple, peeled, cored and diced
½ cup golden seedless raisins or seedless grapes
½ teaspoon ground ginger
½ teaspoon salt
⅛ teaspoon freshly ground black pepper
½ cup water

1. In a large skillet, melt butter. Add celery and onion; sauté for 5 minutes.

2. Stir in apple, raisins, ginger, salt, pepper and water. Heat to boiling, cover, reduce heat and simmer until celery is just crisp-tender, about 3 to 5 minutes, stirring occasionally. Add more water if necessary. Good with roast pork, chicken or ham.

BRAISED CELERY WEDGES

MAKES 8 SERVINGS

2 stalks celery, washed
1 chicken-bouillon cube or 1 envelope instant chicken bouillon
1¼ cups boiling water
1 teaspoon onion powder
⅛ teaspoon salt
Dash ground white pepper
1 tablespoon diced pimiento

1. Cut celery stalks crosswise about 6 inches from the base. (Save tops of stalks for between-meal munching, soups or garnishes.)

2. Cut each stalk lengthwise into 4 wedges. Arrange celery wedges in a large skillet.

3. Dissolve bouillon in water. Add to skillet along with onion powder, salt and white pepper. Bring to boiling point, reduce heat, cover and simmer 12 to 15 minutes, or until celery is just crisp-tender.

4. Arrange celery wedges in serving dish. Scatter pimiento over celery and serve. (Leftover celery may be served cold.)

LOW-CALORIE GREEK YOGURT DIP

MAKES 1¾ CUPS

1 medium cucumber, peeled
1 cup plain yogurt, chilled
1 clove garlic, crushed
2 tablespoons finely chopped
  parsley

¼ teaspoon salt
Few twists freshly ground
  black pepper
Crisp ribs of celery, chilled

1. Finely chop or shred cucumber. Combine cucumber with yogurt, garlic, parsley, salt and pepper. Cover and refrigerate 1 to 2 hours to let flavor develop.
2. Use as a dip for celery ribs or as a salad dressing.

PEANUT BUTTER AND CELERY SNACKS

MAKES ABOUT 24 SMALL SERVINGS

1 stalk celery
1⅓ cups (12 ozs.) chunky or
  creamy peanut butter

½ cup coarsely grated carrots
2 tablespoons raisins

1. Trim tops from celery (use in soup, stews, etc.); separate into ribs, rinse.
2. Cut each rib into 3-inch lengths.
3. In medium bowl, combine peanut butter, carrots and raisins. Use mixture to spread on celery.

June

Oh, the wonder and golden warmth of June. With the scent of roses combined with honeysuckle, it has always been a nostalgic time of the year—a month of graduations, commencements, reunions, showers and weddings.

Parties are the order of the day from breakfasts, brunches, lunches, receptions and dinners. We can all find ourselves caught up in the flow, one way or another, if we want to extend ourselves to others.

Party-planning is easy with our selection of tempting main dishes, delicious salads and sandwiches and glorious desserts.

Our Vegetable of the Month is the familiar green bean. Plain or fancy, green beans are a delight.

Spring and Summer Party Menus

BUFFETS	APPETIZER	SALAD	SOUP	MAIN COURSE
Shower	Golden Cheese Spread Crackers	Sliced Tomatoes Watercress	Fresh Tart Fruit Soup	Ham and Cheese Crepes
Reception	Shrimp Canapes Parmesan Onion Thins Seafood Stuffed Mushrooms	Avocado Festival Salad	Jamaican Squash Soup	Beef Bourguignon
Brunch	Assorted Juices and Drinks	Sangria Mold Fresh Fruit		Eggs Benedict or Cheese Strata
Garden Party	King Crab Pacific Coast	Vegetable-Juice Aspic Carib		Polynesian Chicken Curry

VEGETABLE	ACCOM-PANI-MENTS	BREAD	DESSERTS	BEVERAGE
Lemon Butter Asparagus	Pear Marmalade	Assorted Rolls	Frozen Lemon Dessert	Rose Wine Coffee Tea
Baked Carrots Julienne	Rice Pilaf	French Bread	Golden Blossoms Cake	Citrus Sparkle Punch Coffee
Basket of Fresh Vegetable Sticks	Quick Orange Marmalade	Basket of Bread Sticks	Fresh Fruit Kuchen Cinnamon Walnut Coffeecake	Sparkling Burgundy Coffee
Savory Green Beans and Red Peppers	Fresh Fruit Pickles Curry Accompaniments	Hot Herb Bread	Strawberry Cheese Cake	Sangria Coffee

Party Main Dishes

HAM AND CHEESE CREPES

MAKES 16 (8-INCH) CREPES

Crepe Batter:
4 tablespoons melted butter
½ teaspoon salt
1 cup cold water
1 cup milk

4 eggs
2 cups sifted all-purpose flour
2 tablespoons cognac, brandy,
sherry, cider or apple juice
Vegetable oil for frying

1. Combine all ingredients in electric blender and blend, covered, until thoroughly mixed. Scrape down sides of blender, cover and blend again until batter is completely smooth.
2. Cover and refrigerate overnight or at least 2 hours. Batter should coat a spoon. If too thick add a slight bit of water.
3. Lightly coat bottom of 8-inch skillet with vegetable oil; heat until hot, but not smoking. Spoon in about 4 tablespoons batter to lightly coat bottom of pan, cook until golden brown on bottom, turn and cook second side quickly.
4. Stack browned crepes with wax paper between. Crepes may be made in advance, securely wrapped (airtight) and frozen until ready to fill.

Filling:
½ cup butter
½ cup sifted all-purpose flour
2 cups light cream
2 cups cubed cooked ham
2 cups cubed natural Swiss
cheese

2 cans (4-oz. size) sliced
mushrooms, undrained
½ teaspoon salt
¼ teaspoon freshly ground
black pepper

1. In medium saucepan, melt butter on medium heat, remove from heat. Stir in sifted flour smoothly.
2. Gradually add light cream, stir until smooth. Cook, stirring until sauce thickens and comes to a boil.

116

January

A trio of pasta favorites with old-country flavor: Manicotti American Style (page 11), Deep Sea Chowder (page 56) and Three Cheese Noodle Casserole (page 6). *(Photo by Gus Francisco/Alan Baillie.)*

February

Hearty, heartwarming Northwestern Bean Cassoulet (page 34), fragrant with herbs and spicy sausage,
makes a great dish for a winter buffet. *(Photo by Willard
Purvis.)*

March

The joy of Easter abounds in this festive holiday dinner
featuring Glazed Ham with Rosé Pears (page 61), Noodles
Romanoff (page 13) and Lemon-Butter Asparagus (page
87). *(Photo by Willard Purvis.)*

April

Roast Spring Lamb with Herbs (page 74) is a succulent choice for a special dinner party. *(Photo by Bill Margerin.)*

May

Watching calories can be fun when this beautiful Mediterranean Garden Salad (page 96) is on the menu. *(Photo by Elmer Moss.)*

June

June is certainly the time to make all the prettiest party foods imaginable: Chocolate Pastry Dessert (page 126), Coffee Charlotte Dessert (page 125), Citrus Sparkle Punch with Strawberry Sherbert (page 282) and Golden-Blossoms Cake (page 130). *(Photo by Walter Storck.)*

July

The fruits of summer temptingly preserved include:
Brandied Desert Fruits (page 152), Santa Rosa Jam and
Jelly (page 154), Grapevine Preserves (page 155),Spiked
Peach Jam (page 154), Peachy-Plum Pie (page 151), Vine-
land Vinegar (page 153), Fresh Fruit Pickles (page 153),
Solar Plum Leather (page 156), Polynesian Papaya Mar-
malade (page 156) and Spirited Raisins (page 157). *(Photo
by Fred Lyon.)*

August

A summer salad showcase that's sure to please are these four beauties: Starburst Lettuce Salad (page 159), Fresh Fruit Hawaiian Salad (page 148), Genoa Potato Salad (page 240) and Avocado Festival Salad (page 158). *(Photo by Larry Lubeck.)*

September

Stick-to-the-ribs dishes for hungry camper appetites: Chuck Wagon Favorite Stew (page 207), Pan Biscuits (page 207), Skillet Pintos (page 206) and Basque Soup (page 205). *(Photo by William Holland.)*

October

Cooking for the fair is an American tradition. Our recipes include: Brandied Peaches (page 234), Wine Jelly (page 272), Sweet Cherry Marmalade (page 233), Energy Saver Bars (page 238), Chocolate Surprise Squares (page 235), Aunt Mattie's Maple Joys (page 238), Genuine Dill Pickles (page 232) and Anadama Bread (page 239). *(Photo by Bob Scott Studio.)*

November

A Thanksgiving feast with our favorite foods: Spit-Roasted Turkey (page 250), Uncooked Cranberry-Apple Relish (page 14), Old-Fashioned Pumpkin Pie (page 262) and Cornmeal Spoon Bread (page 228). *(Photo by Walter Storck.)*

December

A memorable Christmas dinner, resplendent with the nostalgia of Currier and Ives: Herbed Standing Rib Roast (page 288), Yorkshire Pudding Puffs (page 288), Tomato Cups with Mushrooms and Peas (page 289), Trifle (page 182) and Orange-Vanilla Liqueur (page 276). *(Photo by Rupert Callender.)*

3. Add ham, Swiss cheese, mushrooms, salt and pepper; heat, stirring, just until cheese is almost melted.

4. To assemble, spoon about ¼ cup filling in center of each crepe, roll and place seam side down in lightly oiled shallow baking dish. Continue filling and rolling until all crepes are filled.

5. Coat crepes with topping. Cover and refrigerate if not serving immediately.

6. To serve, heat, covered, in preheated 350°F. oven for 45 minutes. Place under broiler, 4 inches from heating element, and broil for 3 to 5 minutes until topping is golden brown.

**MAKES ABOUT 6 CUPS FILLING,
ENOUGH FOR 16 (8-INCH) CREPES**

Topping Sauce:
- 2 tablespoons butter
- 2 tablespoons all-purpose flour
- 2 cups light cream
- 2 tablespoons red wine*
- ½ cup shredded natural Swiss cheese

Dash salt
Dash freshly ground black pepper
1 cup shredded natural Swiss cheese
2 to 4 tablespoons water, optional

1. In 1-qt. saucepan, heat butter until melted, remove from heat and stir in flour smoothly. Gradually add cream, return to heat and cook, stirring constantly until mixture thickens and comes to a boil.

2. Stir in wine, ½ cup Swiss cheese, salt and pepper. Simmer, stirring just until cheese melts.** Pour sauce over crepes.

3. Sprinkle 1 cup Swiss cheese over crepes.

**MAKES 3 CUPS TOPPING SAUCE,
ENOUGH FOR 16 (8-INCH) CREPES**

* Or use sherry or cider.
** If sauce is too thick, add 2 to 4 tablespoons water.

ORANGE MOLASSES GLAZED HAM

MAKES 12 TO 14 SERVINGS

2 canned hams (3 lbs. each) or
1 canned ham (7 lbs.)
¾ cup dark molasses
¾ cup orange juice
½ cup apricot preserves

2 teaspoons prepared mustard
½ teaspoon ground allspice
Orange sections and
watercress for garnish

1. Place ham on rack of shallow roasting pan. With knife, score surface. Bake according to label directions or at 325°F., about 20 minutes per pound.
2. In blender combine molasses, orange juice, preserves, mustard and allspice. Cover and blend until smooth.
3. Arrange orange sections down center of ham. Spoon glaze over ham several times during the last half hour of baking.
4. Remove ham to heated platter. Garnish with additional orange sections and watercress. Heat any remaining glaze and serve as sauce

TURKEY AND HAM CASINO

MAKES 12 SERVINGS

1 cup chopped onion
1 cup chopped green pepper
¼ cup butter or margarine
½ cup unsifted all-purpose
flour
2 cups milk
1¾ cups chicken broth
¼ cup dry sherry
1 can (4 ozs.) sliced
mushrooms, drained
2 cups coarsely chopped
cooked turkey

2 cups coarsely chopped
canned ham
½ cup diced pimientos
1 can (8 ozs.) water
chestnuts, drained and
sliced
1 teaspoon salt
¼ teaspoon freshly ground
black pepper
6 to 8 cups hot cooked rice

1. In 4- to 6-qt. Dutch oven, sauté onion and green pepper in hot butter until tender. Add flour all at once and blend in smoothly.
2. Add milk, broth and sherry. Cook, stirring constantly, until mixture begins to boil.
3. Add mushrooms, turkey, ham, pimientos, water chestnuts, salt and pepper.
4. Heat until mixture comes to boiling point. Reduce heat and simmer 5 minutes.
5. Pour Casino mixture into serving dish or chafing dish. Serve mixture over beds of rice.

POLYNESIAN CHICKEN CURRY

MAKES 6 TO 8 SERVINGS

3 or 4 large chicken breasts,
  split
¼ to ½ cup butter or
  margarine
1 tablespoon curry powder
1¼ cups unsweetened
  pineapple juice
¼ cup honey
¼ cup ketchup
1½ teaspoons salt
¼ teaspoon garlic powder
1 tablespoon cornstarch
¼ cup unsweetened
  pineapple juice

1 green pepper, seeded and
  cut in chunks
1 cup halved cherry
  tomatoes
½ cup salted cashews
  Oven-Steamed Rice
  (recipe below)
6 strips crisp-cooked bacon,
  diced
1 cup chopped scallions
1 cup flaked coconut
1½ cups chutney

1. In large skillet, sauté chicken in butter until golden brown. Drain excess fat and reserve 1 tablespoon. Stir in curry powder.
2. Add 1¼ cups pineapple juice, honey, ketchup, salt and garlic powder. Heat to boiling, cover, reduce heat and simmer for 25 to 30 minutes until chicken is tender.
3. Remove chicken to a heated serving platter and keep warm.
4. Combine cornstarch with ¼ cup pineapple juice, and stir into pan juices until sauce boils and thickens.
5. Add green pepper, tomatoes and cashews. Heat throughout, then spoon sauce over chicken.
6. Serve with hot cooked rice. Pass bacon, green onion, coconut and chutney as accompaniments in separate bowls.

OVEN-STEAMED RICE

MAKES 6 TO 8 SERVINGS

1½ cups raw converted
  white rice
1½ teaspoons salt
  Dash freshly ground black
  pepper

2 tablespoons butter or
  margarine
3½ cups boiling water

1. Preheat oven to 350°F.
2. In a 1½-qt. ungreased casserole with tight-fitting lid, combine rice, salt and pepper. Dot top with butter.
3. Pour boiling water over all, stir to melt butter.
4. Cover and bake for 45 minutes (don't peek, don't stir). To serve, fluff up lightly with fork.

SWEDISH MEATBALLS

MAKES 50 MEATBALLS, 3½ CUPS GRAVY

2 to 6 tablespoons butter or margarine
1 cup very finely chopped onion
2 cups tiny fresh bread cubes
¼ cup fine dry bread crumbs
2 eggs
¾ cup milk
2 teaspoons salt
½ teaspoon ground white pepper
¼ teaspoon ground allspice
¼ teaspoon sugar
1 lb. lean ground chuck
1 lb. ground pork

2 to 4 tablespoons solid all-vegetable shortening
¼ cup unsifted all-purpose flour
1 pt. half-and-half
1 can (10½ ozs.) beef consommé, undiluted
¼ cup water
½ teaspoon salt
¼ teaspoon ground white pepper
½ teaspoon liquid gravy seasoning
2 tablespoons water or milk
2 tablespoons chopped parsley

1. In medium skillet, slowly heat 2 tablespoons butter until melted. Stir in onion and sauté 5 minutes over medium heat, stirring frequently.
2. In large bowl combine sautéed onion, bread cubes, bread crumbs, eggs, milk, 2 teaspoons salt, ½ teaspoon pepper, allspice and sugar. Beat with mixing fork or large wire whisk until well blended.
3. Add meat to seasoning mixture and stir well, until smoothly combined. (For final mixing, your own well-scrubbed hands do a fine job!) Cover, refrigerate about 1 to 2 hours, until thoroughly chilled. (Chilling makes shaping meatballs easier.)
4. Using about 1 tablespoon of meat mixture, shape into ball about 1½ inches in diameter.
5. In medium skillet slowly heat 2 tablespoons butter and 2 tablespoons shortening until hot. Fry meatballs, 7 or 8 at a time, over medium-high heat, shaking pan frequently to keep round shape for even browning. Remove from pan when meatball feels firm and is cooked through.
6. Continue frying until all are browned. Add butter and shortening to skillet as necessary.
7. Make gravy: Pour off all but ¼ cup pan drippings. Stir flour into pan drippings smoothly. Gradually stir in half-and-half, consommé and water. Bring to a boil, stirring constantly.
8. Season to taste with ½ teaspoon salt, ¼ teaspoon pepper and liquid gravy seasoning.

9. To freeze: Place meatballs in plastic freezer container. Cover securely, label, date, freeze. Pour gravy into 1-qt. freezer container. Cover securely, label, date, freeze.*

10. To serve: Allow meatballs and gravy to thaw in refrigerator 5 to 8 hours.

11. Heat gravy slowly in large skillet, stirring until smooth and bubbly. Add meatballs. Heat to boiling; reduce heat and simmer, covered, 15 to 20 minutes, until heated through. If gravy appears too thick, stir in 2 tablespoons water or milk.

12. Carefully spoon meatballs into casserole or chafing dish. Sprinkle with chopped parsley. Place over candle warmer or other buffet warmer, set on buffet table.

* If serving right away, eliminate steps 9 and 10, and proceed with steps 11 and 12.

Party Sandwiches and Salads

SHRIMP CANAPÉS

MAKES 2 CUPS SPREAD,
32 CANAPÉS

1 lb. frozen, peeled shrimp	1 tablespoon lemon juice
4 tablespoons butter or margarine, softened	2 tablespoons sherry
1 package (8 ozs.) cream cheese, softened	1 teaspoon seasoned salt Dash hot pepper sauce
1½ teaspoons grated lemon rind	32 slices thin party rye bread 32 slices stuffed green olives

1. Cook shrimp as package label directs; drain well.
2. Blend shrimp a little at a time in blender or food processor until finely ground.
3. With electric mixer, blend butter and cream cheese until smooth. Blend in shrimp.
4. Add lemon rind, lemon juice, sherry, seasoned salt and hot pepper sauce. Beat until smooth. (Steps 3 and 4 may be done in food processor.)
5. Using a heaping tablespoon for each canapé, spread shrimp mixture on rye bread. Garnish center with slice of stuffed olive. Serve immediately or cover with plastic film and refrigerate.
6. Shrimp spread can be made day before and canapés assembled just before serving.

COOL CUCUMBER SANDWICHES

MAKES 24 TRIANGULAR SANDWICHES

1 medium cucumber	12 slices thinly sliced white bread, crusts removed
1 teaspoon salt	
½ cup butter or margarine, softened	Ground white pepper Chopped parsley

1. Peel cucumber and slice paper-thin with sharp knife. Toss in small bowl with 1 teaspoon salt. Cover and refrigerate ½ hour. Drain well and dry on paper towels.

2. Spread the butter on the bread. Place a thin layer of cucumber on 6 slices bread. Sprinkle with white pepper and chopped parsley. Top each with a slice of bread. Cut each sandwich diagonally into 4 triangles.

3. Cover with plastic film and refrigerate until serving time.

PEANUT BUTTER-CELERY SANDWICHES

MAKES 6 SANDWICHES

1 cup cream-style peanut butter
½ cup chopped celery

12 slices thinly sliced white bread, crusts removed

1. In small bowl blend the peanut butter and chopped celery.

2. Using about 2 tablespoons mixture per sandwich, make 6 sandwiches. Cut in halves or triangles.

SANGRIA MOLD WITH FRESH FRUIT

MAKES 6 SERVINGS

2 envelopes unflavored gelatin
1 cup cold water
½ cup sugar
3 cups bottled Sangria wine

2 navel oranges, peeled and sliced
1 pt. strawberries, hulled and halved
3 bananas, peeled and sliced
2 peaches, peeled and sliced

1. Sprinkle gelatin over water in 2-qt. saucepan.

2. Place over low heat. Stir constantly until gelatin dissolves, about 5 minutes. Remove from heat.

3. Add sugar; stir until dissolved. Stir in Sangria.

4. Pour into 4-cup mold or bowl or individual dishes. Chill until set.

5. Unmold on attractive serving plate. Garnish with some of the prepared fruit. Serve remaining fruit with Sangria Mold.

VEGETABLE-JUICE ASPIC CARIB

MAKES 7 CUPS, 14 SERVINGS

4 envelopes unflavored gelatin	2½ teaspoons Worcestershire sauce
1 can (1 qt. 14 ozs.) vegetable juice	½ teaspoon hot pepper sauce
¼ cup dill-pickle juice	½ cup lemon juice
1¼ teaspoons salt	Crisp chicory leaves
2¼ teaspoons sugar	Carrot sticks
	Pitted black olives
	Mayonnaise, optional

1. In 2-qt. saucepan sprinkle gelatin over about ⅓ of the vegetable juice. Heat slowly, stirring constantly, until gelatin dissolves (takes 3 to 5 minutes).
2. Add remaining vegetable juice, dill-pickle juice, salt, sugar, Worcestershire sauce, hot pepper sauce and lemon juice; stir to blend.
3. Pour into 2-qt. mold, cover with foil or plastic wrap. Refrigerate 4 to 5 hours or overnight, until thoroughly jelled.
4. Unmold onto attractive serving platter. Surround with chicory leaves. Thread slender carrot sticks through holes in black olives, place here and there on greens. Serve with mayonnaise if desired. Refrigerate before serving.

MIXED GREEN SALAD WITH WALNUT DRESSING

MAKES 6 TO 8 SERVINGS

1 head romaine lettuce, washed and torn	½ cup vegetable oil
2 bunches watercress	½ cup lemon juice
3 heads Boston, Oakleaf or Simpson lettuce	1 teaspoon salt
1 head Belgian endive	¼ teaspoon coarse black pepper
1 cup coarsely chopped walnuts	1 tablespoon grated Romano or Parmesan cheese

1. Wash and dry greens. Combine greens in salad bowl. Sprinkle with walnuts.
2. Make dressing: In bowl, blend oil, lemon juice, salt, pepper and Romano cheese.
3. Pour dressing over greens at table; toss.

Party Desserts

COFFEE CHARLOTTE DESSERT

MAKES 8 TO 10 SERVINGS

2 tablespoons instant coffee powder
¾ cup hot water
32 regular marshmallows, cut in small pieces
2 cups (4½-oz. container) frozen whipped topping, thawed

1 package (3 ozs.) ladyfingers, split
1½ cups (¾ of 4½-oz. container) frozen whipped topping, thawed
1 square unsweetened baking chocolate

1. In medium saucepan, dissolve instant coffee in hot water. Add marshmallows. Stir over low heat until marshmallows are completely melted. Chill until slightly thickened.

2. Fold 2 cups whipped topping into coffee mixture smoothly.

3. Line an 8-inch-square pan with double thickness of wax paper, extending paper above top of pan.

4. Arrange half of ladyfingers in single layer on bottom of pan. Top with half of coffee mixture. Cover with another layer of ladyfingers and top with remaining coffee mixture. Freeze until firm (takes about 2 hours).

5. Overwrap with foil, seal with freezer tape, label, date, return to freezer.

6. To serve: Lift dessert out of pan with wax paper. Carefully remove wax paper from dessert, place on serving platter.

7. Spoon 1½ cups whipped topping into pastry bag with Number 7 star tip. Pipe scallops and rosettes around edge of the dessert. Refrigerate until serving time.

8. To make chocolate curls: Allow chocolate square to soften slightly in warm oven about 2 minutes. Make curls with a vegetable peeler, scraping carefully across surface. Place on dessert.

REGAL ALMOND CAKE

MAKES 1 (10-INCH) CAKE

Butter or margarine
¾ cup sliced almonds
1 tablespoon sugar
¾ cup butter or margarine, softened
1½ cups sugar
1½ teaspoons pure vanilla extract
¼ teaspoon almond extract
1 teaspoon grated lemon rind
3 eggs, separated
2½ cups sifted cake flour
3 teaspoons baking powder
1 teaspoon salt
1 cup milk

1. Preheat oven to 325°F. Generously butter bottom and sides of a 10-inch tube pan; press almonds into butter on both bottom and sides; sprinkle with 1 tablespoon sugar.
2. In large bowl with electric mixer, beat butter until creamy; gradually add sugar, beating until light.
3. Add vanilla, almond extract and lemon rind. Beat in egg yolks and continue beating at high speed until light and fluffy.
4. Sift together flour, baking powder and salt. Add to creamed mixture alternately with milk, beating at low-medium speed after each addition.
5. With clean beaters, beat egg whites until stiff but not dry. Gently fold into batter. Carefully pour into prepared pan.
6. Bake about 1 hour and 10 minutes, or until cake tester inserted in center comes out clean.
7. Let cool in pan about 10 minutes, then invert onto wire rack to cool completely.

CHOCOLATE PASTRY DESSERT

MAKES 8 SERVINGS

1 package (11 ozs.) piecrust mix
2 tablespoons sugar
1 tablespoon water
1 envelope unflavored gelatin
¼ cup water
2 squares unsweetened chocolate
½ cup sugar
⅛ teaspoon salt
1 tablespoon rum or 1 teaspoon pure vanilla extract
4 cups (9-oz. container) frozen whipped topping, thawed
1 tablespoon confectioners' sugar
¼ cup chopped pistachio nuts, walnuts or almonds

1. In medium bowl combine piecrust mix and sugar; prepare piecrust mix with 1 tablespoon more water than directed on package.

2. Place dough directly on outside bottom of 15- x 10- x 1-inch jelly-roll pan. Roll dough to completely cover outside bottom of pan.

3. Preheat oven to 450°F. Measuring across long side of dough mark off 4 sections 3¾ inches wide and 10 inches long. Pierce with fork.

4. Measuring down on one section, mark off eight 1¼ x 3¾-inch strips. Pierce with fork.

5. Bake 8 to 10 minutes. Cool completely on rack. When cool, cut with sharp knife into sections on pierced lines.

6. Combine gelatin and ¼ cup water in saucepan; let stand 5 minutes to soften. Add chocolate, sugar and salt.

7. Stir over low heat until chocolate and sugar are melted. Cool slightly; blend in rum.

8. Spoon whipped topping into a large bowl, fold in gelatin-chocolate mixture thoroughly.

9. Spread 1 cup chocolate mixture over each of two large pastry strips; stack. Top with third large pastry strip.

10. Spoon remaining chocolate mixture into pastry bag with Number 8 star tip. Make 8 rosettes on top of pastry, spacing evenly in pairs.

11. Place pastry on foil-covered cardboard; freeze until firm. Remove from freezer, overwrap with foil, seal with freezer tape, label, return to freezer.*

12. Place small pastry strips on foil-covered cardboard, overwrap with foil, seal with freezer tape, label, date, freeze.

13. About 1½ to 2 hours before serving, remove pastry and pastry strips from freezer. Remove foil, refrigerate about 1½ hours to thaw.

14. When ready to serve, arrange pastry strips on top of pastry between rosettes. Cut 2 pastry strips in half and place lengthwise between rosettes. Sprinkle with confectioners' sugar and chopped nuts.

15. Place on plate. Serve immediately or refrigerate until serving time.

* Or assemble dessert completely without freezing, refrigerate until serving time.

DELICIOUS BUNDT CAKE

MAKES 1 LARGE CAKE

½ cup butter or margarine (1 stick)
½ cup shortening
2 cups sugar
4 eggs, room temperature
1 teaspoon pure vanilla extract
1 teaspoon lemon extract
½ teaspoon almond extract

3 cups sifted all-purpose flour
1 tablespoon baking powder
1 cup milk, room temperature
Confectioners' sugar, optional
Whipped Cream-Apricot Sauce, optional

1. Grease a 3-qt. Bundt pan or 10-inch tube pan. Preheat oven to 325°F. (Set oven at 300°F. if using a Teflon-lined pan.)
2. In large bowl with electric mixer at high speed, beat butter and shortening together. Add sugar gradually, beating until fluffy.
3. Beat in eggs one at a time; scrape sides of bowl frequently. Beat in extracts.
4. Sift flour with baking powder. Add in thirds to creamed mixture alternately with milk, beating at low speed, beginning and ending with flour.
5. Pour batter into prepared pan. Bake for 1 hour and 10 minutes, or until cake tester poked in center comes out clean. Cool in pan 10 minutes, invert onto cake rack and cool completely.
6. Sift confectioners' sugar over surface, if desired; or serve with Whipped Cream-Apricot Sauce (recipe below).

WHIPPED CREAM-APRICOT SAUCE

MAKES 3 CUPS

8 pitted unpeeled apricots, quartered
2 tablespoons pineapple juice

3 tablespoons sugar
1 cup heavy cream, whipped

1. Place apricot quarters and pineapple juice in electric blender container. Blend covered 30 to 60 seconds until smooth (makes about 1¼ cups purée).
2. Add sugar to purée, blend.
3. Fold purée into whipped heavy cream, until just blended. Refrigerate covered, until ready to serve.
4. Serve as a sauce with plain cake.

CINNAMON-WALNUT COFFEE CAKE

MAKES 1 (2-LB.) CAKE

Topping:
½ cup walnuts or pecans
½ cup sugar
1 tablespoon ground
cinnamon

Batter:
½ cup (1 stick) butter, cut in
4 or more pieces
1 cup sugar

1 teaspoon pure vanilla
extract
2 eggs
1 cup sour cream
1½ cups unsifted all-purpose
flour
1½ teaspoons baking powder
1 teaspoon baking soda
⅛ teaspoon salt

1. Make topping: With metal blade in place, add walnuts, ½ cup sugar and cinnamon to bowl of food processor.
2. Process, turning on and off, until mixture is combined and nuts are coarsely chopped. Turn mixture onto sheet of waxed paper.
3. Make batter: Again using metal blade, add butter, 1 cup sugar and vanilla to bowl and process until combined, about 30 seconds.
4. Add eggs and sour cream. Process until thoroughly mixed.
5. Combine flour, baking powder, baking soda and salt. Stir to mix, then add to butter mixture. Turn on and off 3 or 4 times until flour disappears.
6. Grease and flour a 7- to 9-cup tube pan (an 8-inch springform pan will work, too).
7. Place half of batter in pan and top with half of cinnamon mixture. Add remaining batter and sprinkle top evenly with remaining cinnamon mixture.
8. Bake in a preheated, 350°F. oven for 45 to 50 minutes. Cool for 10 minutes in pan; turn out on rack, turning again so topping side is up, to cool completely.

GOLDEN-BLOSSOMS CAKE

MAKES 1 (4-LAYER) CAKE,
ABOUT 20 SERVINGS

1 package (18.5 ozs. or 18½ ozs.) yellow or white cake mix
1 envelope whipped topping mix

4 large eggs
1 cup cold water
Sunny Butter Frosting (recipe below)

1. Combine cake mix, whipped topping mix (do not whip; use right from envelope), eggs and water in large bowl of electric mixer.
2. Blend at low speed until moistened. Beat at medium speed for 4 minutes, scraping sides of bowl occasionally with spatula. Timing is important here, do not under-beat.
3. Preheat oven to 350°F. Spoon the following amounts of batter into the greased and floured pans:

9-inch pan—3 cups batter
7¼-inch pan—2¼ cups batter
5½-inch pan—1¼ cups batter
3¼-inch pan—remaining batter

4. Bake the two larger layers for 30 to 35 minutes and the two smaller layers for 25 to 30 minutes, or until cake tester inserted in center of each comes out clean.
5. Cool cakes in pans 10 minutes; then remove from pans and finish cooling on racks.
6. Frost tops of layers with Sunny Butter Frosting; stack and frost sides of cake. Use a small spatula to achieve smooth effect.
7. Spoon remaining frosting into pastry bag with Number 32 star tip. Make shell design at edges of layers.
8. Place cake on 9-inch foil-covered cardboard circle. Place in freezer until frosting is firm.
9. Remove cake from freezer, cover with plastic bag. Seal to cardboard with freezer tape, label, date, return to freezer.
10. To serve: Remove plastic bag from cake. Allow to thaw at room temperature 2 to 3 hours.
11. Place cake on serving plate or cake stand. Garnish with flowers, if desired. Always place flowers on a doily, never directly on cake.

SUNNY BUTTER FROSTING

MAKES 3½ CUPS FROSTING

⅓ cup orange-flavored instant breakfast drink
⅓ cup water
¾ cup butter, softened

½ teaspoon salt
1½ lbs. unsifted confectioners' sugar

1. Dissolve instant breakfast drink in water. In large bowl of electric mixer combine butter and salt.
2. At low speed, gradually add about half of the sugar, blending well. Scrape sides of bowl and beaters occasionally with rubber spatula.
3. At low speed, add remaining sugar alternately with liquid, beating after each addition until mixture is smooth.
4. At medium speed, beat until of proper spreading consistency.

BANANAS LAGOON CLUB

MAKES 8 TO 10 SERVINGS

¼ cup light or dark rum
1 cup water
4 tablespoons light molasses
1½ cups light brown sugar, packed
½ cup lime juice

2 tablespoons butter or margarine
9 medium-ripe bananas
1½ qts. vanilla ice cream
¼ cup light or dark rum

1. In a skillet, combine ¼ cup rum, water, molasses, brown sugar, lime juice and butter. Heat to boiling, stirring until sugar dissolves. Reduce heat and simmer uncovered (about 3 minutes, or until syrupy).
2. Slice bananas diagonally in 2-inch chunks; add to syrup. Spoon syrup over bananas.
3. Cook over medium heat while stirring (about 5 minutes, or until bananas are just tender and glazed all over).
4. Place a scoop of vanilla ice cream into each of 8 to 10 dessert dishes.
5. Heat remaining ¼ cup rum over candle warmer at table; ignite with match. Pour flaming rum over bananas. Spoon bananas and sauce over ice cream.

Vegetable of the Month: Green Beans

MUSHROOMS AND GREEN BEANS A LA CHEDDAR

MAKES 4 TO 6 SERVINGS

1 lb. fresh mushrooms or 2 cans (6- to 8-oz. size) sliced mushrooms

5 tablespoons butter or margarine

2 tablespoons flour
Milk

1½ cups shredded Cheddar cheese

4 drops hot pepper sauce

1 package (10 ozs.) frozen cut green beans, cooked and drained, or 1 can (1 lb.) cut green beans, drained, or ¾ lb. fresh green beans, cooked and drained

2 to 3 slices toast, cut in triangles

2 tablespoons toasted slivered almonds, optional

1. Rinse, pat dry and slice fresh mushrooms (makes about 5 cups) or drain canned mushrooms, reserving ½ cup of the liquid.
2. In large skillet melt 3 tablespoons of the butter. Add mushrooms and sauté 5 minutes, stirring frequently. Set aside.
3. In a medium saucepan melt remaining 2 tablespoons butter. Stir in flour; cook and stir 1 minute.
4. Gradually blend in 1 cup milk if using fresh mushrooms or, if using canned mushrooms, ½ cup milk and the reserved ½ cup mushroom liquid. Bring to boiling point, stirring constantly.
5. Remove from heat and stir in 1 cup of the cheese and hot pepper sauce. Stir in reserved mushrooms and green beans. Reheat until just heated through.
6. Spoon into a shallow 1½-qt. ovenproof serving dish. Sprinkle with remaining ½ cup cheese. Broil 4 inches from source of heat about 3 minutes, or until cheese is melted.
7. Garnish with toast points and almonds. Delicious served with ham.

132

GREEN BEANS WITH BASIL

MAKES 4 SERVINGS
---

1 tablespoon corn oil
3 tablespoons water
1 lb. green beans, tipped and rinsed, or 1½ packages (10-oz. size) frozen green beans

½ teaspoon salt
½ teaspoon dried basil leaves or 3 fresh basil leaves
Dash pepper

1. Pour oil and water into medium saucepan with a tight-fitting cover. Add rest of ingredients, cover. Cook over low heat about 10 to 12 minutes, just until vegetables are tender. Shake pan several times to prevent sticking.
2. If using frozen green beans, turn block frequently during first few minutes of cooking and separate vegetables with a fork. Cook, covered, 5 minutes.

GREEN BEAN AND CARROT DILLY

MAKES 4 TO 6 SERVINGS
---

1 lb. green beans
4 medium carrots
1 cup white wine or cider vinegar
6 tablespoons sugar

½ teaspoon salt
1 tablespoon fresh chopped dill
½ teaspoon caraway seed

1. Rinse beans, snap off ends. Pare carrots and cut into thin strips about 3 inches long.
2. Combine beans and carrots in saucepan, add boiling water to depth of 2 inches. Cover and cook just until crisp-tender, about 8 to 10 minutes.
3. Drain, reserving ½ cup cooking liquid. Place vegetables in shallow refrigerator container or dish.
4. Combine reserved cooking liquid with remaining ingredients in a small pan. Heat until sugar dissolves. Pour over beans and carrots; cover and refrigerate at least 3 hours. Serve as a salad or drain and serve as cocktail finger-food.

SAVORY GREEN BEANS AND RED PEPPERS

MAKES 6 SERVINGS

2 lbs. fresh whole green
  beans, stemmed
1½ cups boiling water
½ teaspoon salt
2 red peppers, seeded and
  cut in strips

2 tablespoons butter or
  margarine
Few twists freshly ground
  black pepper

1. Cook green beans in boiling, salted water about 10 to 15 minutes, or until as tender as you like. Toss beans once during cooking to cook evenly.
2. Add pepper strips and cook 2 minutes longer. Drain, save liquid, either to drink or to use in soups or gravy.
3. Add butter and pepper, tossing until well combined. Serve immediately.

COLACHE—A VEGETABLE STEW

MAKES 4 TO 6 SERVINGS

2 tablespoons vegetable oil
1 cup finely chopped onions
1 teaspoon minced garlic
2 lbs. young zucchini,
  scrubbed, unpeeled and cut
  crosswise into ¼-inch slices
1 lb. green beans, cut
  crosswise into 1½-inch slices
⅛ teaspoon hot green chilies,
  finely chopped

4 medium-firm tomatoes, ripe,
  peeled, seeded and coarsely
  chopped (or 1½ cups
  canned tomatoes, drained
  and chopped)
2 teaspoons salt
¼ teaspoon freshly ground
  black pepper
1 cup corn kernels, fresh or
  frozen

1. In a flameproof casserole, heat the oil. Add onions and garlic. Sauté, stirring, until they are soft and translucent.
2. Add the zucchini, green beans and chilies. Sauté for 3 minutes.
3. Add the tomatoes, salt and pepper. Cover and cook for 15 minutes.
4. Add corn, fresh or defrosted. Simmer until zucchini and green beans are tender but crisp.
5. Taste for seasoning and serve at once.

July

July swings open with the celebration of the Fourth of July. It's a wonderful weekend to honor our country with fireworks, parades and picnics.

The bubbly beat of summertime is with us. Our garden is coming into its own with all the seasonal fruits and vegetables we planted and faithfully tended. Our feature chart shows many ways to use the garden produce as it comes into harvest.

Enjoyable also are the fruits that say summer—strawberries, raspberries, peaches and plums. Delicious by themselves, they are delightful combined.

Our Vegetables of the Month—tomatoes and zucchini—are virtually impossible to separate, so we serve and preserve them in endless fashion.

This Summer's Garden: Next Winter's Table

VEGETABLE	SOUP	BREAD
Sweet Corn	Vegetable Beef Soup	Corn Fritters
Cabbage	Russian Sauerkraut Soup	
Carrots	Mediterranean Minestrone Fresh Vegetable-Beef Soup Russian Sauerkraut Soup	Carrot Bread
Celery	Mediterranean Minestrone Gourmet Mushroom Vegetable	
Cucumbers	Chilled Cucumber Soup	
Eggplant		
Green Beans	Vegetable Beef Soup	

MAIN DISH	SALAD	DESSERT	OTHER
Baked Corn Pudding			All Seasons Corn Relish
Stuffed Cabbage Rolls	Sweet 'N' Simple Cole Slaw	Chocolate Surprise Squares	Hodgepodge Relish
Glazed Carrots and Bananas Carrot Mold Baked Carrots Julienne	Marinated Vegtables	Crunchy Bumpy Munchy Cookies; Frosted Carrot Cake; Golden Carrot Cake	
Braised Celery Wedges	Celery Antipasto		Peanut Butter and Celery Snacks
Cucumber Sandwiches	Cucumbers with Yogurt		Genuine Dill Pickles
Easiest Eggplant Ratatouille Baked Stuffed Eggplant	Eggplant Salad		
Green Beans and Peppers Mushrooms and Green Beans Cheddar	Marinated Vegetables a la Grecque		

VEGETABLE	SOUP	BREAD
Peppers	Gazpacho	
Leeks	Vichyssoise	
Lettuce	Cream Lettuce Soup	
Onions	French Onion Soup	Onion Fritters
Potatoes	Vichyssoise Potato & Leek Soup	Potato Yeast Rolls
Yams		
Pumpkin		Pumpkin Bread
Spinach	Gourmet Mushroom Soup	
Zucchini		Zucchini Carrot Bread
Tomatoes	Gazpacho Fresh Vegetable-Beef Soup	

MAIN DISH	SALAD	DESSERT	OTHER
Ratatouille Spanish Skillet Chicken	Marinated Vegetables a la Grecque		Hodgepodge Relish
Braised Leeks	Marinated Vegetables a la Grecque		
	Italian Meatball Salad Mixed green salad Korean Lettuce Supper salad		
Chicken and Onion Stew	Baked Onions Vinaigrette		Parmesan Onion Thins
	Hot German Potato Salad Herbed Potato Salad	Chocolate Potato Torte	
Baked Yams Amalie Candied Yam Casserole		Fresh Sweet Potato Pie	
		Old-Fashioned Pumpkin Pie Pumpkin Torte	
Quadrettini Casserole Florentine Rice Quiche Spinach Souffle Crepes	Spinach Salad Gribiche Dressing Good Earth Salad		
Ratatouille			
Spaghetti/Fresh Tomato Sauce	Avocado Festival Salad Starburst Lettuce Salad		Baked Stuffed Tomatoes

Fourth of July Favorites

MARILYN'S SECRET BARBECUED CHICKEN

MAKES 8 SERVINGS

5 lbs. chicken parts
Salt

1 can (6 ozs.) frozen orange-
juice concentrate, thawed
¼ cup Worcestershire sauce

1. Sprinkle chicken lightly with salt.
2. Arrange on rack about 4 inches above slow-burning charcoal; broil 30 minutes, turning once. Or place on rack under a preheated broiler, 4 inches from source of heat; broil for 30 minutes, turning once.
3. Make Secret Sauce: Combine orange juice-concentrate with Worcestershire sauce and blend well.
4. After chicken has cooked for 30 minutes, baste it every 5 minutes. Turn chicken often until tender, about 15 minutes. Total broiling time: approximately 45 minutes.
5. Leftover sauce may be refrigerated in covered container. Secret Sauce may be used on spareribs, hamburgers, ham steaks, etc.

ALL-AMERICAN FRIED CHICKEN

MAKES 8 SERVINGS

2 (2½- to 3-lb. size) broiler-
fryer chickens, cut in
serving pieces
1½ cups unsifted all-purpose
flour
1½ teaspoons salt
2 teaspoons thyme leaves

2 teaspoons paprika
1 egg
⅓ cup milk or evaporated
milk, undiluted
2 tablespoons lemon juice
Vegetable oil or solid all-
vegetable shortening

1. Wash chicken; do not dry. Combine flour, salt, thyme and paprika in pie plate. Beat egg in another pie plate, add milk and lemon juice and mix well.

2. Roll chicken pieces lightly in seasoned flour, dip in egg mixture and then roll again in seasoned flour. Place on waxed paper. Let chicken stand at least 30 minutes for coating to dry; roll in flour again if coating is moist.

3. To fry: Pour vegetable oil to depth of ½ inch in 1 very large skillet or 2 medium skillets. Heat oil to 375°F. or shortening to 365°F. Add chicken pieces, skin side down. Cook until golden brown on one side, about 10 minutes. Turn and brown other side, 5 to 10 minutes. Reduce heat, cover skillet, and cook 25 minutes, or until done. Drain on absorbent paper.

GOLDEN-APRICOT BARBECUED RIBS

MAKES 4 TO 6 SERVINGS

1½ qts. water
12 whole black peppercorns
1 onion stuck with 2 whole cloves
2 teaspoons salt
3½ to 4 lbs. pork spareribs, cut in large serving pieces
1 can (17 ozs.) apricot halves
⅓ cup light brown sugar, packed
3 tablespoons vinegar
1 clove garlic, crushed
4 teaspoons soy sauce
⅛ teaspoon ground ginger

1. In 6-qt. Dutch oven, bring water, peppercorns, onion and 1 teaspoon of salt to boiling.

2. Wipe spareribs with paper towel, add to boiling water; return to boiling, cover, reduce heat and simmer 1 hour to 1 hour and 30 minutes, until tender.

3. Drain apricots, reserving ⅓ cup syrup. Purée apricots in electric blender with reserved syrup. Pour into small saucepan, adding brown sugar, vinegar, garlic, soy sauce, and ginger. Stir.

4. Heat sauce over medium heat to boiling, stirring to dissolve sugar. Reduce heat and simmer uncovered for 10 to 15 minutes.

5. Drain spareribs. Brush with apricot sauce. Place on grill about 4 or 5 inches from hot coals. Grill 10 to 15 minutes on each side until well browned, brushing several times with sauce.

6. Cut into strips with scissors. Serve any remaining sauce as dip for ribs. Delicious with rice and a green salad.

TEXAS RANCH BEANS

MAKES 6 TO 8 SERVINGS

1½ cups dried pink or pinto beans
5 cups water
1 teaspoon salt
2 tablespoons butter, margarine or vegetable oil
½ cup chopped onion
½ cup diced green pepper
2 cloves garlic, crushed
2 cans (8-oz. size) tomato sauce
1 can (8 ozs.) tomatoes and jalapeño pepper
2 teaspoons chili powder
1 teaspoon salt
⅛ teaspoon freshly ground black pepper
1 teaspoon Worcestershire sauce
¼ cup dark molasses
1 can (12 ozs.) whole kernel corn, drained
1 can (1 lb.) chick-peas, drained
2 cups (8 ozs.) cubed Monterey Jack cheese

1. Wash and sort beans. Place in 3-qt. saucepan with 3 cups water. Bring to boiling; cover and remove from heat. Let stand 1 hour.
2. Add remaining 2 cups water to beans. Bring to boil; reduce heat. Simmer, covered, 30 minutes. Add 1 teaspoon salt; simmer, covered, 30 minutes, until just tender, drain.
3. Meanwhile, prepare sauce: In medium skillet, in hot butter, sauté onion, green pepper and garlic 5 minutes, stirring occasionally.
4. Add tomato sauce, tomatoes and jalapeño pepper, chili powder, 1 teaspoon salt, pepper, Worcestershire sauce and molasses. Bring mixture to boiling. Reduce heat and simmer 5 minutes.
5. In 3-qt. casserole place beans, corn and chick-peas. Add sauce and mix well. (May be made ahead up to this point; cover and refrigerate.)
6. When ready to bake, preheat oven to 350°F. Bake, covered, for 1 hour, or until bubbly throughout. Remove cover and stir in cheese. Serve immediately.

RED, WHITE AND BLUE PIE

MAKES 1 (9-INCH) PIE, 8 SERVINGS

1 9-inch baked graham cracker pie shell
2 eggs
1 can (15 ozs.) sweetened condensed milk
½ teaspoon grated lime peel
½ cup fresh lime juice
2 tablespoons confectioners' sugar
½ pt. heavy cream, whipped
1 pt. fresh strawberries, hulled
1 cup fresh blueberries
1 tablespoon silver dragées

1. Make graham cracker pie shell and refrigerate.

2. Beat eggs, milk and lime peel together in bowl. Gradually blend in lime juice. Continue beating until the mixture is thickened; pour into pie shell. Chill 2 or 3 hours.

3. Stir confectioners' sugar into cream. Spread cream on top of pie.

4. Make row of upstanding strawberries around rim of pie. Scatter blueberries and dragées between strawberries. Refrigerate.

AMERICAN FLAG CAKE

MAKES 1 (13- x 9- x 2-INCH)
CAKE, 12 SERVINGS

1 package (18½ ozs.) yellow cake mix	2 tablespoons confectioners' sugar
1 package (3¾ ozs.) vanilla instant pudding mix	1 cup blueberries
½ cup vegetable oil	1 pt. strawberries, hulled and sliced in half
1 cup water	3 bananas
4 eggs	2 tablespoons orange or lemon juice
½ teaspoon almond extract	½ cup apple jelly, melted
1 cup (½ pt.) heavy cream, whipped	

1. Preheat oven to 350°F. Grease and flour a 13 x 9 x 2-inch pan. In large bowl, combine cake mix, pudding mix, oil, water, eggs and almond extract.

2. At low speed of electric mixer, blend all ingredients; beat at medium speed for 2 minutes.

3. Pour batter into prepared pan and bake for 40 to 50 minutes or until center springs back when touched lightly.

4. Cool right side up in pan for 20 minutes, then turn out onto serving plate or foil-covered cardboard if desired. Cool completely.

5. Blend whipped cream with confectioners' sugar. Spread evenly on cake.

6. Mark off blue field in upper left hand corner of cake and place blueberries in rows.

7. Make stripes by lining up rows of sliced strawberries and bananas. (Dip banana slices in orange juice before placing on cake.)

8. Brush melted apple jelly onto fruit. Refrigerate cake if not serving immediately.

Picnic Basket Fare

ANDALUSIAN SALAD

4 cups cold, cooked white
  rice
¼ cup chopped green pepper
¼ cup pimiento, diced
¼ cup finely chopped
  scallions
2 tablespoons finely chopped
  parsley
1 head Boston or leaf lettuce
5 small tomatoes

5 large stuffed green olives,
  chopped
2 hard-cooked eggs, chopped
2 tablespoons vinegar
1½ teaspoons salt
½ teaspoon freshly ground
  black pepper
½ teaspoon ground mustard
½ clove crushed garlic
1 cup salad oil
1 teaspoon oregano leaves

1. Combine cold rice with green pepper, pimiento, scallions and parsley.
2. Line a heavy, chilled salad bowl with lettuce. Spoon in rice mixture. Circle salad with tomatoes. Top with olives and eggs; cover with foil. Refrigerate.
3. In jar, combine all remaining ingredients. Cover and shake well. Refrigerate until ready to pour over salad.

LAYERED CHICKEN CURRY SALAD

6 cups shredded lettuce
2 packages (10-oz. size)
  frozen peas, cooked,
  drained and chilled
3 cups chopped cooked
  chicken or turkey
3 cups chopped tomatoes

2 cups seeded cucumber
  slices, halved
3 cups mayonnaise
1 tablespoon sugar
1½ teaspoons curry powder
3 cups croutons

1. Layer lettuce, peas, chicken, tomatoes and cucumber in 5-qt. salad bowl.
2. Combine mayonnaise, sugar and curry; mix well. Spread over salad. Cover with plastic film; refrigerate overnight.
3. Before serving, sprinkle with croutons.

COLD BEAN SALAD

MAKES ABOUT 10 SERVINGS

1 can (1 lb.) whole green beans, drained
1 can (1 lb.) red kidney beans, drained
1 can (1 lb.) garbanzos or chick-peas, drained
⅓ cup chopped pimiento
½ cup chopped onion
1 red onion, sliced into rings
1 cup wine vinegar
½ cup salad oil
½ cup sugar
2 teaspoons salt
½ teaspoon freshly ground black pepper

1. In large bowl, combine green beans, kidney beans, garbanzos, pimiento and onions.
2. Combine remaining ingredients in small bowl. Stir well and pour over bean mixture, tossing gently. Cover: refrigerate to chill and blend flavors. Transfer to tightly covered container to take to picnic.

CHEF'S INSPIRATION SALAD

MAKES 6 SERVINGS

1 qt. crisp, torn iceberg lettuce leaves
1 qt. crisp, torn chicory leaves
2 qts. crisp, torn romaine leaves
1 medium red onion, thinly sliced
2 cups cherry tomatoes, halved
½ lb. sliced salami, julienne cut
¼ lb. sliced Swiss cheese, julienne cut
2 cups chicken chunks or 2 cans (5-oz. size) boneless chicken
2 cups king-size corn chips
⅓ cup bottled herb-and-garlic salad dressing, or your own

1. In large salad bowl combine greens and toss. Add onion rings, cherry tomatoes, salami, Swiss cheese and chicken. Cover tightly with foil or plastic film and refrigerate if not serving immediately.
2. Just before serving add corn chips and salad dressing. Toss well.

PIPERADE IN PITA

MAKES 6 SERVINGS

6 round individual Syrian
pita breads
4 tablespoons vegetable or
olive oil
3 medium onions, thinly
sliced
3 medium tomatoes, peeled,
seeded and chopped
2 cloves garlic, crushed

1½ teaspoons marjoram leaves
1½ teaspoons salt
½ teaspoon freshly ground
black pepper
1 green pepper, seeded and
chopped
9 eggs, lightly beaten
Salt and freshly ground
black pepper, optional

1. Preheat oven to 350°F. Place pita breads on baking sheet and bake about 2 minutes or until heated through.
2. In large skillet, heat oil; add onion and sauté, stirring until soft but not brown. Add tomato, garlic, marjoram, salt and pepper and cook for 15 minutes or until thick and pulpy; add the green pepper and cook 5 minutes more.
3. Add the eggs and cook, stirring slowly until cooked as well as you like, as for scrambled eggs. Taste for seasoning, adding more salt and pepper if desired.
4. Slit the tops of breads, spoon the hot mixture into the breads; wrap each in foil to carry.

STUFFED FRENCH BREAD

MAKES 6 TO 8 SERVINGS

½ lb. bacon
¼ cup bacon drippings
½ cup butter or margarine
¾ cup chopped onion
1 teaspoon thyme leaves
½ teaspoon marjoram leaves
¾ teaspoon coarse ground
black pepper

2 lbs. (Braunschweiger)
liverwurst, cubed
1 package (8 ozs.) cream
cheese, softened
2 loaves French or Italian
bread
2 tablespoons butter or
margarine

1. In large skillet, fry bacon until crisp. Drain on paper towels and chop fine.
2. In same skillet, combine bacon drippings and butter. Heat until butter melts; add onion, thyme, marjoram and pepper. Cook, stirring until onion is limp, about 5 minutes.
3. In large bowl with electric mixer at medium speed, blend liverwurst and cream cheese until smooth. Add bacon.

4. Add onion-herb-butter mixture to liverwurst and blend.

5. Cut loaves of French bread in half lengthwise. Pull out soft center, leaving a ½-inch-thick "shell." (Use removed bread for stuffings, bread crumbs, etc.)

6. Spoon filling evenly into the four halves. Spread butter on cut edges of bread. Place filled top half of loaves on top of filled bottom half, pressing edges together to seal. Wrap in foil and refrigerate. To serve, cut into ½-inch-thick slices.

PICNIC PICKLE BEEF ROLL

MAKES ABOUT 8 TO 10 SANDWICHES

1 flank steak, about 2½ lbs.
Prepared mustard
Seasoned salt
Seasoned pepper
6 to 8 dill pickles, quartered
   lengthwise
4 to 5 carrots, quartered
   lengthwise
6 to 8 scallions
¼ cup vegetable shortening
2 cups water
1 beef bouillon cube

¼ cup vinegar
1 cup dry red wine
1 teaspoon whole black
   peppercorns
2 bay leaves
4 sprigs parsley
2 stalks celery, cut in 2-inch
   pieces
8 to 10 seeded rolls, split
   Butter or margarine,
   softened

1. Spread steak liberally with mustard and sprinkle with seasoned salt and pepper. Starting at narrow side, alternate rows of pickles, carrots and scallions on top of steak. Roll up in jelly-roll fashion and tie securely with string at 1-inch intervals.

2. Heat shortening in Dutch oven. Brown steak on all sides; pour off drippings.

3. Add water, bouillon cube, vinegar, wine, peppercorns, bay leaves, parsley and celery. Cover; bring to boiling. Reduce heat and simmer 2½ to 3 hours, or until meat is tender. Chill in liquid in covered bowl.

4. To serve, take meat from liquid and remove strings. Place on serving platter and cut diagonally into slices about ½ inch thick. Spread rolls with butter and mustard; fill with meat slices to make sandwiches.

Fruits of Summer

FRESH TART FRUIT SOUP

MAKES ABOUT 2 QUARTS, 8 TO 10 SERVINGS

1½ lbs. Santa Rosa plums, halved and pitted (about 9)
3 cups water
¾ cup sugar
Dash salt

1½ cups seedless grapes, pulled from stem
1½ cups fresh apple or pineapple chunks
1½ cups fresh peach or pear slices
Vodka as desired, optional

1. In saucepan, mix plums, water, sugar and salt. Bring to boil and simmer, covered, for 10 minutes or until plums are tender. Cool slightly.
2. Pour plums and juices into blender container. Whirl smooth. Pour into 3-qt. serving bowl. Chill.
3. At serving time add fruits and vodka to taste. Ladle into dessert bowls or punch cups.
4. Serve with cheese and crackers as a first course or dessert.

FRESH FRUIT HAWAIIAN SALAD

MAKES 2 SERVINGS

1 fresh Hawaiian pineapple
2 bananas, sliced
1 can (11 ozs.) mandarin orange sections, drained
½ cup strawberry halves
½ cup blueberries

2 tablespoons orange juice
½ cup mayonnaise-type salad dressing
½ cup heavy cream, whipped
Toasted coconut

1. Cut pineapple in half lengthwise through crown. Using curved serrated knife, remove fruit, leaving shells and fronds intact.

2. Core and chunk fruit; toss lightly with bananas, oranges, strawberries, blueberries and orange juice.

3. Spoon fruit mixture into pineapple shells. Combine salad dressing and whipped cream; mix well. Spoon over fruit mixture.

4. Garnish with coconut and additional fruit, if desired.

STRAWBERRY CHEESECAKE

MAKES 1 (9-INCH) CAKE,
12 SERVINGS

1 cup graham cracker crumbs

¼ cup firmly packed light-brown sugar

¼ cup butter or margarine, melted

¼ teaspoon ground nutmeg

5 packages (8-oz. size) cream cheese, room temperature, softened

1¼ cups sugar

3 tablespoons all-purpose flour

1½ teaspoons pure vanilla extract

1½ teaspoons grated orange rind

¼ cup milk

6 eggs, room temperature

2 pts. fresh strawberries, washed and hulled

⅔ cup strawberry or red-currant jelly, melted

1 tablespoon kirsch or rum

1. Preheat oven to 375°F. In medium bowl, toss graham cracker crumbs, brown sugar, butter and nutmeg together. Press mixture onto bottom of 9-inch springform pan. Bake for 10 minutes. Cool in pan on rack.

2. Make filling: Preheat oven to 500°F. In large bowl, with electric mixer at high speed, beat together cream cheese and sugar until light and fluffy.

3. Blend in flour, vanilla, orange rind and milk until mixture is smooth. Beat in eggs, one at a time, beating thoroughly after each addition.

4. Pour mixture over baked crumb crust in pan. Bake in preheated oven for 15 minutes. Reduce heat to 250°F. Bake 1 hour longer.

5. Leave cake in oven, with heat turned off and door shut, about 20 minutes. Remove from oven.

6. Cool on rack until room temperature, then refrigerate cake 3 hours or longer.

7. Prepare strawberry topping: Slice enough dry strawberries to garnish. Arrange sliced and whole strawberries on top of cake.

8. To glaze: Combine melted strawberry jelly and kirsch, cool slightly. Brush strawberries with glaze. Refrigerate until ready to serve.

FRESH BLUEBERRY COBBLER

MAKES 6 SERVINGS

½ cup sugar
1 tablespoon cornstarch
4 cups fresh blueberries or peaches
1 teaspoon lemon juice
Dash ground nutmeg
1 tablespoon sugar

1 cup unsifted all-purpose flour
1½ teaspoons baking powder
½ teaspoon salt
3 tablespoons vegetable shortening
½ cup milk

1. Heat oven to 400°F. Blend ½ cup sugar and cornstarch in medium saucepan. Stir in blueberries, lemon juice and nutmeg. Cook, stirring constantly, until mixture comes to boil. Boil and stir 1 minute.
2. Pour hot fruit mixture into ungreased 2-qt. casserole. Place in oven to keep hot while preparing biscuit topping.
3. Combine 1 tablespoon sugar, flour, baking powder and salt in bowl. Add shortening and milk. Cut through shortening 6 times; mix until dough forms a ball. Drop dough by 6 large spoonfuls onto hot fruit. Bake 25 to 30 minutes, until biscuits are golden-brown.

CLASSIC OLD-FASHIONED STRAWBERRY SHORTCAKE

MAKES 1 (9-INCH) CAKE, 10 TO 12 SERVINGS

3 cups unsifted all-purpose flour
3¼ teaspoons double-acting baking powder
2 tablespoons sugar
1¼ teaspoons salt
½ cup soft all-vegetable shortening
1 egg, beaten

⅔ cup plus 2 tablespoons milk
3 pts. strawberries, washed
¾ to 1 cup sugar
2 cups (1 pt.) heavy cream
2 tablespoons sugar
½ teaspoon pure vanilla extract
1 tablespoon butter or margarine

1. Preheat oven to 450°F. Heavily grease a 9-inch round layer-cake pan.
2. In large bowl sift together: flour, baking powder, 2 tablespoons sugar and salt. With pastry blender, cut shortening into flour mixture until crumbly.
3. Add egg and milk, stirring with fork to make a soft dough. Gather dough together with hands. Knead 15 to 20 times on lightly floured board.

4. Pat dough into pan evenly with fingers. Bake for 15 to 20 minutes or until a cake tester inserted in center comes out clean.

5. Reserve 3 perfect strawberries for garnish. Slice remainder into large bowl, toss with ¾ to 1 cup sugar, depending on taste and sweetness of berries.

6. In large chilled bowl whip cream with chilled beaters until cream holds a soft shape. Stir in 2 tablespoons sugar and vanilla. Refrigerate, covered, until ready to use.

7. Cool shortcake biscuit on wire rack. When cool, make two layers by carefully cutting in half with a serrated bread knife.

8. Lightly spread cut side of bottom layer with butter. Spoon on about 3 cups sliced strawberries. Top with 2 cups whipped cream.

9. Cover with top shortcake layer, cut side down. Spoon on remaining berries and top with remaining whipped cream. Garnish center with reserved strawberries.

PEACHY-PLUM PIE

MAKES 1 (8-INCH) PIE,
6 TO 8 SERVINGS

Pastry for double 8-inch pie crust
1 (8-inch) pan frozen Peach-Plum Pie Filling (recipe below)

1 egg yolk
1 teaspoon water
2 tablespoons sugar
Heavy cream, optional

1. Preheat oven to 425°F. Roll out half of pastry and line the bottom of an 8-inch pie pan.

2. Slide pie filling out of foil pan into pastry-lined pie pan.

3. Roll out remaining pastry; cut into strips and make a lattice top.

4. Beat egg yolk with water. Brush lattice with egg glaze and sprinkle with sugar.

5. Bake for 60 to 70 minutes, until fruit is fork tender and crust is golden. Crust should be covered with aluminum foil when brown to prevent burning. Serve warm or cold with heavy cream if desired.

PEACH-PLUM PIE FILLING
MAKES FILLING FOR 3 PIES

2¼ lbs. fresh peaches
2¼ lbs. fresh plums
   Boiling water
¼ cup lemon juice
2 cups sugar

¼ cup quick-cooking tapioca
½ teaspoon salt
3 (8-inch size) foil cake or
   pie pans

1. To peel peaches: Drop peaches into boiling water for 30 seconds; transfer with slotted spoon to cold water. Skins will slip right off.
2. Halve and remove pits from peaches and plums. Slice into large bowl (there should be about 8 cups); add lemon juice and toss to coat.
3. Combine sugar, tapioca and salt; add to fruit. Let stand for 15 minutes.
4. Divide fruit mixture evenly among 3 (8-inch) foil cake or pie pans.
5. Double-wrap in freezer paper or heavy-duty aluminum foil; label; freeze.
6. When needed, remove from freezer and unwrap.

BRANDIED DESERT FRUITS

MAKES 2 QUARTS

1 pkg. (1 lb.) light brown
   sugar
3 cups water
1½ lbs. Thompson seedless
   grapes, in small clusters
1 pkg. (6 ozs.) dried apricots

1 pkg. (10 ozs.) pitted dates
1 cup raisins
½ cup blanched whole
   almonds
1 cup brandy

1. Combine sugar and water in a saucepan and bring to a boil. Reduce heat and simmer for 5 minutes.
2. While syrup is simmering, arrange fruit and almonds in hot, sterilized jars.
3. Remove syrup from heat and add brandy. Pour over fruit and seal jars.
4. Place each jar as it is filled onto rack in canner or deep kettle half filled with hot water. When canner is filled, add hot water to cover jars 1 to 2 inches.
5. Cover canner and bring water to boil. Reduce heat to hold water at a steady boil. Start processing time when water reaches a full boil. Process 20 minutes.

VINELAND VINEGAR

MAKES 1 PINT

1½ cups white wine vinegar
1 tablespoon honey
½ cup Thompson seedless
  grapes

1 thin slice fresh pineapple
Peel of one small orange

1. Warm the wine vinegar and honey in a small saucepan.
2. Place grapes, pineapple and orange rind in a pint bottle and pour in the warmed vinegar. Cap and let stand for several days. (Variation: Omit pineapple and orange peel; add sprigs of favorite fresh herb.)

FRESH FRUIT PICKLES

MAKES 2 QUARTS
---

2 cups cider vinegar
3½ cups sugar
2 cups water
2 bay leaves
1 tablespoon pickling spice
4 fresh peaches, peeled

½ lb. fresh plums, halved and
  pitted
1 small cantaloupe, peeled
  and cut into slices
½ lb. seedless grapes

1. Combine vinegar, sugar, water, bay leaves and pickling spice in a large saucepan. Bring to a boil; reduce heat and simmer for 15 minutes.
2. Arrange fruit in hot, sterilized jars and pour pickling mixture over fruit. Seal immediately.
3. Place each jar as it is filled onto rack in canner or deep kettle half filled with hot water. When canner is filled, add hot water to cover jars 1 to 2 inches.
4. Cover canner and bring water to boil. Reduce heat to hold water at a steady boil. Start processing time when water reaches a full boil. Process 25 minutes.

SANTA ROSA JAM AND JELLY

MAKES 1½ PINTS JAM, PLUS
4 TO 5 HALF PINTS JELLY

1¼ lbs. fresh red Santa Rosa
plums (about 8)
¼ cup water
1 box (1 pt.) fresh
strawberries

7½ cups sugar
3 tablespoons lemon juice
½ bottle (6 ozs. per bottle)
liquid pectin

1. Slice and pit plums. Put plums and water in large, heavy kettle. Bring to a boil. Reduce heat and simmer for 5 minutes.
2. Halve strawberries (there should be about 2 cups); add to plums, along with sugar and lemon juice. Mix well.
3. Bring mixture to a full, rolling boil, stirring constantly; boil for 1 minute.
4. Remove from heat immediately, stir in pectin. Skim off foam with metal spoon. Stir and skim for 5 minutes.
5. Cover large bowl with several thicknesses of cheesecloth. Secure with large rubber band.
6. Pour hot jam through cloth, stirring gently to allow most of juice to strain through.
7. Spoon pulp mixture out of cheesecloth (there should be about 2 cups). Mix in ¾ cup of the strained jelly.
8. Ladle jam into hot, sterilized jars, filling to within ⅛ inch of top; seal with 2-piece metal caps.
9. Place each jar as it is filled onto rack in canner or deep kettle half filled with hot water. When canner is filled, add hot water to cover jars 1 to 2 inches.
10. Cover canner and bring water to boil. Reduce heat to hold water at a steady boil. Start processing time when water reaches a full boil. Process 15 minutes.
11. For jelly, fill hot sterilized jars and process in boiling water bath as above or seal with paraffin.

SPIKED PEACH JAM

MAKES 6 TO 7 CUPS

3 lbs. fresh ripe peaches
2 tablespoons lemon juice
1 package (1¾ ozs.)
powdered fruit pectin

5½ cups sugar
1 tablespoon port, bourbon,
brandy or rum, optional
Paraffin

1. Peel peaches; drop peaches into boiling water for 30 seconds.
2. Transfer with a slotted spoon to cold water; slip off skins. Halve and remove pits.
3. Finely chop or grind peaches to make 4 cups; add lemon juice.
4. In a 6- to 8-qt. saucepan thoroughly mix peaches with powdered fruit pectin.
5. Over high heat, cook, stirring constantly, until mixture comes to a full boil.
6. Add sugar; bring to a full rolling boil and boil for 1 minute, stirring constantly.
7. Remove from heat; skim off foam with metal spoon. Stir and skim for 5 minutes.
8. Into clean, hot jars, pour 1 tablespoon liquor if desired.
9. Add hot jam, leaving ½-inch space at top. Cover jam immediately with 2-piece lids.
10. Place each jar as it is filled onto rack in canner or deep kettle half filled with hot water. When canner is filled, add hot water to cover jars 1 to 2 inches.
11. Cover canner and bring water to boil. Reduce heat to hold water at a steady boil. Start processing time when water reaches a full boil. Process 15 minutes.

POLYNESIAN PAPAYA MARMALADE

MAKES 2 HALF PINTS

1 jar (10 ozs.) orange marmalade
2 cups chopped Hawaiian papaya (1½ papayas)
1 cup chopped fresh peaches (2 small)
2 tablespoons lemon juice
Dash salt

1. Combine all ingredients in heavy skillet or saucepan. Cook over medium heat, stirring for about 15 minutes, just until juices have thickened slightly.
2. Pour into 2 sterilized half-pint jars. Seal.
3. Place each jar as it is filled onto rack in canner or deep kettle half filled with hot water. When canner is filled, add hot water to cover jars 1 to 2 inches.
4. Cover canner and bring water to boil. Reduce heat to hold water at a steady boil. Start processing time when water reaches a full boil. Process 15 minutes.

GRAPEVINE PRESERVES

MAKES 2½ PINTS

1 lb. (about 3 cups) seedless grapes, pulled from stems
2 small oranges, peeled and sliced
2 tablespoons lemon juice
2 teaspoons orange or lemon peel (optional)

1 drop green food coloring (optional)
1 cup light corn syrup
2¼ cups sugar
¾ cup water
1 pkg. (1¾ ozs.) powdered fruit pectin

1. Chop grapes in blender, a few at a time, at low speed. (Do not purée.)
2. Repeat for oranges. Measure 2 cups fruit with juices into bowl. Stir in lemon juice, peel; add food coloring if desired.
3. Thoroughly mix corn syrup and sugar into fruit; let stand for 10 minutes.
4. Mix water and pectin in saucepan. Bring to boil and boil for 1 minute, stirring constantly.
5. Stir pectin mixture into fruit; continue stirring for 3 minutes.
6. Ladle quickly into sterilized freezer jars or container, allowing ¼-inch head space.
7. Seal according to manufacturer's directions. Let stand at room temperature for 24 hours. Store in freezer.
8. If used in 2 or 3 weeks, store in refrigerator.

SOLAR PLUM LEATHER

MAKES 2 SHEETS ABOUT
12x15-INCHES EACH

2 lbs. fresh plums (about 14 to 16)*

¼ cup light corn syrup

1. Slice plums thinly (there should be 5 cups); discard pits.
2. Turn plums into large saucepan; add corn syrup and bring to a boil, stirring. Boil for 3 minutes.
3. Pour mixture into blender container; blend until smooth. Set aside to cool.

* Peaches, apricots or prunes may also be used.

4. Prepare a smooth, level drying surface in full sunlight. Cover cookie sheets or baking pans with clear plastic wrap.

5. Pour strained purée onto prepared surface and spread to ¼-inch thickness.

6. Let dry in sunlight. (Drying may take up to 24 hours.) Bring pans inside at end of day and finish drying second day.**

7. Fruit is dry when purée can be peeled off plastic easily.

8. For storing, roll up Leather in plastic wrap and seal tightly.

9. Leather will keep at room temperature about 1 month, in refrigerator about 4 months or 1 year in freezer.

** Drying may be finished indoors. Set cookie sheets in 150°F. oven. Leave door open. Leather can be dried completely indoors. Set pans of purée in oven. Heat to 200°F. and turn oven off. Reheat oven several times a day to maintain a temperature of 200°F. Leather will dry in about 24 hours.

SPIRITED RAISINS

MAKES 1 HALF PINT

1 cup dark seedless or golden raisins
½ cup warmed brandy, rum, orange liqueur, coffee-flavored liqueur, chocolate-based liqueur, sherry or tequila

1. Place raisins in sterilized ½-pint jar. Pour warmed liquor or liqueur over them; seal.

2. Let stand for 24 hours or more, shaking occasionally.

3. When using Spirited Raisins in a recipe, take out desired amount, straining liquor back into jar. To replenish, add more raisins and liquor to the jar, estimating proportions.

Vegetables of the Month: Tomatoes and Zucchini

GAZPACHO

MAKES 4 CUPS

Soup purée:
½ large cucumber, peeled and seeded
4 large tomatoes, peeled and quartered
½ onion
½ clove garlic
2 tablespoons vegetable oil
⅓ cup wine vinegar

1 teaspoon salt
¼ teaspoon freshly ground black pepper

Accompaniments:
1 cup chopped, peeled tomato
¼ cup chopped green pepper
¼ cup chopped onion
½ cup tiny crisp croutons

1. In container of electric blender, place all ingredients for soup purée. Cover and blend slowly until puréed. Cover and chill 2 hours. Cover and process at high speed.
2. Pour into bowl and stir in accompaniment ingredients or serve separately in small bowls.

AVOCADO FESTIVAL SALAD

MAKES 6 TO 8 SERVINGS

2 qts. washed, torn, assorted salad greens
2 avocados, peeled and sliced
8 tomato slices
½ cup chopped dill pickle

⅓ cup green onion slices
6 crisply cooked bacon slices, crumbled
Bottled French salad dressing

1. Place greens onto a large serving platter. Arrange avocado slices and tomato slices on greens. Top with pickles, green onion and bacon.
2. Serve with French dressing.

158

STARBURST LETTUCE SALAD

MAKES 6 SERVINGS
---

1 head iceberg lettuce, cut into 6 wedges

2 cups carrot slices, partially cooked

1½ cups thinly sliced raw zucchini

1 cup fresh mushroom slices

½ cup sliced pitted ripe olives

1 cup sour cream

½ cup bottled Italian salad dressing

1. Arrange lettuce wedges in salad bowl. Combine carrots, zucchini, mushrooms and olives; toss lightly. Sprinkle over lettuce wedges. Cover and refrigerate.

2. In small bowl or blender, combine sour cream and Italian dressing, mixing until blended. Serve with salad.

GARDEN VEGETABLE CASSEROLE

MAKES 6 SERVINGS
---

1 lb. (1 medium) eggplant, sliced

1 lb. (3 large) tomatoes, sliced

¾ lb. (2 medium) green peppers, cut in strips

¾ lb. (5 medium) zucchini, sliced

1 teaspoon salt

¼ teaspoon freshly ground black pepper

½ teaspoon basil leaves

2½ cups chicken broth

4 ozs. sliced Swiss cheese

3 tablespoons grated Parmesan cheese

6 poached eggs

1. Preheat oven to 400°F. In 2-qt. shallow casserole layer vegetables, sprinkling each layer with salt, pepper and basil.

2. Pour chicken broth over all. Top with Swiss cheese slices and Parmesan cheese.

3. Bake for 1 hour, or until vegetables are fork-tender.

4. Spoon vegetables and broth into soup bowls. Top each serving with poached egg.

ZUCCHINI ROMANO

MAKES 8 SERVINGS

8 small zucchini (about 1½ lbs.)
1 egg, lightly beaten
⅓ cup shredded mozzarella cheese
3 tablespoons Italian salad dressing

1/16 teaspoon freshly ground black pepper
2 tablespoons melted butter or margarine
½ lb. ground ham or veal
½ cup Salsa Italiana (recipe below)

1. Wash zucchini and trim ends. Slice off a narrow lengthwise strip. Using an apple corer remove seeds to make a hollow about ¾ inch deep in each zucchini. Cover with boiling water, simmer about 5 minutes, and drain well.
2. Meanwhile, combine egg, cheese, dressing, pepper and butter in a bowl. (If using veal, add ¼ teaspoon salt.) Lightly mix in meat. Fill zucchini with meat mixture using about 3 tablespoons in each hollow.
3. Arrange zucchini, stuffed side up, in a single layer in an oiled shallow 1½-qt. baking dish; spread tops with Salsa Italiana. (Or omit Salsa Italiana and brush tops with olive or cooking oil.)
4. Bake at 375°F. about 15 minutes, or until meat is cooked. Serve hot.

SALSA ITALIANA

MAKES ABOUT 3 CUPS SAUCE

1 cup chopped onion
¼ cup olive oil or cooking oil
1 clove garlic, minced
¼ cup grated carrot
1 tablespoon finely snipped parsley
¼ teaspoon basil leaves, crushed

⅛ teaspoon thyme leaves, crushed
2 cans (8-oz. size) tomato sauce
½ cup beef broth (dissolve ½ beef bouillon cube in ½ cup boiling water)

1. Add onion to hot oil in saucepan and cook until tender. Stir in the garlic, carrot, and parsley; cook about 3 minutes, stirring frequently.
2. Blend in basil, thyme, tomato sauce, and beef broth. Simmer gently until flavors are blended, about 10 minutes.

Editor's Note: Sauce may be stored in tightly covered container in refrigerator a few days; for a longer period, freeze.

QUADRETTINI CASSEROLE

MAKES 6 SERVINGS

2 tablespoons butter or margarine
2 tablespoons vegetable oil
1 cup finely chopped carrot
1 cup finely chopped onion
1 cup finely chopped celery
2 cloves garlic, crushed
1 lb. ground beef chuck
1 can (6 ozs.) tomato paste
3 cups chopped, peeled, fresh tomatoes or canned tomatoes in purée
2 teaspoons salt

1½ teaspoons oregano leaves
1 teaspoon basil leaves
½ teaspoon thyme leaves
½ teaspoon hot pepper sauce
1 package (8 ozs.) narrow regular or spinach noodles
1 package (10 ozs.) frozen chopped spinach
½ cup grated Parmesan cheese
Tomato Sauce (recipe below), optional

1. In 3-qt. saucepan melt butter and add oil. Add carrot, onion, celery and garlic; cook, stirring, until tender, about 10 minutes.
2. Add ground beef and cook, stirring with cooking spoon, until meat loses its red color. Add tomato paste, tomatoes, salt, oregano, basil, thyme and hot pepper sauce. Simmer, uncovered, 1 hour, stirring occasionally.
3. Preheat oven to 350°F. Cook noodles according to package directions; drain well. Cook spinach according to package directions and drain well.
4. Add noodles and spinach to sauce. Turn into a 2-qt. casserole, sprinkle with cheese and bake for 30 to 40 minutes, until bubbly. Serve with Tomato Sauce if desired.

TOMATO SAUCE

MAKES 2 CUPS

2 cans (8-oz. size) tomato sauce
½ teaspoon oregano leaves
½ teaspoon basil leaves

¼ teaspoon sugar
1 bay leaf
Few twists freshly ground black pepper

1. Combine all ingredients in small saucepan. Heat to boiling, stirring. Reduce heat and simmer 5 to 10 minutes covered.

ZUCCHINI-STUFFED TOMATOES

MAKES 8 SERVINGS

8 medium tomatoes
¼ cup butter or margarine
3 medium zucchini (about 1 lb.), diced
½ lb. mushrooms, sliced
1 medium onion, chopped
1 clove garlic, minced

1 teaspoon salt
½ teaspoon sugar
¼ teaspoon basil leaves
Few twists freshly ground black pepper
1 cup toasted croutons

1. Preheat oven to 350°F.
2. Cut a thin slice from top of each tomato; scoop out pulp, leaving a ¼-inch shell. Chop pulp and set aside.
3. In large skillet, melt butter; add tomato pulp, zucchini, mushrooms, onion, garlic, salt, sugar, basil and pepper. Cook over low heat, stirring frequently, until most of the liquid has evaporated (about 15 minutes). Stir in croutons.
4. Spoon mixture into tomato shells. Place tomatoes in shallow baking dish. Bake for 20 minutes.

BAKED STUFFED TOMATOES, GREEK STYLE

MAKES 6 SERVINGS

6 large, ripe tomatoes
1 cup chopped onion
2 tablespoons olive or vegetable oil
1 teaspoon sugar
⅓ cup raw white rice
1 lb. finely ground lamb or beef
⅛ teaspoon ground nutmeg
¼ teaspoon ground cinnamon
1 small clove garlic, crushed

1 tablespoon finely chopped parsley
1 teaspoon chopped mint or 1 teaspoon dry mint, if available
¼ cup pine nuts
1 teaspoon salt
¼ teaspoon freshly ground black pepper
¼ cup fine dry bread crumbs
2 tablespoons olive or vegetable oil

1. Preheat oven to 375°F.
2. Remove pulp and seeds from each tomato; discard seeds. Chop pulp and set aside. Place tomatoes on foil-covered baking pan.
3. In large skillet, cook onions with 2 tablespoons oil for 5 minutes, stirring. Add sugar, rice, lamb, spices, herbs, chopped tomato pulp, pine nuts, salt and pepper.

4. Heat mixture to boiling, cover and reduce heat, simmer 30 minutes, stirring once or twice. Spoon off any fat if necessary.
5. Fill tomatoes with rice mixture to within ¼ inch of tops.
6. Toss bread crumbs with olive oil. Sprinkle crumbs on top of filling. Bake 20 to 25 minutes until tender and bubbly.

SPAGHETTI WITH ZUCCHINI SAUCE

MAKES 3 TO 4 SERVINGS

8 ozs. thin spaghetti
1 medium zucchini, shredded (1½ to 2 cups)
2 scallions, thinly sliced
2 tablespoons finely chopped parsley

¼ cup vegetable oil
1 teaspoon salt
¼ teaspoon garlic powder
¼ teaspoon oregano leaves, crushed
Dash cayenne pepper

1. Cook spaghetti as package label directs.
2. In large serving bowl, combine zucchini, scallions, parsley, oil and seasonings.
3. After spaghetti has cooked, drain in colander.
4. Add hot spaghetti to zucchini mixture, toss lightly. Serve immediately.

SPAGHETTI WITH FRESH TOMATO SAUCE

MAKES 3 TO 4 SERVINGS

8 ozs. thin spaghetti
¼ cup olive oil
2 medium tomatoes, peeled and finely diced
1 large clove garlic, crushed
¼ cup chopped parsley

1¼ teaspoons salt
½ teaspoon basil leaves, crushed
Few twists freshly ground black pepper

1. Cook spaghetti as package label directs.
2. In large serving bowl combine oil with tomatoes, garlic, parsley, salt, basil and pepper.
3. When spaghetti is cooked, drain well.
4. Add hot spaghetti to tomato mixture, toss lightly. Serve immediately.

ZUCCHINI-CARROT BREAD

**MAKES 1 LARGE LOAF
OR 2 SMALL LOAVES**

3 eggs
1 cup vegetable oil
1½ cups dark brown sugar,
  packed
1 cup grated zucchini
1 cup grated carrots
2 teaspoons pure vanilla
  extract

2½ cups whole wheat flour
½ shredded bran cereal
1 teaspoon salt
1 teaspoon baking soda
3 teaspoons ground
  cinnamon
1 cup chopped unblanched
  almonds

1. Preheat oven to 350°F. Grease and flour a 9- x 5- x 3-inch loaf pan or two 7½- x 3½- x 2-inch loaf pans.
2. In large mixing bowl, beat eggs with oil. Stir in sugar, zucchini, carrots and vanilla.
3. Mix together flour, bran cereal, salt, baking soda and cinnamon. Stir into zucchini mixture. Add almonds and mix well.
4. Bake for 1 to 1½ hours or until a pick inserted in center comes out dry.
5. Allow to cool for 15 minutes in pan; then invert and cool on wire rack. Wrap well to store. (This bread stays moist for several days. It also freezes well.)

August

The steady golden hum of August is upon us with its humid heat and incessant growth. Yes, growth does seem to happen almost overnight, especially if we water regularly.

We feature still more ways to use fruits and vegetables in our special chart, How to Make Fresh Fruit and Vegetable Gelatin Salads.

August is summer in its heyday, and outdoor grills across the country are asizzle. We've got barbecue and go-with ideas to satisfy both the chefs and their guests. For those who prefer sand and spray cooking, there are directions for a Maine-style Clambake and New England Steamed Clams and Lobsters.

To help you keep cool during the long August evenings, we have included a collection of refrigerator and freezer desserts.

With the corn and cucumbers ripening daily, they are our Vegetables of the Month, and we include recipes to use this bounty. There is also a bonus on using and preserving fresh garden herbs.

Fresh Vegetable and Fruit Gelatin Salads

VEGETABLE/FRUIT	GELATIN	SALT	COLD LIQUID
APPLE	orange or raspberry	Dash	¾ cup water
AVOCADO/ ORANGE	lemon, lime or orange	½ tsp.	¾ cup water
BANANA	strawberry	¼ tsp.	¾ cup water
CABBAGE/ APPLE	lemon	1 tsp.	¾ cup water
CARROTS	lemon or lime	¼ tsp.	¾ cup water
CARROTS/CABBAGE	lemon	1 tsp.	¾ cup water
CAULIFLOWER/ TOMATO	lemon	1 tsp.	¾ cup water
CHEESE/ CELERY	lemon, orange or orange-pineapple	½ tsp.	1 cup tomato sauce or tomato juice
CITRUS/ CABBAGE	lime or lemon	⅛ tsp.	¾ cup fruit juice plus water
COTTAGE CHEESE/ VEGETABLE	lemon or lime	¾ tsp.	¾ cup water
GRAPEFRUIT	lemon	⅛ tsp.	¾ cup fruit juice plus water
ORANGES/ ONION	orange, lemon or orange-pineapple	none	¾ cup water
PEACHES	lime or lemon	none	¾ cup ginger ale
TOMATO	lemon	½ tsp.	¾ cup water

BASIC METHOD FOR MAKING GELATIN SALADS

Dissolve 1 package (3 oz.) gelatin and the salt in 1 cup boiling water. Add cold liquid and vinegar or lemon juice. Chill until thickened, about 1 hour. Fold in prepared vegetable or fruit. Chill until firm in a 3- or 4-cup mold, individual molds or square pan. Unmold and serve with lettuce and mayonnaise, if desired. Makes about 3 cups or 6 servings.

VINEGAR OR LEMON JUICE	PREPARED VEGETABLE/FRUIT
1 tbsp.	¾ cup diced unpeeled apple ¼ cup each chopped nuts and celery
2 tsp.	1 cup diced peeled avocado 1 cup diced orange sections ¼ cup sliced red onion
1 tbsp.	1 medium banana, sliced ¼ cup each chopped celery and nuts
2 tbsp.	¾ cup each finely shredded cabbage and diced unpeeled apple 1 tablespoon prepared horseradish
2 tsp.	1 cup shredded carrots ¼ cup diced celery 2 tablespoons sliced olives
2 tbsp.	1 cup each grated carrots and finely shredded cabbage
2 tbsp.	¾ cup each cauliflower florets and diced tomatoes 2 tablespoons each chopped green pepper and scallions
1½ tbsp.	1 cup grated Cheddar cheese ½ cup finely diced celery
1 tbsp.	Sections from 1 large orange and 1 medium grapefruit, diced 1 cup shredded cabbage 1 tablespoon sliced scallions
1 tbsp.	1 cup creamed cottage cheese ¼ cup diced celery 2 tablespoons chopped green pepper 1 teaspoon grated onion
none	1 cup diced grapefruit sections ¾ cup diced celery ¼ cup diced olives
2 tsp.	Sections from 3 oranges ½ cup thin red onion rings ¼ cup chopped celery
none	1 cup diced sweetened peaches ¼ cup chopped nuts ¼ cup chopped celery
1 tbsp.	1 tomato, cut in thin wedges ¼ cup each sliced celery and sliced quartered cucumber

Barbecues and Clambakes

HERB-AND-WINE BARBECUED STEAK

MAKES 8 SERVINGS

3 lb. round or shoulder steak, 2½ inches thick
2 cups dry red wine
½ cup salad oil
2 tablespoons instant minced onion
1½ tablespoons marjoram leaves
1 tablespoon salt
½ teaspoon instant minced garlic
¼ teaspoon freshly ground black pepper

1. Wipe meat with damp paper towel. Place meat in heavy-duty plastic bag.
2. Combine remaining ingredients. Pour over meat in bag. Seal securely with twister. Refrigerate about 24 hours, turning meat 2 or 3 times to marinate evenly.
3. When ready to grill, drain marinade from meat. Reserve marinade.
4. Grill steak over hot charcoal 4 to 5 inches from source of heat for about 20 to 30 minutes, until of desired doneness, turning and basting with marinade every 8 minutes.
5. To serve, slice thinly on the diagonal.

GRILLED LEG OF LAMB NUGGETS

MAKES 6 TO 8 SERVINGS

1 (5½ to 6 lbs.) leg of lamb, boned
Juice of 2 fresh lemons
2 teaspoons salt
1 teaspoon crushed black peppercorns
3 cloves garlic, split
1 teaspoon thyme leaves
1 teaspoon oregano leaves
1 bay leaf
2 onions, sliced
2 cups red or white wine

168

1. Have butcher bone lamb and remove skin or fell. With sharp, small knives, separate lamb-leg meat into the individual shape nature gives, removing all fat, membrane and as much sinew as possible. You now have a variety of sizes of meat: "nuggets."
2. In large, shallow earthenware or glass pan combine lemon juice, salt, peppercorns, garlic, thyme, oregano, bay leaf and onions. Mix well.
3. Coat lamb "nuggets" with marinade on all sides. Allow to marinate for 24 hours, covered in refrigerator, turning meat once or twice.
4. On day of serving, remove from refrigerator and allow to marinate at room temperature several hours.
5. To grill, preheat charcoal grill until gray coals form. Place lamb "nuggets" on grill until cooked to desired doneness.

BARBECUED CHICKEN HICKORY

MAKES 6 TO 8 SERVINGS, 2 DRUMSTICKS PER SERVING

12 to 16 (2½ to 3 lbs.) drumsticks
2 tablespoons butter or margarine, melted

Hickory Barbecue Sauce (recipe below)

To broil chicken:
1. Preheat broiler if necessary. Place drumsticks in shallow foil-lined pan, brush with butter.
2. Place drumsticks 5 inches below source of heat. For gas range, set thermostat at 450°F.; leave door slightly open. Broil for 20 to 25 minutes. For electric range, broil 20 to 25 minutes.
3. Turn drumsticks; broil 15 to 20 minutes. Brush with Barbecue Sauce; broil 5 minutes; turn and brush again. Continue broiling about 5 minutes, or until chicken is browned.

To grill chicken:
1. Preheat grill or prepare and light charcoal grill. Brush drumsticks with melted butter.
2. Place drumsticks on grill 5 inches above source of heat. Grill for 20 to 25 minutes. Turn drumsticks; grill 15 to 20 minutes. Brush with Barbecue Sauce; grill 5 minutes; turn and brush again. Continue grilling about 5 minutes, or until chicken is browned.

BARBECUED BEEF-ON-A-BUN

MAKES 24 BUNS

1 (8 to 9 lbs.) fresh beef brisket
2 qts. water
1 teaspoon salt
4 whole black peppercorns
1 onion stuck with 2 cloves
1 bay leaf
1 carrot
Hickory Barbecue Sauce (recipe below)
24 sesame seed buns

1. Place brisket in large kettle or covered roaster. Add 2 qts. water, salt, peppercorns, onion, bay leaf and carrot. Bring to boil. Reduce heat and simmer, covered, 2 to 2½ hours, or until fork-tender. Drain, discard herbs and vegetables.

2. To oven-glaze brisket: Preheat oven to 375°F. Trim excess fat from brisket. Place in shallow foil-lined baking pan. Brush brisket with Barbecue Sauce.

3. Bake for 20 to 30 minutes, basting occasionally with sauce until glazed.

4. To grill brisket: Preheat grill or prepare and light charcoal grill. Trim excess fat from brisket. Place brisket on grill. Brush with Barbecue Sauce.

5. Grill about 10 to 15 minutes per side, basting occasionally with sauce until glazed.

6. To serve: Place brisket on a wooden cutting board. Cut across grain into ¼-inch-thick slices.

7. Place slice of meat on split buns. Pour a little extra warm Hickory Barbecue Sauce on meat.

BARBECUED RIBS HICKORY

MAKES 6 TO 8 SERVINGS

4½ to 5 lbs. spareribs (½ to ¾ lb. per person)
Hickory Barbecue Sauce (recipe below)

To roast spareribs:

1. Preheat oven to 450°F. Place spareribs in shallow foil-lined pan.

2. Roast spareribs 30 minutes. Pour off excess drippings. Reduce temperature to 350°F. and continue roasting 45 minutes.

3. Brush spareribs with Barbecue Sauce and roast 10 to 15 minutes, or until browned. Cut into strips to serve.

To grill spareribs:

1. Preheat grill or prepare and light charcoal grill. Cut most of excess fat off the ribs.

2. Place ribs on grill about 5 inches from source of heat and grill slowly for about 45 minutes, basting ribs with lightly salted water and turning frequently.

3. Brush with Barbecue Sauce and grill slowly 20 to 30 minutes longer, until glazed and tender. (This method keeps the sauce from burning excessively. It also allows more smoke flavor to penetrate through the ribs.)

4. Heat Hickory Barbecue Sauce and serve as a dip for ribs.

HICKORY BARBECUE SAUCE

MAKES ABOUT 4 CUPS

¼ cup butter, margarine or vegetable oil
½ cup finely chopped onion
1 clove garlic, crushed
1 can (1 lb. 12 ozs.) tomatoes, broken up
1 can (6 ozs.) tomato paste
1 cup water
¼ cup cider vinegar
½ cup ketchup
¼ cup dark molasses
1 tablespoon chili powder

1 tablespoon hickory-smoked salt
½ teaspoon charcoal seasoning, optional
1 teaspoon ground mustard
1½ teaspoons Worcestershire sauce
¼ teaspoon freshly ground black pepper
1 bay leaf
3 drops hot pepper sauce

1. In large saucepan heat butter until hot. Add onion and garlic, and sauté 5 minutes, stirring occasionally.

2. Stir in remaining ingredients.

3. Bring mixture to boil. Reduce heat and simmer, uncovered, 30 minutes. Stir occasionally. Strain.

4. If not using immediately, store sauce in covered jar in refrigerator. It will keep well for 2 or 3 weeks.

Editor's Note: Sauce may be frozen.

SURPRISE SEAFOOD PACKETS

MAKES 6 SERVINGS

Per Serving:

⅛ lb. haddock fillet
½ lobster tail (cut completely through shell lengthwise with scissors)
4 clams in the shell, scrubbed

4 mussels in the shell, scrubbed
3 large shrimp in the shell
Garlic-Herb Sauce (recipe below)
Hot Italian bread in foil

1. Place haddock fillet, lobster tail, clams, mussels and shrimp on large square of heavy-duty aluminum foil. Make up as many as you need.
2. Sprinkle each seafood arrangement with 3 to 4 tablespoons Garlic-Herb Sauce. Wrap foil around seafood, sealing securely with double fold across top and at ends.
3. Place on preheated foil-lined barbecue grill over medium-hot coals and grill about 15 to 20 minutes. (Or bake in preheated oven at 425°F. about 25 minutes.) Packets are ready when fish and lobster are tender and clams and mussels steam open.
4. Heat foil-wrapped Italian bread 10 minutes on grill or 5 minutes in (425°F.) oven.
5. Place packets on individual serving plates. Open at table and serve with hot Italian bread to "sop up" the fantastic seafood broth.

GARLIC-HERB SAUCE

3 cloves garlic, crushed
1 cup butter or margarine
½ teaspoon tarragon leaves
½ teaspoon rosemary leaves
½ teaspoon thyme leaves

¼ cup lemon juice
2 teaspoons salt
Few twists freshly ground black pepper

1. In saucepan combine garlic, butter, tarragon, rosemary, thyme, lemon juice, salt and pepper. Heat, stirring, until butter melts.

GRILLED ITALIAN LOAF

MAKES 8 SANDWICHES, 4 SERVINGS

1 (½ lb.) loaf Italian bread
1 cup (¼ lb.) shredded
  mozzarella cheese
⅓ cup mayonnaise
2 tablespoons prepared
  mustard

1 to 2 tablespoons finely
  chopped hot cherry peppers
8 slices (8 ozs.) capicollo or
  boiled ham
1 tablespoon melted butter or
  margarine

1. Cut crusts from ends of bread. Make 15 slashes ½ inch apart, cutting to, but not through, bottom crust.
2. In small bowl combine cheese, mayonnaise, mustard and peppers.
3. Fill every other slash with cheese mixture and capicollo.
4. Brush top and sides of loaf with butter; wrap securely in heavy-duty aluminum foil.
5. Bake in preheated 300°F. oven for 30 minutes, or until hot. Or heat 4 inches from glowing coals for 30 minutes, turning loaf every 10 minutes.
6. To serve: Cut through bottom crust of unfilled sections, serve hot!

CHEESE-GRITS CASSEROLE

MAKES 6 TO 8 SERVINGS

1 teaspoon salt
4½ cups water
1 cup quick grits
½ cup (1 stick) butter or
  margarine
½ lb. grated sharp Cheddar
  cheese
2 cloves garlic, crushed

2 eggs
⅔ cup milk
Dash hot pepper sauce
2 tablespoons butter or
  margarine
2 cups cornflake crumbs
Paprika

1. Add salt to water; bring to a rapid boil. Slowly add grits and continue boiling 3 to 5 minutes.
2. Remove from heat, add ½ cup butter, cheese and garlic, stir until butter melts.
3. Beat eggs; stir in milk. Add to grits mixture. Add pepper sauce; mix and pour into greased 2½-qt. casserole.
4. Dot top with 2 tablespoons butter. Sprinkle with cornflake crumbs and paprika.
5. Bake in preheated 350°F. oven about 1 hour.

MAINE-STYLE CLAMBAKE

Good sized rocks	white baking potatoes
Split cordwood (hickory is good)	Quartered, pre-browned chickens
Wet seaweed	Cubes of fish steak
Clean sheeting or tarpaulin	Clams, 6 to 12 per person
Partially husked corn	Lobsters, 1 per person
Peeled white onions	1½ cups clarified butter
Scrubbed unpeeled sweet or	(recipe below)

1. Dig a saucer-shaped pit, line with good-sized rocks, cover with wood (hickory lends a wonderful smoky flavor) and start a good hot fire. The rocks must get very hot so allow up to several hours, depending on size of pit.

2. When the fire has burned down, rake the glowing coals and ashes over the rocks, pushing the coals to the windside, leaving a breathing hole for the fire so the embers can smolder.

3. Top the rocks with wet seaweed and cover with clean sheeting or tarpaulin.

4. Lay on the steaming cloth partially husked corn and peeled white onions tied in separate cheesecloth bags; do the same with scrubbed but unpeeled sweet or white baking potatoes; quartered, pre-browned chickens; cubes of fish steak.

5. Next add to the bake, clams tied in cheesecloth for easy handling; allow 6 to 12 per person. (Mail order and most market-purchased clams will have been washed. If you dig them yourself, or know they have not been cleaned, do this by changing their water several times before baking. This will cleanse them of sand within their shells. Use salt water or fresh water to which cornmeal has been added.)

6. Top the bake with 1 lobster per person; cover with another piece of sheeting or tarpaulin. Weight down with sand, soil or rocks.

7. Relax; let bake steam the necessary length of time. The bake is done when lobsters turn a bright red and clams open. A small bake will take 1 to 2 hours, one for a crowd of 100 needs 5 hours.

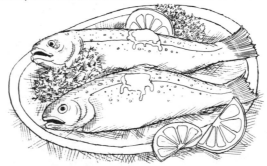

NEW ENGLAND STEAMED CLAMS AND LOBSTERS

MAKES 4 SERVINGS

Salted water
12 small new potatoes, scrubbed
4 ears corn, husked and cut into 2-inch chunks
4 (1½-lb. size) fresh live lobsters
24 to 32 fresh live steamer clams, well scrubbed
1½ cups clarified butter (recipe below)
Lemon wedges

1. In a very large saucepot or wash boiler, place 2 inches of salted water; bring to the boiling point.
2. Add potatoes and return to boiling. Reduce heat and simmer, covered, until parboiled, about 12 minutes.
3. Add corn and lobsters. Return to the boiling point. Reduce heat and steam, covered, for 5 minutes.
4. Add clams; steam, covered, until clams open, about 4 minutes.
5. Place clams in a bowl; serve each portion with a cup of the broth from the saucepot and some clarified butter.
6. Arrange lobsters, corn and potatoes on platters garnished with lemon wedges. Serve with clarified butter.
7. To eat clams, remove clam from shell; holding the neck, dip first into the broth and then into the butter. The broth helps to clean off sand that may still be clinging to the clam.

CLARIFIED BUTTER

MAKES ABOUT 1½ CUPS

1 lb. butter

1. Heat butter in small heavy saucepan over moderate heat until melted.
2. Skim off the top foam. Slowly pour off the clear yellow fat which is the clarified butter and discard the milky residue at the bottom of the pan.
3. Serve clarified butter hot.

Herbs for Now and Later

DRYING OR FREEZING HERBS

Here's how to *dry* herbs for future use. Cut the stems when the plant is ready. Don't cut too close to the ground. Separate into small bunches; tie with string and hang in a warm, dry, dark place until the leaves are crisp and brittle. In the summer drying takes from three to ten days. Strip the leaves and buds and put as whole as possible into a jar with a tight lid to preserve the flavor. Check during the first few days to be sure the herbs are dry; otherwise mold might develop.

To *freeze* herbs, gather as for drying, wash if dusty, pat off excess water, place into plastic bags and put into the freezer immediately. When it's time to use, snip or chop the herbs without thawing because they mince easily. Also, put chopped herbs into an ice-cube tray, fill with water and freeze. Cubes can be popped into soups or stews as needed.

BASIL BLOCKS
MAKES 8 TO 12 CUBES

12 to 14 fresh basil leaves
6 sprigs fresh parsley
2 cloves garlic
1 teaspoon salt

3 tablespoons grated
Parmesan cheese
1½ cups salad oil

Wash and drain 12 to 14 fresh basil leaves and 6 sprigs fresh parsley. Place in electric blender container with garlic, salt, Parmesan cheese and salad oil. Cover container and blend until smooth. Pour mixture into ice-cube tray. Freeze overnight. When frozen solid remove Basil Blocks from tray. Place blocks in plastic bag; keep frozen until needed.

Use a few melted blocks for pesto sauce when cooking pastas. Also very good to add 1 or 2 blocks to soups, stews and beans.

HERB BOUQUET GARNI

Cut 4- x 6-inch squares of double cheesecloth. Cut heavy string into 1-foot lengths. Into center of each piece of cheesecloth place: 1 bay leaf, 3 peppercorns, ½ teaspoon dried oregano leaves, 1 teaspoon dried basil leaves, pinch of rosemary, thyme, 1 teaspoon dried parsley flakes, 1 teaspoon onion flakes, 1 teaspoon dried celery flakes. Bring up cheesecloth around herbs and tie securely with string. Store in attractive containers (with lids on securely).

Excellent flavor addition for stews, soups, beans, pot roast and sauces for pastas. (Tie string to pot handle for easy removal.)

Bouquets Garnis make nice gifts, especially for new chefs.

TABBULI

MAKES 6 CUPS

1 cup bulgur wheat, rinsed
2 cups boiling water
2 cups peeled, diced tomatoes
1 cup finely chopped scallions
3 tablespoons chopped fresh mint or 2 teaspoons dried mint flakes, crumbled

1 cup finely chopped parsley
½ cup olive oil
½ cup lemon juice
2½ teaspoons salt
¼ teaspoon freshly ground black pepper
Romaine lettuce leaves or cucumber slices

1. Place bulgur into medium bowl and pour boiling water over it. Allow to sit for at least 1 hour to absorb moisture.
2. Drain bulgur, turn into large bowl and add tomatoes, scallions, mint, parsley, olive oil, lemon juice, salt and pepper.
3. Cover and chill well.
4. Tabbuli can be eaten with romaine leaves or cucumber slices. Also great with pita bread.

Refrigerator and Freezer Delights

PRALINE ICE-CREAM RING WITH STRAWBERRIES

MAKES 6 TO 8 SERVINGS

Butter
¾ cup unblanched almonds
1½ cups sugar
½ teaspoon cream of tartar
2 qts. vanilla ice cream,
 slightly softened

1 qt. strawberries, preferably
fresh with stems, or just-
thawed whole*
Mint sprigs

1. Butter a 13- x 15-inch sheet of heavy-duty foil lightly and fold up edges ½ inch.
2. In medium-size heavy skillet place almonds, sugar and cream of tartar. Cook over medium heat, stirring, until sugar liquefies and becomes a rich caramel-amber color. (Almonds will be toasting.) Pour hot caramelized syrup onto prepared foil. Let cool.
3. Break into large chunks with mallet or wooden spoon. Pulverize to medium-fine consistency between two sheets of foil. Or blend medium-fine in blender.
4. In large bowl combine slightly softened ice cream with ½ of praline powder.** No need to combine smoothly; leave ripples of praline in ice cream.
5. Pack ice cream firmly into foil-lined 6-cup ring mold. Cover with foil, freeze until firm.
6. Unmold onto plate just before serving. (A silver or glass plate would be an excellent choice.) Place strawberries in center and around outside. Garnish with small bouquet of mint sprigs.

* Frozen raspberries may be used instead.

** Store remaining praline powder in tightly covered jar.

FROZEN CHOCOLATE CHARLOTTE

MAKES 10 TO 12 SERVINGS

1 tablespoon butter or margarine
2 tablespoons sugar
2 packages (3-oz. size) fresh ladyfingers
1/4 cup white crème de menthe
2 packages (6-oz. size) semisweet chocolate pieces

3 tablespoons instant coffee powder
1/2 cup boiling water
6 eggs, separated
1/2 cup sugar
1 teaspoon pure vanilla extract
1 1/2 cups heavy cream
1 cup heavy cream
1 bar (4 ozs.) sweet baking chocolate

1. Butter a 9-inch round spring-form pan and then sprinkle with 2 tablespoons sugar, set aside.
2. Split ladyfingers but do not separate into individual pieces. Brush flat surfaces with crème de menthe.
3. Line sides of prepared spring-form pan with ladyfingers, rounded sides against pan.
4. Separate remaining ladyfingers and line bottom of pan overlapping and piecing to fit.
5. Melt chocolate in top of double boiler, stirring occasionally. Dissolve coffee in boiling water.
6. Beat egg yolks in small bowl with electric mixer until foamy. Beat in sugar gradually until thick.
7. At low speed, beat in melted chocolate, coffee and vanilla.
8. With clean beaters, beat egg whites in large bowl until stiff peaks form.
9. Stir 1 cup beaten whites into chocolate mixture. Fold chocolate mixture back into remaining egg whites.
10. Beat 1 1/2 cups heavy cream until stiff, and fold into chocolate mixture. Pour into ladyfinger lined pan. Freeze until firm.
11. Whip remaining 1 cup heavy cream until stiff. Using a Number 8 star tip, decorate surface of Charlotte with whipped cream rosettes.
12. Allow semisweet chocolate bar to soften slightly in low oven; make chocolate curls with vegetable peeler, firm curls in refrigerator and use to decorate.
13. Allow to thaw 1 hour at room temperature before serving. Remove springform ring; cut into wedges.

CRANBERRY MOUSSE WITH RASPBERRY SAUCE

MAKES 8 TO 10 SERVINGS

3 cups fresh or fresh frozen cranberries, rinsed
1 cup sugar
1 cup cranberry juice cocktail
3 envelopes unflavored gelatin

1 cup cranberry juice cocktail
2 cups cranberry juice cocktail
⅓ cup kirsch or light rum
2 cups (1 pt.) heavy cream, whipped

1. In medium saucepan combine cranberries, sugar and 1 cup cranberry juice. Heat to boiling, reduce heat and simmer 5 minutes uncovered.
2. Stir gelatin into 1 cup cranberry juice to soften. Stir gelatin mixture into hot cranberry mixture. Add 2 cups cranberry juice and kirsch. Refrigerate until slightly thickened.
3. Fold whipped cream into slightly thickened gelatin mixture. Pour mixture into 2-qt. mold. Chill until firm.
4. When ready to serve, dip mold into lukewarm water for a few seconds, tap to loosen and invert onto a serving platter.
5. Serve each portion of Cranberry Mousse with a little Cranberry Sauce.

Raspberry Sauce:
1 package (10 ozs.) frozen raspberries, thawed

1 jar (12 ozs.) raspberry preserves
¼ cup kirsch or light rum

1. Press raspberries and juice through a sieve, discard seeds. Stir in preserves and kirsch, mix well. Refrigerate, covered.

FROZEN LEMON DESSERT

MAKES 12 SERVINGS

6 eggs, separated
1 cup sugar
1 teaspoon grated lemon rind

10 tablespoons lemon juice
2 cups heavy cream
45 vanilla wafers, crushed

1. In large bowl, beat egg whites until stiff. Gradually beat in sugar, beating until whites are a thick, shiny meringue.
2. In medium bowl, beat egg yolks until thick and light-colored. Beat in lemon rind and lemon juice. Fold egg yolk-lemon mixture into egg whites.
3. Beat cream in chilled bowl until it holds a shape. Fold cream into egg white mixture.
4. Sprinkle half of vanilla wafer crumbs in bottom of buttered 13½- x 8¾- x 2-inch baking dish.
5. Pour in lemon mixture. Lightly smooth with spatula. Sprinkle surface with remaining crumbs. Put in freezer overnight.
6. To serve, cut into squares. Serve with forks.

COCONUT LIME PIE

MAKES 8 SERVINGS

1 9-inch baked graham-cracker pie shell
1 package (8 ozs.) cream cheese, softened
1 can (14 ozs.) sweetened condensed milk

1 can (6 ozs.) frozen limeade concentrate, thawed
1 container (4½ ozs.) frozen nondairy whipped topping, thawed
1 can (4 ozs.) flaked coconut

1. Prepare graham-cracker pie shell and cool.
2. In large bowl with electric mixer at high speed, beat cream cheese until creamy. Add condensed milk and beat until blended; continue beating until thoroughly mixed.
3. Add limeade concentrate and beat until smooth.
4. At low speed, add whipped topping, beating just until blended. Pour into pie shell. Top with coconut.
5. Refrigerate about 3 hours or until firm. Also may be frozen and served as a frozen pie.

TRIFLE

MAKES 8
SERVINGS

3 packages (3-ozs. each) lady fingers, split
1 cup sweet sherry
2 cups strawberry jam
⅓ cup honey
1 teaspoon grated lemon rind
3½ cups Custard Sauce (recipe below)

1 cup (½ pt.) heavy cream
¼ cup confectioners' sugar
1 teaspoon pure vanilla extract
Additional strawberry jam
Fresh strawberries
Mint leaves
2 tablespoons chopped walnuts

1. In 2-qt. glass serving bowl, arrange a layer of lady fingers. Sprinkle them with about ⅓ cup sherry.
2. In a bowl, combine strawberry jam, honey and lemon rind.
3. Spoon a layer of strawberry mixture over lady fingers and then add a layer of Custard Sauce. Continue layering, ending with sauce.
4. Whip cream until stiff. Fold in sugar and vanilla.
5. Spoon whipped cream around outer edge of bowl.
6. Drizzle additional strawberry jam over cream and top with fresh strawberries, mint leaves and sprinkle of walnuts.
7. Refrigerate several hours before serving. Refrigerate leftovers.

CUSTARD SAUCE

MAKES ABOUT 3½ CUPS

6 egg yolks
½ cup sugar
⅛ teaspoon salt

3 cups milk
1½ teaspoons pure vanilla extract

1. In double boiler over hot, not boiling water, with wire whisk, beat egg yolks, sugar and salt until blended.
2. Gradually stir in milk and cook, stirring constantly, until mixture thickens and coats a spoon; about 25 minutes.
3. Stir in vanilla extract. Cover surface with lightly buttered waxed paper and refrigerate.

Vegetables of the Month: Corn and Cucumbers

CORN FRITTERS

MAKES 6 FRITTERS

Vegetable oil for frying
1 tablespoon vegetable oil
2 cups whole-kernel corn: 4 or 5 large ears, scraped, or 1 package (10 ozs.) frozen cut corn or 1 can (12 or 16 ozs.) corn, drained
1 cup unsifted, all-purpose flour
¼ cup milk
2 eggs
1 teaspoon double-acting baking powder
½ teaspoon salt
Maple or maple-blended syrup

1. Pour vegetable oil into electric skillet to ½-inch depth. Heat oil to 400°F. on deep-frying thermometer.
2. Using fork, stir together 1 tablespoon oil, corn, flour, milk, eggs, baking powder and salt in medium bowl.
3. Drop batter by large tablespoonfuls into hot oil and fry for 3 to 5 minutes until golden brown. Turn each fritter once.
4. With slotted spoon, remove fritters to paper towels.
5. Serve hot with syrup. Delicious by themselves or with fried chicken, crisp bacon or baked ham.

ALL-SEASONS CORN RELISH

MAKES 4 TO 5 PINTS

6½ cups whole-kernel corn, yellow or white shoe-peg, or 4 cans (12-oz. size) corn, drained
1½ cups chopped celery
1 cup chopped green pepper
1 cup choped white onion
1 jar or can (4 ozs.) pimiento, drained and chopped
2 teaspoons celery seed
2 teaspoons mustard seed
½ teaspoon crushed red pepper

2 teaspoons non iodized salt
1 large clove garlic
2 cups white vinegar
1¼ cups sugar
1½ tablespoons ground mustard
3½ tablespoons all-purpose flour
¾ cup water
2 or 3 tablespoons hot water or vinegar, optional
Sugar, optional
Salt, optional
Vinegar, optional

1. Put corn, celery, green pepper, onion, pimiento, celery seed, mustard seed, crushed red pepper, salt, garlic and vinegar in 6-qt. kettle or Dutch oven. Bring to a boil, stirring, then let boil 5 minutes, uncovered.

2. In 1-qt. saucepan blend sugar, mustard and flour, then slowly add ¾ cup water. Heat to boiling over moderate heat, stirring constantly. Stir into corn mixture.

3. Bring corn mixture to boiling and cook, stirring now and then, until celery, green pepper and onion are tender, about 10 minutes.

4. If mixture becomes too thick, add 2 or 3 tablespoons hot water or vinegar. Mixture should be moist, but not soupy. Taste for seasoning; add sugar, salt or vinegar if necessary.

5. Ladle boiling-hot relish to ⅛ inch of top of hot sterilized jars; wipe off anything spilled on tops or threads of jars with clean, damp cloth.

6. Put sterilized lids on jars, screw sterilized bands tight. As each jar is filled, stand it on rack in a canner full of hot, not boiling, water. Water should cover jars 1 to 2 inches.

7. Put cover on canner, bring water to a boil, process jars in boiling-water bath 15 minutes.

8. Remove jars from canner. Let cool for about 12 hours. Label. Store in cool place.

CHILLED CUCUMBER SOUP

MAKES ABOUT 5 CUPS,
6 TO 8 SERVINGS

1 cup chicken broth	1 teaspoon grated lemon rind
2 tablespoons lemon juice	1 cup sour cream
¼ cup finely chopped onion	1 cup plain yogurt
1 teaspoon salt	2 cups peeled, seeded,
½ teaspoon dried dill leaves,	chopped cucumber
crushed	Cucumber slices
Dash garlic powder	Lemon slices

1. In electric blender container combine broth, lemon juice, onion, salt, dill, garlic and lemon rind. Blend covered 1 to 2 minutes, or until smooth.

2. Add sour cream and yogurt. Blend covered 15 to 30 seconds, until just blended. Stir in chopped cucumber. Cover; refrigerate at least 1 hour, until very cold.

3. Pour into chilled 1½-qt. tureen. Float cucumber and lemon slices on surface.

CUCUMBERS WITH YOGURT

MAKES 3 CUPS

2 large cucumbers, peeled and thinly sliced	½ teaspoon ground cumin
Salt	½ teaspoon ground coriander
¼ teaspoon freshly ground	1 tablespoon lemon or lime
black pepper	juice
1 cup (½ pt.) plain yogurt	¼ to ½ teaspoon salt

1. Layer cucumber slices in shallow, flat pan and salt lightly. Cover with plastic film and refrigerate for at least 1 hour or longer.

2. Drain off liquid from cucumbers.

3. In medium bowl blend pepper, yogurt, cumin, coriander and lemon juice. Add cucumbers, and ¼ to ½ teaspoon salt, toss well. Serve as an accompaniment to curries, roasted meats, fish or chicken.

HODGEPODGE RELISH

MAKES 5 TO 7 PINTS

2 cups washed, ½-inch-thick sliced cucumbers
1 cup washed, trimmed, 1½-inch pieces green beans
1 cup washed, peeled, 1½-inch carrot sticks
1 cup washed, 1½-inch celery sticks
1 cup washed, quartered, small green tomatoes
2 cups washed, 2-inch cauliflowerets
2 cups chopped onions
2 cups coarsely chopped red peppers
1 hot red pepper
1 cup non iodized salt
Water
3 tablespoons mustard seed
2 tablespoons celery seed
1 teaspoon ground mustard
1 teaspoon ground ginger
2 cups sugar
5 cups white vinegar
Boiling vinegar, optional
Boiling water, optional

1. Turn vegetables into nonmetal bowl. Add salt, mix well and cover with ice-cold water (takes about 4 qts.). Let stand 12 to 18 hours, refrigerated. Stir several times during first hour or two to be sure salt hasn't settled at bottom of bowl.

2. Drain vegetables. If too salty, rinse in cold water and drain again. Set aside.

3. Put all remaining ingredients into large kettle. Heat, stirring, for 3 minutes.

4. Add the drained vegetables; simmer vegetables until heated through. If more liquid is necessary, add more mixture of equal amounts of boiling vinegar and water.

5. Spoon hot relish to ¼ inch of top of sterilized jars. Wipe tops and threads of jars with clean, damp cloth.

6. Put sterilized lids on jars; screw sterilized bands tight. As each jar is filled, stand it on rack in a canner full of hot, not boiling, water. Water should cover jars 1 to 2 inches.

7. Put cover on canner, bring water to a boil, and process jars in boiling-water bath for 15 minutes.

8. Remove jars from canner. Let cool for about 12 hours. Label. Store in cool place.

September

September's air is softer now, and its blue sky has a warm serenity after the hot fever of late summer.

Apples and pears are coming into picking ripeness, and our feature chart shows the varied ways they can be enjoyed. Check the recipe section for your favorites.

It's back to school for the youngsters and the not-so-young. We have some ideas for school lunches, cookies and favorite foods that should appeal to just about everyone.

Many families may be taking that last lingering visit with summer on a late camping trip. We have a knapsack full of recipes to add to the pleasure of the excursion.

Our Vegetables of the Month are eggplant and spinach without which we wouldn't have Ratatouille or Eggs Florentine. Think of it.

Using the Apple and Pear Harvest

	SOUP	BREAD	MAIN DISH
APPLE	Fresh Tart Fruit Soup	Apple Tea Bread	Bavarian Apple Pot Roast Fresh Fruit Stuffing Apple/Sage Stuffing
PEAR	Fresh Tart Fruit Soup		Baked Ham with Rosé Pears

SALAD	DESSERT	OTHER
Green Apple Chicken Salad Waldorf Salad	Granny's Green Apple Cake Caramel Apples Baked Apples with Raisins	Apple Chutney Hot Spiced Apple Juice with Roasted Apples
Pear, Pineapple and Cottage Cheese Salad	Fresh Fruit Kuchen Baked Fruit Compote Baked Bosc Pears Half Shell	Pear Honey Lemon-Pear Marmalade

Apple and Pear Favorites

GREEN APPLE CURRIED CHICKEN SALAD

MAKES 6 TO 8 SERVINGS

2 large Granny Smith or Greening apples
2 tablespoons lime or lemon juice
3½ cups cooked, cubed, chicken or turkey
1⅓ cups cooked rice
1 cup mayonnaise
½ cup slivered toasted almonds

1 tablespoon chopped onion
3 teaspoons curry powder
1¼ teaspoons salt
⅛ teaspoon ground black pepper
Crisp salad greens
2 limes, cut into wedges
Chutney

1. Core and dice apples. In large bowl, combine diced apple and lime juice.
2. Stir in chicken and rice. Blend mayonnaise, almonds, onion, curry powder and salt; stir into apple mixture. Cover and chill.
3. Mound salad on greens; sprinkle with a little curry powder. Garnish with lime and chutney.

HOT SPICED APPLE JUICE WITH ROASTED APPLES

MAKES 8 SERVINGS

8 very small apples
Whole cloves
2 tablespoons melted butter or margarine
2 tablespoons sugar
2 qts. apple juice

½ cup firmly packed dark or light brown sugar
2 whole nutmegs
4 cinnamon sticks
16 whole cloves
16 whole allspice

1. Preheat oven to 350°F. Core apples and remove skin from top ⅓ of each apple. Place in baking pan. Insert cloves in peeled portion. Brush with butter; sprinkle with sugar.

2. Bake 30 to 45 minutes. Baking time will depend on size and variety of apple, but they should be almost as tender as baked apples.

3. In 3-qt. saucepan combine apple juice and brown sugar. Tie spices in cheesecloth bag; crush with hammer or mallet and add to saucepan. Bring to boiling. Cover; reduce heat and simmer 15 minutes. Remove spice bag; discard.

4. To serve, pour hot spiced apple juice into tureen. Float hot roasted apples on surface. Ladle into mugs and top each serving with a roasted apple.

GRANNY'S GREEN APPLE CAKE

MAKES 1 (9- OR 10-INCH) CAKE

3 cups unsifted all-purpose flour
2 cups sugar
1 teaspoon baking soda
1 teaspoon salt
½ teaspoon ground cinnamon
1 cup vegetable oil
½ cup milk
3 eggs

1 teaspoon pure vanilla extract
3 Granny Smith or Greening apples, peeled, cored and diced
1 cup chopped walnuts
½ cup raisins
Lemon Glaze (recipe below)

1. In large bowl of electric mixer, blend flour, sugar, baking soda, salt, cinnamon, oil, milk, eggs and vanilla. Beat on low speed of electric mixer 3 minutes.

2. Fold in diced apples, nuts and raisins. Pour batter into greased and floured 9- or 10-inch tube pan.

3. Bake in preheated 350°F. oven for 1 hour and 15 minutes or until cake tester inserted in center comes out clean.

4. Cool cake in pan on wire rack for 10 minutes; remove from pan and cool completely. Spoon Lemon Glaze over cake.

LEMON GLAZE

MAKES ½ CUP GLAZE

1 cup confectioner's sugar   2 tablespoons lemon juice

1. In a small bowl, blend confectioners' sugar and lemon juice until smooth.

FRESH FRUIT KUCHEN

MAKES 2 CAKES

¾ cup unsifted all-purpose flour
2 tablespoons sugar
½ teaspoon salt
1 package active dry yeast
½ cup milk
¼ cup water
¼ cup plus 2 tablespoons margarine
1 egg at room temperature

¼ cup unsifted all-purpose flour
1 to 1½ cups unsifted all-purpose flour
4 cups sliced fresh apples, pears, nectarines, peaches or plums
⅔ cup sugar
1½ teaspoons ground cinnamon
2 tablespoons margarine

1. In a large bowl, thoroughly mix ¾ cup flour, 2 tablespoons sugar, salt and undissolved active dry yeast.

2. Combine milk, water and ¼ cup margarine in a saucepan. Heat over low heat until liquids are very warm (120°-130°F.). Margarine does not need to melt. Gradually add to dry ingredients and beat 2 minutes at medium speed of electric mixer, scraping bowl occasionally.

3. Add egg and ¼ cup flour. Beat at high speed 2 minutes, scraping bowl occasionally. Stir in enough additional flour to make a stiff batter.

4. Cover; let rise in warm place, free from draft, until doubled in bulk, about 1 hour. If desired, let dough rise in refrigerator. Cover tightly and refrigerate 2 hours or overnight.

5. Stir batter down. Turn into any 2 of the following greased pans: 9-inch square, 9-inch round, 2-qt. shallow baking dish, 12-inch pizza pan or 9-inch ovenproof skillet. Use lightly floured fingers to spread batter to edge of pans.

6. Arrange fruit slices evenly over batter. Combine ⅔ cup sugar, cinnamon and 2 tablespoons margarine; mix until crumbly. Sprinkle over fruit. Cover; let rise in warm place, free from draft, until doubled in bulk, about 1 hour.

7. Just before rising time is up preheat oven to 375°F. Bake about 25 to 30 minutes or until done.

BAKED APPLES WITH RAISINS

MAKES 6 SERVINGS

Clear cooking wrap with foil edges
6 (2½ to 3 lbs.) medium Rome Beauty or Greening apples, washed and cored
6 tablespoons dark brown sugar
6 tablespoons raisins
6 teaspoons butter or margarine
¾ cup orange juice, apple juice or cider

1. Preheat oven to 400°F. Line a 2½-inch-deep baking dish with enough cooking wrap to enclose apples, plus 3-inch overlap.
2. Place apples on wrap; fill centers with 1 tablespoon each of brown sugar and raisins, and 1 teaspoon butter. Pour orange juice over all.
3. Double-fold plain edges, making 3-inch overlap; double-fold foil edges to seal; pierce top of wrap 6 times with meat fork. Bake 25 to 30 minutes, or until apples are fork-tender.
4. Serve warm with syrup from pan.

BAKED BOSC PEARS HALF SHELL

MAKES 6 SERVINGS

3 fresh Bosc pears
Lemon juice
Choice of Fillings (see below)
½ cup water
½ cup packed dark brown sugar
1 tablespoon butter or margarine
½ teaspoon cinnamon

1. Preheat oven to 350°F. Halve and core pears. Brush with lemon juice.
2. Place pears in shallow baking pan. Fill centers with your choice of filling.
3. Combine water, sugar, butter and cinnamon. Heat to boiling, stirring until sugar dissolves. Pour over pears.
4. Bake pears for about 30 to 40 minutes until tender. Baste once with syrup. Serve as accompaniment dish at dinner or as dessert.

Fillings:

Raisin: Combine 2 tablespoons raisins, 2 tablespoons chopped almonds and 2 tablespoons orange marmalade.

Mincemeat: Use ½ cup prepared mincemeat.

Cranberry: Combine 2 tablespoons chopped fresh cranberries and ½ cup strawberry jam.

NORTHWESTERN APPLE CANDY

MAKES 16 (2-INCH) SQUARES

4 to 5 apples, unpeeled
1 cup water
2 envelopes unflavored
  gelatin
½ cup cold water
2 cups sugar

1 tablespoon cornstarch
Dash salt
1 cup coarsely chopped
  walnuts
1 teaspoon grated lemon rind
1 tablespoon lemon juice
Confectioners' sugar

1. Wash apples; without peeling or coring, cut into small pieces. Cook in water 10 minutes until tender.
2. Put through food mill or sieve and measure 2 cups pulp into a heavy, 2-qt. saucepan. Cook until thick, stirring often.
3. Soften gelatin in cold water. Mix sugar, cornstarch and salt; add to apple pulp. Cook over low heat, stirring constantly, until mixture thickens. Add gelatin; cook over low heat, stirring until gelatin is dissolved and mixture is a thick purée. Remove from heat.
4. Stir in walnuts, lemon rind and juice. Turn into an 8-inch-square shallow glass dish. Refrigerate overnight.

CARAMEL APPLES

MAKES 4 TO 5 APPLES

49 (14-oz. bag) caramels
2 tablespoons water
4 or 5 medium-sized apples,
  washed and dried
Wooden sticks

Topping: chopped walnuts,
cinnamon red hots, flaked
coconut, chocolate bits,
puffed rice cereal, chopped
peanuts

1. Melt caramels with water in the covered top of a double boiler, or in a heavy saucepan, over low heat. Stir occasionally until sauce is smooth.
2. Insert a wooden stick into stem end of each apple. Dip into hot caramel sauce and turn until coated. (Allow apples to stand at room temperature before dipping.)
3. Scrape off excess sauce from bottom of apples. Leave plain, or roll in desired toppings.
4. Place on greased waxed paper and chill until firm. Keep in cool place, but do not refrigerate.

APPLE CHUTNEY

MAKES 3 PINTS

2 qts. peeled, sliced, tart, hard-ripe apples
3 tablespoons salt
2½ qts. cool water
1 cup grated or finely chopped onion
¾ cup chopped crystallized ginger
½ cup chopped candied orange or grapefruit peel
1 pod chili pepper, seeded and chopped, or ½ teaspoon crushed red pepper

3 large cloves garlic, finely chopped
3 cups sugar
½ teaspoon ground ginger
½ teaspoon ground allspice
2 cups red wine vinegar or cider vinegar
¾ cup Worcestershire sauce
2 teaspoons non iodized salt
1¼ cups raisins
1½ cups lime juice
Sugar, optional
Salt, optional

1. Cut apple slices into 2 or 3 crosswise pieces. Drop apples into a nonmetallic container of brine made by dissolving 3 tablespoons salt in 2½ qts. cool water. Cover container and refrigerate for 2 days. Apples will discolor and shrivel a bit.

2. Put all ingredients except brined apples into a large kettle. Bring to boiling and boil rapidly, uncovered, stirring often, for 20 minutes.

3. Add well-drained apples and boil gently, uncovered, until mixture thickens; stir occasionally. Mixture should be neither dry nor soupy. Taste for seasoning; add sugar or salt if desired.

4. Keep chutney boiling as you fill hot sterilized jars. Pour boiling chutney to ⅛ inch of top of sterilized jars.

5. Wipe off anything that is spilled on tops or threads of jars with a clean, damp cloth.

6. Place each jar as it is filled onto rack in canner or deep kettle. When canner is filled, add hot water to cover jars 1 to 2 inches.

7. Cover canner and bring water to boil. Reduce heat to hold water at a steady boil. Start processing time when water reaches a full boil. Process 15 minutes.

PEAR HONEY

MAKES 4 PINTS

4½ lbs. fresh pears (9 cups),
    peeled and diced
1 cup diced fresh or canned
    pineapple

Grated peel and juice of
1 lime
5 cups sugar

1. Combine all ingredients in large saucepan.
2. Heat to boiling, stirring, until sugar dissolves. Reduce heat and let boil gently for about 30 to 45 minutes, until thickened.
3. Ladle hot mixture into hot sterilized jars and seal.
4. Put filled and sealed home-canning jars into a water bath canner or kettle filled with hot water. Add hot water if needed to bring water 2 inches over tops of jars.
5. Bring water to a rolling boil and boil gently for 5 minutes.
6. Remove jars from canner after processing. Cool away from drafts.

LEMON-PEAR MARMALADE

MAKES 3 PINTS

4 lemons
2 cups water

3 lbs. fresh pears (7 cups),
    peeled and diced
3½ cups sugar

1. Thinly slice and seed lemons. Place in 3-qt. saucepan or 6-qt. Dutch oven with water. Bring to boil and boil 10 minutes, or until lemon peel is tender.
2. Add pears and sugar to lemon-water mixture. Heat to boiling, stirring, until sugar dissolves. Reduce heat and let boil gently for about 30 minutes, stirring frequently to prevent scorching.
3. Ladle boiling mixture into hot sterilized jars and seal.
4. Put filled and sealed canning jars into a water bath canner or kettle filled with hot water. Add hot water if needed to bring water 2 inches above tops of jars.
5. Bring water to a rolling boil and boil gently for 5 minutes.
6. Remove jars from canner after processing. Cool away from drafts.

Back-to-School Lunch Treats

PEANUT BUTTER SANDWICH SPECIALS

Special No. 1
1 cup peanut butter
½ cup finely chopped celery
½ cup shredded carrot
¼ cup raisins
8 slices whole wheat bread
1½ cups shredded lettuce

1. In small bowl, combine peanut butter, chopped celery, carrot and raisins.
2. Divide filling between 4 slices whole wheat bread, top with shredded lettuce and remaining bread slices. Cut into halves.

MAKES 4 SANDWICHES

Special No. 2
1 cup peanut butter
½ cup coconut
¼ cup honey
6 slices toasted whole wheat bread
2 bananas
2 tablespoons orange juice

1. In small bowl, combine peanut butter, coconut and honey.
2. Divide filling evenly between 3 slices toasted whole wheat bread. Top with remaining toasted slices and cut in quarters.
3. Top each quarter with a banana slice that has been dipped in orange juice.

MAKES 3 SANDWICHES

HE-MAN LIVERWURST SANDWICHES

¼ lb. liverwurst
1 package (3 ozs.) cream cheese, softened
¼ cup chopped peanuts or celery
1 tablespoon ketchup

1 tablespoon pickle relish
¼ teaspoon onion powder
6 slices pumpernickel bread
Crisp lettuce leaves
3 small tomatoes

1. In medium bowl, blend liverwurst and cream cheese with fork until smooth. Add peanuts, ketchup, relish and onion powder.

2. Spread mixture on three slices of bread. Top with lettuce and remaining bread. Wrap in waxed paper or plastic bag. Place two sandwiches in lunch box with tomatoes.

DEVILED-EGG SANDWICHES

6 hard-cooked eggs
1 can (4½ ozs.) deviled ham
1 tablespoon finely chopped onion or 1½ teaspoons instant minced onion
½ cup finely chopped celery
½ cup mayonnaise
¾ teaspoon Worcestershire sauce

½ teaspoon ground mustard
Dash freshly ground black pepper
Butter or margarine
20 slices bread: enriched white, whole wheat or rye
10 crisp lettuce leaves

1. Mash eggs finely with fork on a sheet of waxed paper. Turn mashed eggs into a medium bowl and blend with deviled ham, onion, celery, mayonnaise, Worcestershire sauce, mustard and pepper.

2. Lightly butter bread. On one slice of bread place about ¼ cup egg mixture, spread smooth with spatula. Top with lettuce leaf and one slice bread. Cut sandwich in half. Repeat until all sandwiches are made.

JACK-IN-THE-BOX

MAKES 1 JACK-IN-THE-BOX
SANDWICH, 2 SERVINGS

1 slice square sandwich bread
1 slice round sandwich bread
2 teaspoons prepared mustard
  or margarine
1 slice round Edam or
  Cheddar cheese
2 slices stuffed green olive
1 (1-inch round) circle
  pimiento

1 curved sliver bologna or
  pimiento
½ can (4½ ozs.) deviled ham
1 small celery leaf
1 (4 inch) celery stick
1 (2 inches x ½ inch) strip
  pimiento
2 slices stuffed green olive

1. Spread both slices of bread with mustard. Place round cheese on round sandwich bread, making "face"; place on plate.
2. Place 2 olive slices, pimiento circle and sliver of bologna on bread, making "eyes," "nose" and "mouth."
3. Cut 2¼-inch triangle from side of square sandwich bread, making "hat" and "box." Spread each with deviled ham. Place "hat" at top and "box" at bottom of sandwich face.
4. Finish decorations with celery-leaf "feather" on hat, celery-stick "bow tie" centered with pimiento strip, and olive-slice "buttons."

THE BUG

MAKES 1 BUG
SANDWICH,
1 SERVING

1 slice round sandwich bread
½ teaspoon prepared mustard
  or margarine
1 slice round Edam or
  Cheddar cheese

1 slice round bologna,
  quartered
2 large slices carrot
3 slices stuffed green olive
2 (4 inch) celery sticks

1. Spread sandwich bread with mustard. Cover bread with round cheese; place on plate.
2. Place 2 bologna quarters on sandwich at top, 1 inch apart at edge; points almost touching. Place 2 quarters bologna on top of each other, and place on sandwich at bottom, with point in, 1¾ inches at edges from other two bologna quarters.
3. Place carrot slices topped with 2 olive slices on cheese, making "eyes." Place remaining olive slice on bottom of bologna quarter, making "mouth." Finish "bug" with celery stick "antennae," centering sticks between "eyes."

CHOO-CHOO TRAIN

MAKES 1 CHOO-CHOO
TRAIN, 2 SERVINGS

2 slices square sandwich
  bread
5½ tablespoons cream-style
  peanut butter
3 (1¼ inch) celery sticks
8 (¼-inch thick) banana
  slices
1 (½-inch thick) banana
  slice

1 whole Maraschino cherry
1 (2 inch) piece carrot,
  peeled
1 small celery leaf
1 tablespoon raisins or
  currants
2 (3½ inch) carrot sticks
4 Maraschino cherries,
  quartered

1. Spread each slice bread with 2½ tablespoons peanut butter; cut in half.
2. Arrange sandwich halves in a row, ends 1 inch apart, on foil-covered cardboard or tray. Place celery sticks between train "cars," making "couplings."
3. Place the 8 banana slices on bottom of "cars," making "wheels." Top thick banana slice with whole Maraschino cherry and attach with peanut butter to front "car," making "engine light." Place 2-inch piece of carrot on engine, making "stack," and place celery leaf on top, making "smoke."
4. "Fill" the first train "car" with raisins: "coal"; the second with carrot sticks: "logs"; the third with quartered cherries: "apples."

SAILBOAT

MAKES 1 SAILBOAT
SANDWICH, 1 SERVING

1 slice square sandwich bread
2 tablespoons whipped cream
  cheese
2 tablespoons process cheese
  spread, softened

1 (6 inch) celery stick
1 slice carrot, cut on diagonal
6 to 8 slices stuffed green olives

1. Cut bread in half on the diagonal. Spread cream cheese on one triangle. Spread cheese spread on remaining triangle.
2. Place cream-cheese triangle on plate, cut side vertically straight, up and down, making "sail." Place celery stick alongside, making "mast." Top with carrot, making "flag."
3. Place cheese-spread triangle across bottom of "sail," making "boat." Decorate top of "boat" triangle with row of sliced olives.

PARTICIPATION PIZZA

MAKES 2 PIZZAS, 4 HEFTY SERVINGS

1 package active dry yeast
1¼ cups warm water
¼ cup olive or vegetable oil
4½ cups (about) unsifted all-
purpose flour
½ teaspoon salt
½ teaspoon coarse ground
black pepper
2 cups Pizza Tomato Sauce
(recipe below)
½ lb. shredded mozzarella
½ lb. grated provolone
2 tablespoons olive or
vegetable oil

Pizza Topping
Suggestions:
¼ lb. thinly sliced pepperoni
¼ lb. thinly sliced salami
½ lb. precooked ground beef
½ lb. precooked Italian
sausage, sliced
1 cup onion rings
1 cup green-pepper chunks
1 cup sliced mushrooms
1 can (2 ozs.) anchovies,
drained

1. In large bowl sprinkle yeast over ¼ cup warm water. Stir to dissolve. Add remaining water and olive oil.
2. With large spoon, beat in 1½ cups flour until smooth; continue beating 2 minutes. Add salt, pepper and enough remaining flour to make a stiff dough.
3. Turn out onto lightly floured board. Knead until smooth and elastic, about 8 to 10 minutes. Place in oiled bowl, turning to oil top. Cover; let rise in warm place, free from draft, until doubled in bulk, about 1½ hours.
4. Punch dough down; divide in half. Press onto a lightly oiled pizza pan or large baking sheet, making 12-inch circles with ½-inch-high borders.
5. Preheat oven to 400°F. Spread each round with 1 cup tomato sauce. Top with cheese mixture. Add pizza toppings of choice. Sprinkle with oil.
6. Bake 20 to 25 minutes, until crust is golden brown.

PIZZA TOMATO SAUCE

MAKES ABOUT 2 CUPS

1 can (15 ozs.) tomato sauce
or 2 cans (8-oz. size) tomato
sauce
1 teaspoon oregano leaves

½ teaspoon basil leaves
½ teaspoon sugar
2 tablespoons water

1. Combine all ingredients in small saucepan. Heat to boiling; reduce heat and simmer, uncovered, 5 minutes.

CHILI DOGS FOR A GANG

MAKES 32 SERVINGS

1 cup finely chopped onion
½ cup chopped green pepper
1 garlic clove, crushed
3 tablespoons vegetable oil
2 lbs. ground beef (chuck)
3 cans (8-oz. size) tomato
    sauce
2½ teaspoons chili powder

2 teaspoons salt
¼ teaspoon freshly ground
    black pepper
¼ cup light molasses
2 cans (16-oz. size) red kidney
    beans, drained
32 frankfurters
32 frankfurter buns, split

1. In large skillet, sauté onion, green pepper and garlic in hot oil. Add beef and cook, stirring until beef loses its red color.
2. Add tomato sauce, chili powder, salt, pepper and molasses; simmer, uncovered, for 15 minutes. Add kidney beans and heat well.
3. Meanwhile, add frankfurters to boiling water, simmer for 5 minutes, drain. Heat frankfurter buns in preheated 350°F. oven for 5 minutes.
4. Place a frankfurter in each bun and top with chili.

WHEAT AND RAISIN CHOCOLATE CHIP COOKIES

MAKES 45 LARGE COOKIES

1½ cups regular margarine or
    solid all-vegetable
    shortening
1½ cups firmly packed dark
    brown sugar
1½ cups sugar
2 teaspoons pure vanilla
    extract
4 eggs
2½ cups unsifted all-purpose
    flour

2½ cups unsifted whole wheat
    flour
½ teaspoon salt
2 teaspoons baking soda
2 tablespoons hot water
1 cup chopped nuts
1 cup raisins
1 package (12 ozs.) semi-sweet
    chocolate bits

1. Preheat oven to 350°F.
2. Beat margarine in large bowl until soft. Gradually add sugars, beating until light and fluffy. Add vanilla.
3. Add eggs one at a time, beating well.
4. Blend both kinds of flour and salt on sheet of waxed paper. Gradually add flour mixture to sugar mixture, beating at low speed until well-mixed.

5. Dissolve baking soda in hot water and add to sugar-flour mixture.

6. Stir in nuts, raisins, and chocolate bits.

7. Using 1 generous tablespoon of dough for each cookie, place on greased cookie sheet, flattening dough to a 2½-inch circle.

8. Bake for 10 to 12 minutes. Allow to cool.

WALNUT JUMBOS

MAKES 12 (5-INCH) COOKIES

1¼ cups sifted all-purpose flour
¾ teaspoon salt
½ teaspoon baking powder
½ teaspoon soda
½ teaspoon ground cinnamon
½ teaspoon ground ginger
½ cup butter or margarine, softened
1 cup light or dark brown sugar, packed
1 large egg
⅓ cup light molasses
2 cups uncooked quick oats
¾ cup chopped walnuts
¼ cup chopped walnuts

1. Preheat oven to 350°F. Lightly grease cookie sheets. Resift flour with salt, baking powder, soda and spices.

2. In large bowl with electric mixer, beat butter, sugar and egg together well.

3. Blend in molasses, then flour mixture and oats. Stir in ¾ cup walnuts.

4. Drop by quarter cupfuls onto lightly greased baking sheets, allowing room for spreading, and flatten slightly. Sprinkle top with ¼ cup walnuts.

5. Bake above oven center for 13 to 15 minutes, until lightly browned. Let stand on sheets about 5 minutes, then use broad spatula to lift onto wire racks to cool.

Camping Go-Alongs

BEEF JERKY

MAKES ¾ POUND

1½ lbs. flank steak, partially
frozen
1 teaspoon salt
1 teaspoon liquid smoke
⅓ teaspoon garlic powder
⅓ teaspoon freshly ground
black pepper

⅓ teaspoon monosodium
glutamate
1 teaspoon onion powder
¼ cup soy sauce
¼ cup Worcestershire sauce

1. Slice flank steak in thin slices diagonally across the grain.
2. Combine seasoning mixture and brush on both sides of meat.
Arrange meat slices on two 10- x 15- x 1-inch jelly-roll pans.
3. Place in preheated, very low 200°F. oven for 8 to 12 hours, turning
meat several times to dry out evenly. Or hang outside on string, away
from animals, in cool, airy place to dry.
4. Store in plastic bags in refrigerator or freezer.

QUICK ENERGY GORP

MAKES 4 CUPS

1 handful (½ cup) raisins
1 handful (½ cup) cashews
1 handful (½ cup) candy-
coated chocolate
1 handful (½ cup) cut-up
dried apricots

1 handful (½ cup) sunflower
seeds
1 handful (½ cup) cut-up
dried apples
2 handfuls (1 cup) granola

1. Mix ingredients in bowl. Divide between several plastic bags and
seal with twisters.

GRANOLA

MAKES ABOUT
3 QUARTS

1 cup soy flour
1 cup shredded or flaked
 coconut
1 cup slivered almonds
1 cup cashews
2 cups wheat germ
6 cups rolled flakes (oatmeal,
 barley, wheat or rye flakes)

½ cup sesame seeds, preferably
 unhulled
2 tablespoons brewer's yeast
1 teaspoon salt
1 cup vegetable oil
1 cup honey
4 cups cut-up dried fruit:
 apricots, prunes, dates,
 cherries, apples, raisins, etc.

1. In large 4- to 6-qt. pot, mix all dry ingredients, except dried fruit.
2. Pour oil and honey over all and mix until well combined.
3. Spread mixture evenly on three 10- x 15- x 1-inch jelly-roll pans. Bake in slow, preheated 250°F. oven for 1½ hours or until as crunchy as you like. Stir every half-hour for even baking. Cool granola.
4. Cut up dried fruit and mix into granola thoroughly. Spoon into plastic bags; seal with twister. Keep some at room temperature, some in refrigerator and freeze remaining.

BASQUE SOUP

MAKES 6 SERVINGS

1 cup chopped green pepper
1 cup chopped onion
1 teaspoon paprika
3 tablespoons butter or
 margarine
2 cans (10¾-oz. size) condensed
 chicken broth

2 cans (11-oz. size) condensed
 tomato bisque soup
2 cans (16-oz. size) chick peas,
 drained
8 ozs. sliced hard salami,
 slivered

1. In 3-qt. saucepan, cook green pepper and onion with paprika in butter until tender.
2. Add all remaining ingredients. Heat to boiling, cover, reduce heat and simmer for 15 minutes.

CHICKEN STEW

MAKES 4 QUARTS

1 (2½ lbs.) broiler-fryer, cut up
1 qt. water
1 onion, peeled and quartered
Salt
5 to 6 large onions (2 lbs.), chopped
5 to 6 potatoes (2 lbs.), peeled and diced
2 cans (17-oz. size) cream-style corn
1 can (8 ozs.) tomato sauce
1 can (6 ozs.) tomato paste
2 tablespoons vinegar
½ teaspoon freshly ground black pepper
1 cup water
Hot pepper sauce, optional

1. In 3-qt. saucepan place chicken, 1 qt. water, quartered onion and 1 teaspoon salt.
2. Heat to boiling, cover, reduce heat and simmer 30 to 40 minutes until chicken is tender.
3. Remove chicken from broth and allow to cool. Save broth.
4. Skin and bone chicken. Coarsely chop chicken and add to broth in 6-qt. kettle or Dutch oven.
5. Stir in chopped onion, diced potato, corn, tomato sauce, tomato paste, vinegar, pepper and 1 cup water.
6. Heat to boiling, cover, reduce heat and simmer 40 to 50 minutes until potatoes are tender. Stir to prevent sticking. Add hot pepper sauce to taste, if desired.
7. Serve in bowls with saltines or spoon over rice. Can be frozen.

SKILLET PINTOS

MAKES 4 SERVINGS

1 can (8 ozs.) sliced peaches
1 can (12 ozs.) luncheon meat, cut in 8 slices
½ cup chopped onion
2 tablespoons butter or margarine
2 cans (16-oz. size) pinto beans in tomato sauce

1. Drain peaches, reserving 2 tablespoons liquid. In skillet, brown luncheon meat and cook onion in butter until tender.
2. Stir in beans, peaches and reserved peach liquid. Heat, stirring often. (Variation: Add ½ teaspoon chili powder.)

CHUCK WAGON FAVORITE STEW

MAKES 8 SERVINGS

3½ lbs. boneless chuck roast (2½ to 3 inches thick)
2 tablespoons vegetable shortening or vegetable oil
1 can (10¾ ozs.) condensed cream of mushroom soup
1 can (10¾ ozs.) condensed cream of onion soup
½ cup water
¼ teaspoon freshly ground black pepper
2 tablespoons prepared white horseradish
6 medium potatoes (about 2 lbs.) peeled and cut in half
2 cups carrots, peeled and cut diagonally in 2-inch pieces

1. Cut meat across grain into 8 slices.
2. In a large, heavy pan, brown meat in shortening over medium-high heat. Pour off fat.
3. Stir in soups, water, pepper and horseradish. Heat to boiling, cover and cook over low heat for 45 minutes.
4. Add potatoes and carrots. Stirring often, cook for 45 minutes more or until done.

PAN BISCUITS

MAKES 18 BISCUITS

½ cup milk
2 tablespoons vegetable oil
1 tablespoon vinegar
½ teaspoon onion salt
1½ cups biscuit mix
½ cup cornmeal
2 tablespoons vegetable shortening or vegetable oil

1. In measuring cup, combine milk, oil, vinegar and onion salt.
2. In bowl, mix biscuit mix and cornmeal. Stir in milk mixture with fork.
3. Form dough into a ball. Turn dough out onto a floured board and knead it about 10 times.
4. Shape into 18 smooth balls about 1½ inches in diameter; flatten with palm of hand to about ¼-inch thickness.
5. In skillet, melt shortening over medium-low heat; add biscuits. Cook until lightly browned on both sides and cooked through. Use more shortening if necessary.

Vegetables of the Month: Eggplant and Spinach

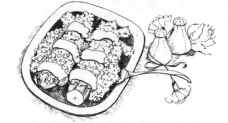

SUPER EASY EGGPLANT

MAKES 4 TO 6 SERVINGS

1 to 2 lbs. 1½-inch chunks
    unpeeled eggplant or
    zucchini
¾ cup vegetable oil
¼ cup vinegar

½ teaspoon salt
½ teaspoon ground mustard
¼ teaspoon freshly ground
    black pepper
1 small clove garlic, crushed

1. Thread chunks of eggplant on skewers or bamboo sticks. Place on grill or broiler rack.
2. Combine oil, vinegar, salt, mustard, pepper and garlic in a small covered jar. Shake well.
3. Brush salad dressing on eggplant chunks. Grill, 4 to 5 inches from hot coals, turning and basting until lightly browned and tender, about 3 to 4 minutes per side.

Editor's Note: Great with grilled meats or chicken.

RATATOUILLE

MAKES 8 SERVINGS

3 cloves garlic
1 lb. (6 medium) zucchini
1 lb. (4 large) green peppers
1 lb. (3 large) yellow onions
1 lb. (1 medium) eggplant
2 lbs. (4 large) tomatoes

¾ cup vegetable oil or olive
    oil
2 teaspoons salt
¼ teaspoon freshly ground
    black pepper

1. Prepare vegetables for sautéing: Slice garlic thinly, cut zucchini into ¼-inch-thick slices, green pepper into ½-inch-wide strips, slice onions thinly, cut unpeeled eggplant into 1-inch cubes and peel and quarter tomatoes.

2. In large skillet, heat ¼ cup oil. Add garlic, zucchini and green pepper. Sauté 5 minutes, stirring. Remove to a bowl.

3. In additional ¼ cup oil, sauté onion and eggplant for 5 minutes, stirring. Add to zucchini-green pepper mixture.

4. In ¼ cup oil, sauté tomato quarters for 2 minutes, stirring.

5. Turn all vegetables into skillet with tomatoes. Season with salt and pepper; stir gently to mix. Heat to boiling. Reduce heat and simmer covered 10 minutes. Uncover and simmer 5 to 10 minutes, stirring once or twice, until liquid is practically all absorbed. Vegetables should be soft and tender, but retain their individual identity. Serve hot or cold.

BAKED STUFFED EGGPLANT

MAKES 4 SERVINGS

1 large eggplant	½ teaspoon salt
Vegetable oil	¼ teaspoon freshly ground
½ lb. lean ground beef	black pepper
1 can (6 ozs.) tomato paste	½ cup dry red wine
1 egg, slightly beaten	½ cup plain whole milk
2 tablespoons finely chopped	yogurt
onion	1 can (8 ozs.) tomato sauce
2 tablespoons finely chopped	½ cup shredded mozzarella
green pepper	cheese
1 garlic clove, minced	

1. Preheat oven to 350°F.

2. Cut eggplant in half, scoop out pulp, leaving shell intact, and finely dice eggplant pulp.

3. In a skillet, brown eggplant in oil and add beef, turning until browned. Drain off any fat if necessary.

4. Stir in tomato paste, egg, onion, green pepper, garlic, salt, pepper, red wine and yogurt. Heat thoroughly, but do not boil. Spoon mixture into eggplant halves, top with tomato sauce and mozzarella cheese. Place in baking dish and bake for 45 to 55 minutes until bubbly and eggplant is tender.

FLORENTINE RICE QUICHE

MAKES 1 (9-INCH) QUICHE,
6 TO 8 SERVINGS

1 egg
2 cups cooked rice
⅔ cup finely grated Swiss
  cheese
1 package (10 ozs.) chopped
  spinach
2 tablespoons butter or
  margarine
3 eggs

½ teaspoon salt
1 cup (½ pt.) cottage cheese
¼ cup grated Parmesan
  cheese
6 tablespoons heavy cream or
  evaporated milk
3 drops hot pepper sauce
¼ teaspoon nutmeg

1. Preheat oven to 350°F. Grease a 9-inch pie pan.

2. In medium bowl beat 1 egg. Add rice and Swiss cheese; stir well. Spread rice mixture evenly in prepared pie pan, making a crust. Refrigerate until ready to fill and bake.

3. Cook spinach as directed on package. Pour into strainer and press out all liquid. Add butter to drained spinach, set aside.

4. In medium bowl beat remaining 3 eggs, stir in salt, cottage cheese, Parmesan cheese, heavy cream, hot pepper sauce and nutmeg. When well blended, stir in spinach.

5. Pour filling into prepared rice crust. Bake for 30 to 35 minutes, or until firm.

6. To serve, cut into wedges.

Editor's Note: To make ahead, 1. Prepare crust early in day and refrigerate until needed. 2. Prepare filling ahead and refrigerate until needed. 3. Assemble pie just before baking. We suggest this make-ahead method to help prevent a soggy crust.

SPINACH SOUFFLÉ CREPES

MAKES 6 SERVINGS

3 tablespoons butter or
  margarine
¼ cup minced onion
¾ cup minced fresh spinach
  leaves
3 tablespoons all-purpose
  flour

1 cup milk, scalded
½ teaspoon salt
⅛ teaspoon ground nutmeg
4 eggs, separated
½ cup grated Swiss cheese
12 Basic Crepes (recipe below)
  Cheese Sauce (recipe below)

1. Preheat oven to 375°F. Melt butter in medium saucepan. Add onion and cook, stirring, 5 minutes, until tender. Add spinach and cook, stirring, about 3 minutes to evaporate most of the moisture.
2. Stir in flour smoothly. Add hot milk and cook, stirring, until mixture comes to boiling. Season with salt and nutmeg.
3. Add egg yolks one at a time, stirring well with wire whisk until blended. Add grated cheese.
4. Beat egg whites until stiff peaks form. Fold into egg-yolk mixture with a light hand. Pour into a well-buttered 1½-qt. soufflé dish.
5. Set dish in a pan containing 1 inch hot water. Bake about 35 minutes, or until knife inserted in center comes out clean.
6. To assemble: Place about ⅓ cup of baked spinach soufflé in center of each crepe. Spread lightly with spatula. Roll up. Place in shallow oven-to-table baking dish. Top with Cheese Sauce.
7. Place dish under broiler about 4 inches from heating element for 2 to 3 minutes, to brown sauce lightly.

BASIC CREPES
MAKES 12
TO 14 CREPES

1½ cups milk   1 cup all-purpose flour
 3 eggs   Vegetable oil
⅛ teaspoon salt

1. Put milk, eggs, salt and flour into electric-blender container. Cover. Blend at top speed for 30 seconds.
2. Scrape down batter on sides of blender with spatula. Batter should be the consistency of heavy cream.
3. Cover and refrigerate. If possible, allow to stand an hour or two before cooking. Batter will thicken as it stands. If you find the batter is too heavy, beat in a few tablespoons water.
4. Before preparing each crepe, brush the crepe pan or small 6-inch skillet with oil to cover entire bottom. Heat pan until hot, but not smoking.
5. Pour in about 2 to 3 tablespoons batter, tilt pan to coat bottom evenly with batter. Cook over medium heat about 1 minute until the top of the crepe is dry and the bottom is lightly browned. Turn crepe with spatula and cook on other side about 20 seconds. Tip out onto plate.
6. Repeat, stacking crepes with waxed paper between each.

CHEESE SAUCE
MAKES 1 CUP

3 tablespoons butter or margarine
3 tablespoons all-purpose flour
1 cup milk
¼ teaspoon salt
Dash pepper
1 cup grated Cheddar cheese

1. Heat butter in small saucepan until melted. Stir in flour smoothly. Gradually add milk, stirring.
2. Heat to boiling, stirring until mixture thickens. Add remaining ingredients, stirring until cheese melts.

FLORENTINE TUNA-NOODLE CASSEROLE

MAKES 4 TO 6 SERVINGS

1 tablespoon salt
3 qts. boiling water
4 cups (8 ozs.) ¼-inch-wide noodles or fettucine noodles
⅓ cup margarine or butter
2 tablespoons instant minced onion
⅓ cup unsifted all-purpose flour
1 packet instant chicken bouillon or 1 cube
¾ teaspoon salt
¼ teaspoon freshly ground black pepper
¼ teaspoon ground nutmeg
¼ teaspoon paprika
3 cups evaporated milk, diluted
1 package (10 ozs.) frozen chopped spinach, cooked and well drained
2 cans (6½ or 7 ozs. each) tuna, drained and flaked
½ cup grated process American or Gruyère cheese
Paprika

1. In 6- to 8-qt. kettle add 1 tablespoon salt to rapidly boiling water. Gradually add noodles so that water continues to boil. Cook uncovered 7 minutes, stirring occasionally. Drain in colander.
2. Meanwhile make Florentine Sauce: In 2-qt. saucepan slowly melt margarine. Remove from heat. Stir in instant minced onion, flour, bouillon, ¾ teaspoon salt, pepper, nutmeg and paprika until smooth.
3. Gradually stir in milk. Bring to boil over medium heat, stirring. Reduce heat; simmer 1 minute.
4. Preheat oven to 375°F. Lightly grease a shallow 2-qt. casserole.
5. Layer half of noodles and all of spinach and tuna in casserole. Top with remaining noodles.
6. Pour Florentine Sauce over casserole. Poke gently with spoon to allow sauce to spread. Sprinkle with cheese and paprika.
7. Bake 40 to 45 minutes, until sauce bubbles and cheese is melted.

October

October is a colorful, spirited month. Vivid blue skies are over-head and sure rays of clear sunshine warm our shoulders. The changing leaves dance in the trees and then drift slowly down to form a multi-colored carpet for our walking pleasure.

There is also a deepening sense of returning indoors on these chilly fall afternoons. We feature a whole bakery full of tea breads to enjoy with a warming hot drink.

Halloween closes this month and we suggest a treasure trove of really good-tasting and good-for-you snack foods.

As the holidays approach, we long for the good foods of our heritage. Our sampling of ethnic favorites should satisfy.

October is country fair time in many parts of our land, and we have a collection of foods to sell or show at a fair.

Our Vegetable of the Month is the potato. This earthy tuber lends itself to soups, salads, side dishes, breads—and desserts.

Tea Breads

TEA BREAD	FLOUR	SWEETNER	LEAVENING	SALT
NUT BREAD	2½ cups unsifted all-purpose flour	1 cup sugar	3½ teaspoons baking powder	1 teaspoon
LEMON BREAD	2½ cups unsifted all-purpose flour	1 cup sugar	3½ teaspoons baking powder	1 teaspoon
MARMA-LADE BREAD	2½ cups unsifted all-purpose flour	¾ cup sugar	4 teaspoons baking powder	1 teaspoon
JAM BREAD	2½ cups unsifted all-purpose flour	¾ cup sugar	4 teaspoons baking powder	1 teaspoon
BANANA BREAD	2½ cups unsifted all-purpose flour	1 cup sugar	3½ teaspoons baking powder ½ teaspoon baking soda	1 teaspoon
CRAN-BERRY BREAD	2½ cups unsifted all-purpose flour	1¼ cups sugar	3½ teaspoons baking powder ½ teaspoon baking soda	1 teaspoon
APPLE	2⅔ cups unsifted all-purpose flour	1 cup sugar	3½ teaspoons baking powder ½ teaspoon baking soda	1 teaspoon
ORANGE DATE/NUT	2½ cups unsifted all-purpose flour	1 cup sugar	3½ teaspoons baking powder	1 teaspoon

BASIC METHOD FOR MAKING TEA BREADS

Preheat oven to 350°F. Oil and flour a 9- x 5- x 3-inch loaf pan or two 8½- x 4½- x 2½-inch loaf pans.

Measure all ingredients into large bowl; beat with mixer at medium speed ½ minute.

Turn batter into pans. Bake 55 to 65 minutes or until wooden pick inserted in center comes out clean.

Loosen from sides of pan; turn out on rack to cool.

Cut in thin slices with serrated knife. Wrap in foil when completely cool. Slices best day after baking. Makes 1 large loaf or 2 medium loaves.

To make Pour Syrup: In small saucepan combine sugar and fruit juice. Heat to boiling, stirring until sugar dissolves. Prick tea bread surface with toothpick and slowly pour syrup over warm bread.

OIL	LIQUID	EGG	ADD	POUR
3 table-spoons	1¼ cups milk	1 egg	1 cup chopped walnuts, pecans or almonds	
3 table-spoons	1¼ cups milk	1 egg	1 tablespoon grated lemon rind	¼ cup sugar ¼ cup lemon juice
3 table-spoons	1 cup milk	1 egg	½ cup marmalade	¼ cup sugar ¼ cup orange juice
3 table-spoons	1 cup milk	1 egg	½ cup jam	
3 table-spoons	½ cup milk plus 2 table-spoons	1 egg	1 cup mashed very ripe banana	
3 table-spoons	1¼ cups milk	1 egg	1 cup chopped cranberries	¼ cup sugar ¼ cup orange juice
3 table-spoons	1¼ cups milk	1 egg	1 cup shredded apple	
3 table-spoons	1¼ cups milk 2 table-spoons orange juice	1 egg	½ cup chopped dates ½ cup chopped nuts 1 teaspoon grated orange rind	¼ cup sugar ¼ cup orange juice

Halloween Treats

MOLASSES CUTOUT COOKIES

MAKES 36 COOKIES

1⅓ cups butter or margarine, softened
1 cup sugar
1 cup light or dark molasses
½ cup boiling water
1 teaspoon salt
1 tablespoon ground cinnamon
2 teaspoons ground ginger
6 cups unsifted all-purpose flour or unbleached flour
1 can (16½ oz.) prepared vanilla frosting
1 can (16½ ozs.) prepared chocolate frosting
Red and Yellow food coloring
Candy corn
Licorice strings
Multicolored chocolate candy

1. In large bowl with electric mixer at medium speed, beat butter until smooth; gradually add sugar, beating until light.

2. At low speed add molasses and boiling water. Beat until smooth, scraping side of bowl with rubber scraper.

3. At low speed add salt, cinnamon and ginger. Add flour, 2 cups at a time, stirring with spoon until blended.

4. Turn dough onto sheet of heavy-duty foil. Wrap securely and refrigerate for at least 2 hours. (Or you can make dough one day and bake cookies a few days later.)

5. Make cardboard patterns for cookies. Draw jack-o'-lantern, owl, ghost, witch's hat and cat, each about 5 inches tall by 3 to 4 inches wide. To make Halloween letters and the fence, roll dough between hands to about the width of a pencil and make desired shapes.

6. Roll out ⅓ of dough at a time, ¼-inch thick, on a lightly floured board. A pastry cloth for the board and a stockinette cover for the rolling pin make rolling very easy.

7. Preheat oven to 375°F. Lay patterns on dough and cut out cookies. Reroll any remaining dough. If dough gets too soft, refrigerate. Place cookies on ungreased cookie sheets. Bake 10 to 12 minutes, or until done. Cool 1 minute, then remove from cookie sheets with spatula to wire rack; cool completely.

8. Decorate cookies with frosting. Color vanilla frosting orange with a few drops of red and yellow food coloring if desired for jack-o'-lantern. Make faces with candy corn, licorice and chocolate candy.

DRIED FRUIT ROLLS

MAKES 4 ROLLS

½ lb. pitted dates
1 lb. dried figs
2 cups chopped walnuts
2 cups chopped almonds
½ cup seedless raisins

1 lb. dried apricots or dried apples
1 teaspoon grated orange rind
Flaked coconut, confectioners' sugar or sunflower seeds

1. Put dates, figs, walnuts, almonds, raisins and apricots through food grinder or electric food processor.

2. In large bowl, with well scrubbed hands, mix ground fruits with orange rind. Divide mixture into four parts.

3. Shape into rolls about 10 inches long by 2 inches in diameter. Roll in shredded coconut, confectioners' sugar or sunflower seeds. Wrap in plastic film. Will keep for several weeks.

NATURAL SWEET TREAT

MAKES APPROXIMATELY ½ POUND

⅓ cup honey
½ cup crunchy peanut butter

¾ cup nonfat dry milk

1. Mix honey and peanut butter in bowl. Stir in nonfat dry milk a little at a time until thoroughly blended.

2. Shape into narrow roll. Wrap in wax paper and chill until firm. Cut into 1-inch pieces and wrap in cellophane.

NATURAL NUT NIBBLE

MAKES ABOUT 9 POUNDS

1 lb. roasted, salted soy nuts
1 lb. salted soy nuts
1 lb. unsalted Virginia peanuts
1 lb. unsalted Spanish peanuts
1 lb. sunflower seeds

1 lb. walnuts
1 lb. natural whole almonds
1 lb. cashews
1 lb. unhulled pumpkin seeds

1. Mix all varieties of nuts in large bowl or kettle. Or mix smaller amounts in equal proportion.
2. Divide into plastic bags. Freeze some for storage; keep others cool and dry.

ICE-CREAM COOKIE
SANDWICHES

MAKES 10 SANDWICHES

½ cup shortening
1 cup packed dark brown sugar
½ teaspoon pure vanilla extract
1 egg
1½ cups sifted all-purpose flour

1 cup finely chopped walnuts
½ cup shredded bran cereal
½ teaspoon grated orange rind
½ teaspoon baking soda
½ teaspoon salt
¼ cup milk
3 cups vanilla ice cream

1. In large bowl with electric mixer at high speed, beat shortening with sugar and vanilla until light and fluffy. Beat in egg.
2. On sheet of waxed paper, mix flour, walnuts, shredded bran cereal, orange rind, baking soda and salt.
3. Blend flour mixture into batter alternately with milk.
4. Make 20 cookies: drop by heaping tablespoonfuls onto lightly greased baking sheet, 4 inches apart.
5. Spread dough to make a cookie 2 inches in diameter and ¼-inch thick. Bake in preheated 400°F. oven 5 to 8 minutes, just until cookies are golden but still soft. Do not overbake.
6. Cool 1 minute, then remove from baking sheet and cool completely.
7. Spread about ⅓ cup ice cream on bottom of 10 cookies. Top with remaining cookies to make sandwiches.
8. Freeze at least 1 hour before serving. For long periods of freezing, wrap well in foil; label and freeze.

QUICK POPS

MAKES 12 POPSICLES

1 can (6 ozs.) frozen orange or grape juice or lemonade

3 cans (6-ozs. each) water
2/3 cup light corn syrup

1. In medium bowl stir together juice and water until juice is reconstituted. Add corn syrup and stir until blended.
2. Pour into popsicle molds; insert sticks and cover. Freeze until firm.

Editor's Note: To prepare in ice-cube trays: pour mixture into deep trays; freeze until firm, inserting a craft stick or a wooden spoon into each when partially set.

SURFER SHAKE

MAKES 4 SERVINGS

3 cups milk
1 cup vanilla ice cream
2 eggs
2 tablespoons vegetable oil
1/2 cup nonfat dry milk

1/4 cup natural-flavored malted-milk powder
1/4 cup molasses
2 tablespoons wheat germ
1 teaspoon pure vanilla extract

1. Place all ingredients in order given in electric blender. Blend at low speed 30 seconds, blend at high speed 1 minute until foamy.
2. Pour into glasses.

BEEF WITH BROCCOLI

MAKES 4 SERVINGS

2 packages (10-oz. size) frozen broccoli spears, partially thawed, or 1 bunch fresh broccoli
1 lb. flank steak, partially frozen, thinly sliced across grain
1 teaspoon cornstarch
¼ teaspoon sugar
¼ teaspoon ground ginger
1 tablespoon soy sauce
1½ teaspoons water
1 clove garlic, crushed
2 tablespoons peanut oil
3 tablespoons peanut oil
1 can (8 ozs.) sliced bamboo shoots, drained
½ cup sliced fresh mushrooms
1½ teaspoons salt
¾ teaspoon sugar
2 tablespoons water
1 teaspoon cornstarch
1 tablespoon water
Hot cooked white rice

1. Cut broccoli flowerets and stems into 1½-inch lengths, about ½-inch wide; set aside. If using fresh broccoli, break flowerets with stems from large stems. Peel skin from large and small stems.
2. Cut steak slices into 2- x 1-inch pieces. In a small bowl combine 1 teaspoon cornstarch, ¼ teaspoon sugar, ginger, soy sauce, 1½ teaspoons water and garlic; blend well. Stir in beef and set aside.
3. Preheat wok or a large, heavy skillet about 3 minutes; pour in 2 tablespoons oil. Add beef; stir-fry 1 minute, until meat loses its red color. Return beef to bowl.
4. Heat remaining 3 tablespoons oil in wok or skillet. Stir in broccoli, bamboo shoots and mushrooms; stir-fry 2 minutes.
5. Add salt, remaining ¾ teaspoon sugar and 2 tablespoons water; mix well. Cook 1 minute, stirring occasionally. Add meat; cook and stir 1 minute.
6. Blend together remaining 1 teaspoon cornstarch and 1 tablespoon water. Add to wok or skillet. Cook, stirring until slightly thickened. Serve with rice.

CHINESE SWEET AND SOUR BEEF

MAKES 5 TO 6 SERVINGS

1 lb. top round steak, ½ to ¾ inch thick
Natural meat tenderizer, seasoned or unseasoned
3 tablespoons vegetable oil
2 tablespoons vegetable oil
1 large onion, cut in thin wedges
1 can (8½ ozs.) water chestnuts, drained and sliced
1 green pepper, cut in squares
1 can (13¼ ozs.) pineapple tidbits or chunks, undrained
2 tablespoons ketchup
1 tablespoon wine vinegar
2 tablespoons soy sauce
½ teaspoon sugar
1 tablespoon cornstarch
3 tablespoons cold water
2 firm, ripe tomatoes, cut in eighths
Hot cooked rice

1. Trim excess fat from beef. Prepare meat, one side at a time, with meat tenderizer as follows: Thoroughly moisten meat with water. Sprinkle tenderizer as evenly as salt over entire meat surface. To insure penetration of tenderizer and retain meat juices, pierce meat deeply with fork at ½-inch intervals.

2. With sharp knife, cut beef diagonally across grain into thin slices.

3. In wok or large skillet heat 3 tablespoons vegetable oil until hot but not smoking.

4. Quickly brown beef over high heat, stirring rapidly 3 to 4 minutes. Remove meat and pan drippings to platter.

5. Heat 2 tablespoons oil in same skillet. Add onion, water chestnuts and green pepper. Stir-fry until tender-crisp, about 3 minutes.

6. Add undrained pineapple, ketchup, vinegar, soy sauce and sugar. Heat to boiling.

7. Mix cornstarch smoothly with cold water. Add to sauce in skillet and heat, stirring, until sauce clears and thickens.

8. Return meat and drippings to skillet and add tomatoes; heat through. Serve over hot cooked rice.

HUNAN BEEF

MAKES 4 SERVINGS

1 lb. flank steak, trimmed
1 tablespoon cornstarch
1 egg white
2 tablespoons dry sherry
1 tablespoon soy sauce
1 tablespoon water
2 teaspoons chili paste with
    garlic (Szechuan paste)*
½ teaspoon sugar

¼ teaspoon sesame oil,
    optional
¼ teaspoon minced garlic
2 teaspoons cornstarch
2 cups peanut oil
1 bunch watercress or parsley,
    stems trimmed
1 tablespoon dry sherry
Hot cooked white rice

1. Cut steak lengthwise into 2½-inch strips. Then cut across the grain into thin slices. Place the meat in a bowl and add 1 tablespoon cornstarch and egg white. Blend well and set aside.
2. Combine 2 tablespoons sherry, soy sauce, water, chili paste with garlic, sugar, sesame oil, if desired, garlic and 2 teaspoons cornstarch.
3. Heat peanut oil in wok to 375°F. Have ready a large strainer with a bowl underneath. Add beef slices to hot oil, stirring until cooked, about 1 minute. Pour oil and beef slices into strainer.
4. Return drained beef to wok over high heat. Add sherry mixture and stir-fry 30 seconds; remove meat.
5. Heat 2 teaspoons of the strained oil in wok over high heat. Add watercress and 1 tablespoon sherry and stir-fry about 45 seconds. Garnish beef with watercress. Serve with rice.

* Szechuan paste substitution: Blend 1 tablespoon ketchup, ¼ teaspoon hot pepper sauce, 2 teaspoons chili powder, 1 clove garlic, crushed.

CHINESE CHICKEN AND PEPPERS

MAKES 4 SERVINGS

2 whole chicken breasts,
    boned and skinned
2 tablespoons dry sherry
2 teaspoons cornstarch
2 teaspoons salt

¼ cup vegetable oil
1 large green pepper, cut into
    strips
½ cup sliced water chestnuts

1. Cut chicken into ½-inch thick slices. Blend sherry, cornstarch and salt. Add chicken, tossing to coat well.

2. Heat oil in wok or large skillet over medium heat. Add chicken; stir-fry until chicken turns white.

3. Add green pepper and water chestnuts; stir 3 minutes or until peppers are tender-crisp.

SUKIYAKI

MAKES 4
SERVINGS

1 lb. boneless lean beef, tenderloin, sirloin or flank steak

1 cup water

1 can (8 ozs.) shirataki (yam noodles), drained, optional

1 bunch scallions, cut in 3-inch pieces

½ lb. mushrooms, rinsed and thinly sliced

¾ lb. spinach leaves

1 yellow onion, peeled and sliced ½-inch thick

1 can (5 ozs.) water chestnuts, drained and thinly sliced

1 can 5 ozs.) bamboo shoots, diced

1 lb. fresh mung bean sprouts or 1 can (1 lb.) bean sprouts, drained

2 cakes fresh or canned tofu (soy bean curd), cut into 1-inch cubes, optional

1 square piece beef suet, about 2 x 2 inches

½ cup soy sauce, preferably Japanese

4 tablespoons sugar

½ cup sake (rice wine) or dry sherry

Cooked white rice

1. Place beef in freezer for about 30 minutes until semi-frozen. (This makes slicing easier.) Using sharp, heavy knife, cut beef across the grain into slices ⅛-inch thick. Then cut slices in half crosswise.

2. Bring 1 cup water to boiling, drop in the shirataki; return to boiling. Drain and cut noodles into thirds.

3. Arrange the meat, shirataki and vegetables and tofu in very neat, separate rows on serving platter. Top with beef suet.

4. To make sauce: Combine soy sauce, sugar and sake in small serving pitcher.

5. Preheat electric skillet for 5 minutes at 425°F. Rub suet over bottom and sides of skillet until there are about 2 tablespoons of melted fat.

6. Add meat and stir-fry without browning for 3 minutes. Pour in half of sauce and push meat to one side.

7. Add vegetables in separate groups, toss-stirring each for 1 minute. Push aside each group as it is cooked and add the next.

8. Add remaining sauce and tofu; heat through.

9. With chopsticks, transfer the Sukiyaki to individual serving bowls. Spoon a little sauce over each. Serve with cooked rice in individual rice bowls.

PASTITSIO—A GREEK FAVORITE

MAKES 6 SERVINGS

2 cups (8 ozs.) elbow macaroni
1 tablespoon salt
3 qts. boiling water
2 eggs, beaten
½ cup milk
1 lb. ground beef
2 tablespoons butter or
  margarine
1 large onion, chopped
2 tablespoons tomato paste
1 teaspoon salt
⅛ teaspoon freshly ground
  black pepper
⅛ teaspoon ground cinnamon
½ cup water
1 cup freshly grated Parmesan
  cheese
2 cups Béchamel Sauce
  (recipe below)

1. Gradually add macaroni and 1 tablespoon salt to rapidly boiling water so that water continues to boil. Cook, uncovered, stirring occasionally until tender. Drain. Mix macaroni with eggs and milk.
2. In large skillet, brown beef in butter, stirring frequently to break up beef. Add onion; cook 2 minutes longer. Stir in tomato paste, 1 teaspoon salt, pepper, cinnamon and ½ cup water. Cook about 5 minutes or until mixture is thick. Remove from heat.
3. Spread half the macaroni mixture in a 13- x 9- x 2-inch baking dish; sprinkle about ¼ cup cheese over top. Cover wtih meat mixture; then remaining macaroni mixture. Sprinkle with ¼ cup cheese.
4. Spread Béchamel Sauce on top; sprinkle with remaining cheese. Bake in preheated 350°F. oven for 40 to 45 minutes or until bubbly. Place under broiler about 1 minute to brown top. Cool about 10 minutes. Cut into squares.

BÉCHAMEL SAUCE

MAKES 2 CUPS

¼ cup butter or margarine
¼ cup flour
1¾ cups milk
1 egg
¼ cup milk
1 teaspoon salt
  Dash freshly ground black
  pepper

1. Melt butter, stir in flour.
2. Add 1¾ cups milk, cook, stirring until sauce thickens and boils, 1 minute.
3. Beat egg with remaining ¼ cup milk, stir into sauce and cook slowly, stirring frequently until thickened. Stir in salt and pepper.

GREEK MOUSSAKA

MAKES 10 TO 12 SERVINGS

4 medium eggplants
Vegetable oil
2 lbs. ground lamb
3 onions, chopped
2 large tomatoes, peeled and
chopped
1/4 cup chopped parsley
1/2 cup dry red wine
1 1/2 teaspoons salt
1/4 teaspoon freshly ground
black pepper
1/4 teaspoon ground
cinnamon
1/2 cup grated Parmesan
cheese

1/4 cup fine, dry bread crumbs
6 tablespoons butter or
margarine
6 tablespoons flour
2 cups milk
1/2 teaspoon salt
1/8 teaspoon freshly ground
black pepper
Dash nutmeg
3 eggs, slightly beaten
1 1/2 cups creamed cottage
cheese
1/4 cup fine, dry bread crumbs
Grated Parmesan cheese

1. Cut eggplants into thick slices and brush both sides with oil. Place a layer of eggplant on broiler and broil until browned on both sides and tender, turning once. Repeat until all eggplant is browned.

2. In large skillet, break up ground lamb with spoon. Add onions and cook until meat is browned and onions are tender.

3. Add tomato, parsley, wine, 1 1/2 teaspoons salt, 1/4 teaspoon pepper and cinnamon. Heat to boiling, reduce heat and simmer, uncovered, until liquid is evaporated. Cool slightly. Stir in cheese and 1/4 cup bread crumbs.

4. In saucepan, melt butter over low heat. Blend in flour and gradually stir in milk. Cook, stirring constantly until sauce thickens and comes to a boil.

5. Add 1/2 teaspoon salt and 1/8 teaspoon pepper and nutmeg.

6. Gradually beat a little sauce into eggs, then stir into remaining sauce in pan. Remove from heat and stir in cottage cheese.

7. Grease a shallow, 3-qt. casserole and sprinkle bottom with 1/4 cup bread crumbs. Cover with a layer of eggplant slices, then a layer of meat and continue until all eggplant and meat are used, ending with a layer of eggplant.

8. Top with sauce; sprinkle with additional grated Parmesan and bake, uncovered, in preheated 350°F. oven for 1 hour.

ENCHILADAS DE POLLO

MAKES 6 SERVINGS

Shortening or vegetable oil
12 or more tortillas, canned
or thawed frozen
2 cups light cream
1 cup strong chicken broth
½ cup chopped onion
2 tablespoons butter or
margarine

2 cups chopped cooked
chicken
1 cup Chile Salsa (recipe
follows)
1 cup sour cream
Salt to taste
1½ cups grated Monterey Jack
cheese

1. Heat shortening and dip tortillas into it for a few seconds to make them hot and pliable. Then dip into cream and broth, which have been combined. Reserve remaining cream and chicken-broth mixture.
2. Make the filling by sautéing onion in butter until tender. Stir in chicken, Chile Salsa and sour cream.
3. Spread filling on tortillas; roll and place seam-side down on a baking dish.
4. Pour reserved liquid over top. Sprinkle with cheese and bake in preheated moderate oven (350° F.) until heated throughout and cheese is melted, about 25 to 30 minutes.

CHILE SALSA

MAKES 2 CUPS

½ cup chopped onion
1 large clove garlic, mashed
2 tablespoons shortening or
olive oil
1 tablespoon all-purpose flour
¼ cup chili powder

½ teaspoon dried oregano
leaves
½ teaspoon ground cumin
1 teaspoon salt
1 cup canned tomato puree
1 cup water or bouillon

1. Cook onion and garlic in shortening until limp, about 8 minutes.
2. Stir in flour; heat to boiling, stirring. Add all remaining ingredients. Heat to boiling, reduce heat and simmer for 10 minutes.

ITALIAN MEATBALLS AND SAUCE HEROES

MAKES 30 MEATBALLS, 3½ QUARTS SAUCE, 6 TO 8 SERVINGS

Meatballs:
- 2 tablespoons salad oil
- 1 cup finely chopped onion
- 1 clove garlic, minced
- 4 cups soft bread crumbs
- 1 cup hot milk
- 2 eggs
- ½ cup chopped parsley
- 2½ teaspoons salt
- ¾ teaspoon freshly ground black pepper
- ¾ cup grated Parmesan or Romano cheese
- 2 lbs. ground chuck

Sauce:
- 2 cups chopped onion
- 4 cloves garlic, minced
- 4 tablespoons vegetable oil
- ½ cup chopped parsley
- 2 tablespoons sugar
- 2 teaspoons salt
- 1 teaspoon freshly ground black pepper
- 1 can (12 ozs.) tomato paste
- 2 cans (1 lb. 12 ozs.) tomatoes
- 2 cups water
- 1 tablespoon oregano leaves
- 1 bay leaf

6 to 8 individual hero rolls

1. In large skillet, heat oil; add onion and garlic and cook, stirring five minutes.

2. In large bowl, combine bread crumbs and hot milk. Add onion-garlic mixture, eggs, parsley, salt, pepper, cheese; beat well with large spoon.

3. Add chuck and mix thoroughly. Chill mixture for easier shaping.

4. Preheat oven to 350°F. Using about ¼ cup meatball mixture, shape into balls. Place on baking pan. Bake 30 minutes.

5. Make sauce: In 6- to 8-qt. Dutch oven cook onion and garlic in oil for 5 minutes, stirring.

6. Add parsley, sugar, salt, pepper, tomato paste, tomatoes, water, oregano and bay leaf. Stir well.

7. Heat to boiling; reduce heat and simmer covered 2 hours. Add meatballs during last half of cooking time. Stir occasionally.

8. Split hero rolls and fill with meatballs and sauce. This tasty recipe can also be used for spaghetti.

HONEST AND TRUE IRISH STEW

MAKES 6 SERVINGS

2 lbs. boneless lamb shoulder or shank, cubed (or 2½ to 3 lbs. bone-in lamb)
1 qt. cold water
2 lbs. medium potatoes, peeled and halved
1 lb. white boiling onions, peeled
1 lb. carrots, peeled, cut in 2-inch chunks

6 ribs celery, cut in 2-inch pieces
2 teaspoons salt
¼ teaspoon freshly ground black pepper
½ teaspoon caraway seeds
2 tablespoons chopped parsley

1. Place meat in 8-qt. Dutch oven, add water. Bring to boiling over high heat; skim off surface foam with slotted spoon.
2. Add potatoes, onions, carrots, celery, salt, pepper and caraway seeds. Bring to boiling. Reduce heat and simmer covered 1 to 1½ hours, or until meat and vegetables are tender.
3. Serve in large, deep soup bowls; sprinkle each serving with parsley.

CORNMEAL SPOON BREAD

MAKES 6 TO 8 SERVINGS

¾ cup yellow cornmeal
1 tablespoon sugar
½ teaspoon salt

2 cups milk
¼ cup butter or margarine
4 eggs, separated

1. Preheat oven to 375°F. Lightly oil a 1½-qt. casserole or soufflé dish.
2. Mix cornmeal, sugar and salt in 3-qt. saucepan. Add milk and butter. Heat mixture to boiling point. Stir constantly until thickened. Remove from heat.
3. Beat egg yolks in small bowl. Gradually stir about ⅓ cup of hot cornmeal mixture into yolks, a tablespoon at a time.
4. Stir egg-yolk mixture into remaining cornmeal mixture; mix thoroughly. Cool to lukewarm.
5. Beat egg whites in large bowl with clean egg beater until stiff peaks form; gradually fold in cornmeal mixture. Pour into prepared casserole.
6. Bake 40 minutes. Serve immediately.

BAKLAVA

MAKES 24 SLICES

4 cups walnuts, finely
  chopped or ground
½ cup sugar
1 teaspoon ground cinnamon
½ teaspoon ground nutmeg

1 cup butter, melted
Honey Syrup (recipe below)
1 lb. filo pastry sheets
1 teaspoon grated lemon rind

1. Preheat oven to 325°F. Lightly grease a 9- x 13- x 2-inch pan.
2. Mix ground walnuts with sugar, spices and lemon rind in medium bowl.
3. Cut filo sheets to fit pan. Keep filo sheets moist and flexible by covering with damp cloth.
4. Brush 12 filo sheets lightly with melted butter and place in bottom of pan.
5. Spread 1 cup of walnut mixture over top sheet. Cover with 4 sheets of filo after brushing each with butter. Then repeat layers.
6. Make top layer with 8 sheets of filo after brushing each with remaining butter.
7. With small, sharp knife, cut lengthwise through first layer to make strips 1½ inches wide. Then make diagonal cuts 2 inches apart in top layer to form diamonds.
8. Bake on rack above center of oven for 1 hour, until well browned.
9. Remove from oven and cut through the first cuts, cutting to the bottom of pan.
10. Spread top with cold Honey Syrup. Let stand until completely cold before removing from pan.

Editor's Note: Filo sheets can be found in refrigerated or freezer section of supermarket or specialty food store.

HONEY SYRUP

MAKES 1½ CUPS

1 cup honey
½ cup sugar

½ cup water
1 tablespoon lemon juice

1. Combine honey, sugar and water in small saucepan. Heat, stirring, until sugar dissolves.
2. Remove from heat and stir in lemon juice. Cool thoroughly before using.

SWEDISH MAZARIN TARTS

MAKES 8 TARTS

1 cup sifted all-purpose flour
¼ cup sugar
⅛ teaspoon salt
⅓ cup butter or margarine
3 talespoons cream
⅓ cup butter or margarine
¾ cup sugar

¼ cup sifted all-purpose flour
⅛ teaspoon salt
2 eggs, separated
½ teaspoon baking powder
1 cup finely chopped
  blanched almonds
½ teaspoon almond extract

1. Preheat oven to 400°F.
2. Mix together 1 cup flour, ¼ cup sugar and ⅛ teaspoon salt in bowl. Cut in ⅓ cup butter with pastry blender or fork until mixture is like coarse meal.
3. Gradually add cream and toss mixture with fork to form stiff dough. Cover and chill for 1 hour.
4. Divide chilled pastry into eight greased 3½-inch fluted tart pans; press with thumb evenly against bottoms and sides.
5. Beat ⅓ cup butter and ¾ cup sugar until creamy; then beat in egg yolks.
6. Combine ¼ cup flour and ⅛ teaspoon salt with baking powder.
7. With electric mixer, beat egg whites until stiff but not dry.
8. Fold flour mixture, egg whites, almonds and almond extract into creamed mixture. Spoon into pastry-lined pans.
9. Bake on low rack for about 25 minutes or until golden brown and almond filling is set. Cool tarts in pans, then gently remove.

VIENNESE MOCHA TORTE

MAKES 1 LARGE CAKE,
12 TO 16 SERVINGS

1¼ cups walnuts
6 large eggs, separated
½ teaspoon salt
½ teaspoon cream of tartar
½ cup sugar
½ cup sugar
¼ cup strong, cold coffee

1 teaspoon pure vanilla
  extract
1 cup sifted cake flour
  Chocolate Buttercream
  Frosting (recipe below)
  Mocha Whipped Cream
  (recipe below)

1. Finely chop ½ cup of the walnuts for cake batter. Chop remainder in medium-size pieces for sides of frosting.
2. Beat egg whites in large bowl with electric mixer until frothy. Add salt and cream of tartar and beat to soft peaks.

3. Gradually beat in ½ cup sugar and continue beating at high speed to a stiff meringue.

4. With same beater, beat egg yolks until thick and light-colored. Beat in another ½ cup sugar. Add coffee and vanilla and beat well.

5. Gently pour flour over meringue and lightly fold until no streaks of white remain. Fold in the ½ cup finely chopped walnuts.

6. Divide batter between two ungreased 9-inch, round layer-cake pans. Bake in preheated 350°F. oven 30 to 35 minutes until lightly browned and cake springs back when touched in center.

7. Remove from oven and invert cakes, resting edges of pans on custard cups, to cool. When cool, loosen edges with small spatula and rap edges of pan on counter to turn out.

8. Spread one layer with ½ cup Chocolate Buttercream, then half of the Mocha Whipped Cream. Top with second layer.

9. Spread Buttercream around sides of cake and up over top of cake to make a narrow border (about ¾ inch) on top.

10. Fill center of top layer with remaining Mocha Cream. Turn remaining Buttercream into pastry bag fitted with fluted tip and make a decorative border around top edge of cake. Pat remaining ¾ cup walnuts around sides of cake. Refrigerate until serving time.

CHOCOLATE BUTTERCREAM FROSTING

MAKES 2 CUPS

⅓ cup soft butter or margarine

2 squares (1-oz size) unsweetened chocolate, melted

1 egg yolk

3 tablespoons light cream or milk

3½ cups sifted confectioners' sugar

1. Beat together butter, chocolate, egg yolk and cream. Add confectioners' sugar, beating until smooth. Add a few drops more cream or milk for good spreading consistency.

MOCHA WHIPPED CREAM

MAKES ABOUT 2 CUPS

1 cup heavy cream

¼ cup confectioners' sugar

1 teaspoon instant coffee powder

1. In chilled bowl, with chilled beaters, beat cream, confectioners' sugar and instant coffee powder together until stiff.

Cooking for the Fair

GENUINE DILL PICKLES

MAKES 8 TO 10 QUARTS

18 to 20 lbs. pickling cucumbers, 3- to 5-inches long
1¾ cups granulated pickling or dairy salt
1½ cups vinegar
3 or 4 tablespoons mixed pickling spice
¼ cup sugar
10 qts. water

2 or 3 bunches dill with fully developed seed
Red peppers, optional
Dill sprigs, optional
Light mustard seed, optional
Fresh garlic cloves, optional
Onion, optional

1. Wash, rinse and drain cucumbers. Make brine by combining salt, vinegar, spice and sugar with water. Stir to dissolve salt.

2. Put one or two layers of cucumbers in a glass jar, stoneware crock or tight, well-sealed, odorless wooden keg.

3. Add some of the dill and, if you have them, 3 or 4 fresh grape leaves. Continue in this manner until all cucumbers are in container. Leave 3 or more inches headroom.

4. Add brine to cover cucumbers. (They will spoil if not completely covered.) Use glass or ceramic plate that will fit inside container to hold cucumbers under brine. Fill a fruit jar with water and use as a weight to hold down plate.

5. Cover container with a thin cloth and put in a dry, well-ventilated place. Check container every day and remove scum which forms on top of brine.

6. Watch depth of brine; if it appears to be evaporating rapidly, add more to keep cucumbers well covered. Pickle usually takes 3 to 4 weeks to develop even color and good flavor.

7. Prepare quart-size canning jars. If desired, a small red pepper or a piece of a large one, a few sprigs of dill and a teaspoon or more of

232

light mustard seed may be added to each quart jar of pickle. Do not add garlic or onion without boiling it 5 minutes.

8. Pack pickle to ½ inch of top of jar. Strain brine;* boil it 5 minutes and pour over pickles. Brine should end about ¼ inch from top of jar.

9. Wipe off anything spilled on top or threads of jar. Put dome lid on jar; screw band tight.

10. Prepare to process. Have water in canner at the just-beginning-to-boil point. Slowly lower jar straight down so the entire bottom of the jar touches the water at the same instant. (That reduces the chance of breakage from thermal shock.)

11. Start counting processing time as soon as water comes to a boil. Allow to boil gently for 15 minutes.

12. Remove jars from canner at end of processing time and let them stand several inches apart, out of a draft, to cool.

* If preferred, fresh brine may be substituted for that used to cure the cucumbers.

SWEET CHERRY MARMALADE

MAKES ABOUT 3 PINTS

4 cups fresh sweet Bing cherries	3 cups water
2 oranges	3½ cups sugar
	⅓ cup lemon juice

1. Pit and chop cherries. Remove peel from oranges in quarters and cut into fine slivers. Chop pulp.

2. Place slivered orange peel and pulp in large saucepan. Cover with 3 cups water and cook until tender.

3. Add cherries, sugar and lemon juice. Cook rapidly to jelly stage, about 25 to 30 minutes, stirring occasionally.

4. Pour into sterilized jars, filling to within ⅛-inch of top. Wipe top and threads of jars with clean damp cloth. Cover with 2-piece lids following manufacturer's directions.

5. Place each jar as it is filled onto rack in canner or deep kettle half filled with hot water. When canner is filled, add hot water to cover jars 1 to 2 inches.

6. Cover canner and bring water to boil. Reduce heat to hold water at a steady boil. Start processing time when water reaches a full boil. Process 15 minutes.

BRANDIED PEACHES

MAKES 6 PINTS OR 3 QUARTS

4½ to 5 lbs. freestone peaches, small to medium in size
2 qts. water
3 tablespoons ascorbic acid powder
2 cups water
1½ teaspoons ascorbic acid powder
1½ cups sugar
4 sticks cinnamon
1 teaspoon whole cloves
2 small oranges, sliced, optional
1½ cups California brandy

1. Peel peaches, leave whole. Place in large bowl containing 2 qts. water and 3 tablespoons ascorbic acid powder.
2. Combine remaining 2 cups water, 1½ teaspoons ascorbic acid powder, sugar, cinnamon and cloves in large saucepan. Heat to boiling, stirring until sugar dissolves.
3. Add peaches, and orange slices if desired, and simmer 5 minutes. Pour ¼ cup syrup into each hot, sterilized pint jar (use ½ cup for a quart jar). Fill with peaches and orange slices.
4. Add ¼ cup brandy for each pint of fruit, then add enough syrup to fill jars to ½ inch from top. Seal jars.
5. When jars are filled, set on rack in deep kettle with boiling water halfway up jars.
6. Add more boiling water to top jars by 2 inches. Reheat to boiling; process 20 minutes after boiling resumes.
7. Remove jars from water bath at once and let stand until cold before storing in cool, dark place.

WHOLE WHEAT ALMOND POUND CAKE

MAKES 1 LARGE CAKE, 12 TO 16 SERVINGS

2 tablespoons soft margarine
1 cup slivered unblanched almonds
1 cup soft margarine
1½ cups packed light or dark brown sugar
4 eggs
1 teaspoon almond extract
1½ cups unsifted whole wheat flour
1½ cups unsifted all-purpose flour
⅓ cup soya flour or whole wheat flour
1 cup ground almonds, unblanched
3 teaspoons baking powder
1 teaspoon salt
1½ cups milk

1. Preheat oven to 350°F. Spread 2 tablespoons margarine against bottom and sides of 10-inch tube-cake pan; press slivered almonds into margarine so that they are scattered evenly around pan.

2. In large bowl with electric mixer at high speed, beat margarine until creamy. Gradually add sugar, beating until fluffy.

3. Add eggs, one at a time, and almond extract; beat.

4. Mix flours with ground almonds, baking powder and salt; beat into creamed mixture alternately with milk.

5. Pour batter into prepared pan. Bake for about 1 hour, 10 minutes or until the top is golden brown and a pick inserted into center comes out dry.

6. Cool 20 minutes in pan; invert and remove.

CHOCOLATE SURPRISE SQUARES

MAKES A 13- x 9-INCH CAKE

Cake:
½ cup butter or margarine
1½ cups sugar
3 eggs
1 teaspoon pure vanilla extract
1½ cups unsifted all-purpose flour
½ cup quick or old-fashioned oats, uncooked
½ cup cocoa powder
1 teaspoon baking powder
1 teaspoon baking soda
¼ teaspoon salt

1 cup water
1 can (8 ozs.) sauerkraut, drained and chopped

Frosting:
½ cup butter or margarine, softened
2 cups confectioners' sugar
¼ cup cocoa powder
2 tablespoons milk
1 teaspoon pure vanilla extract
½ cup chopped walnuts

1. Preheat oven to 350°F. Make cake first: Beat together butter and sugar until light and fluffy; blend in eggs and vanilla.

2. Combine flour, oats, cocoa, baking powder, baking soda and salt. Add flour mixture to butter mixture alternately with water, mixing well after each addition; fold in sauerkraut.

3. Pour batter into greased and floured 13- x 9- x 2-inch baking pan. Bake for about 40 minutes or until a wooden pick inserted into center comes out clean; cool completely.

4. Make frosting: In medium bowl with electric mixer, beat together butter, sugar and cocoa. Blend in milk and vanilla; beat well. Spread over top of cake. Garnish with chopped walnuts. Cut into squares.

SOUR CREAM RAISIN PIE

MAKES 1 (9-INCH) PIE, 8 SERVINGS

Pastry for 2-crust 9-inch pie
1 cup raisins
4 eggs, slightly beaten
3 tablespoons lemon juice
1½ cups sour cream
1 cup sugar
1 teaspoon pure vanilla
extract
⅛ teaspoon salt
1 egg yolk
1 tablespoon water
1 tablespoon sugar

1. Preheat oven to 400°F.
2. Line 9-inch pie pan with half of pastry. Sprinkle raisins evenly on unbaked pie shell.
3. In large bowl beat together eggs, lemon juice, sour cream, 1 cup sugar, vanilla and salt. Pour over raisins.
4. Roll out top pastry very thin. Cover pie with top crust. Flute edge.
5. Beat together egg yolk and water. Brush surface of pie with mixture. Sprinkle with remaining 1 tablespoon sugar.
6. Bake for 20 minutes at 400°F.; lower heat to 350°F. and bake 10 to 15 minutes more.
7. Cool completely. Refrigerate.

THREE-LAYER JAM CAKE

MAKES 1 (9-INCH) 3-LAYER CAKE

3 cups unsifted all-purpose
flour
1 teaspoon baking powder
½ teaspoon baking soda
½ teaspoon salt
1 teaspoon ground
cinnamon
1 teaspoon ground nutmeg
½ teaspoon ground cloves
1 cup butter or margarine,
softened
1½ cups sugar
3 eggs
1 cup thick strawberry jam
1 cup buttermilk
Old-Fashioned White
Frosting (recipe below)

1. Preheat oven to 350°F. Grease three 9-inch layer-cake pans. Line with waxed paper. Grease and lightly flour paper.
2. Sift together flour, baking powder, baking soda, salt, cinnamon, nutmeg and cloves.
3. In large bowl of electric mixer, beat butter until well creamed. Gradually beat in sugar and continue beating until light and fluffy. Add eggs, one at a time, beating after each addition.

4. Beat in jam until well blended.

5. Add sifted dry ingredients in thirds, alternating with buttermilk. Beat after each addition.

6. Turn batter into prepared pans. Bake for 30 to 40 minutes, or until cake tester inserted in center comes out clean.

7. Cool in pans on racks 10 minutes. Loosen around edges and turn out of pans. Cool completely.

8. Fill and frost with Old-Fashioned White Frosting.

OLD-FASHIONED WHITE FROSTING

MAKES ENOUGH TO FILL AND FROST
1 (9-INCH) 3-LAYER CAKE

3 egg whites, room temperature
⅛ teaspoon salt
¾ cup sugar
3 tablespoons water

⅓ cup light corn syrup
1½ teaspoons pure vanilla extract
5 teaspoons strawberry jam

1. In large bowl of electric mixer, beat egg whites and salt until soft peaks form when beater is raised.

2. Mix sugar, water and corn syrup in a 1½-qt. saucepan. Stir constantly; bring mixture to a boil.

3. Boil without stirring until syrup registers 242°F. on candy thermometer, or until it spins a 6- to 8-inch thread. Remove from heat.

4. Beat egg whites again at high speed. Pour hot syrup very slowly in a fine stream into egg whites. Add vanilla. Continue beating just until frosting holds stiff peaks.

5. Frost layers, sides and top of Three-Layer Jam Cake.

6. Spoon 5 teaspoons of jam here and there on top of cake. Spread with back of spoon.

ENERGY SAVER BARS

MAKES 9-INCH SQUARE
PAN OF BARS

2 cups quick or old-fashioned oats, uncooked
3 cups miniature marshmallows
½ cup chunk-style peanut butter

¼ cup honey
3 tablespoons butter or margarine
1 cup raisins

1. Toast oats in shallow baking pan in preheated 350°F. oven about 15 minutes or until golden brown. Line 9-inch square baking pan with aluminum foil; grease.

2. Melt marshmallows with peanut butter, honey and butter in medium-sized saucepan over low heat, stirring constantly; remove from heat.

3. Stir in toasted oats and raisins. Place into prepared pan, spreading evenly. Chill until firm. To serve, remove foil; cut into squares.

AUNT MATTIE'S MAPLE JOYS

MAKES ABOUT 6 DOZEN COOKIES

½ cup butter or margarine
1¼ cups packed light brown sugar
2 cups unsifted all-purpose flour
¾ cup quick or old-fashioned oats, uncooked

1 egg, beaten
2 tablespoons milk
1 teaspoon maple flavoring
1 teaspoon baking soda
½ teaspoon salt
⅛ teaspoon ground ginger

1. In large bowl with electric mixer at medium speed, beat together butter and sugar until light and fluffy.

2. At low speed, add flour, mixing well. Set aside ⅓ cup flour mixture.

3. Add oats, egg, milk, maple flavoring, baking soda and salt; mix well.

4. Shape to form 1-inch balls. Stir ginger into ⅓ cup reserved flour mixture. Roll balls in reserved flour mixture; place on ungreased cookie sheet.

5. Bake in preheated 375°F. oven 10 to 12 minutes.

ANADAMA BREAD

MAKES 2 LARGE LOAVES

7 to 8 cups unsifted all-purpose flour
1¼ cups yellow cornmeal
2½ teaspoons salt
2 packages active dry yeast

⅓ cup softened margarine or butter
2¼ cups very warm tap water (120° F.-130° F.)
⅔ cup molasses (at room temperature)

1. In a large bowl thoroughly mix 2½ cups flour with cornmeal, salt and undissolved active dry yeast. Add margarine.
2. Gradually add water and molasses to dry ingredients and beat 2 minutes at medium speed of electric mixer, scraping bowl occasionally. Add ½ cup flour.
3. Beat at high speed 2 minutes, scraping bowl occasionally. Stir in additional flour to make a stiff dough. Work remaining flour into dough with your own well-scrubbed hands.
4. Turn out onto lightly floured board, knead until smooth and elastic, about 8 to 10 minutes. Place in greased bowl, turning to grease top. Cover; let rise in warm place, free from draft, until doubled in bulk, about 1 hour.
5. Punch dough down; divide in half. Roll each half into a 14 x 9-inch rectangle. Shape into loaves. Place in two greased 9 x 5 x 3-inch loaf pans. Cover; let rise in warm place, free from draft, until doubled in bulk, about 45 minutes.
6. Just before rising time is up, preheat oven to 375°F. Bake about 45 minutes, or until done. Remove immediately from pans and cool on wire racks.

Editor's Note: To test bread for doneness, when baking time is up, remove one loaf and tap bottom or sides with knuckle. It is done if loaf sounds hollow. In breads baked on a baking sheet, tap top crust with knuckle, if it sounds hollow it is done.

Vegetable of the Month: Potatoes

GENOA POTATO SALAD

MAKES 6 SERVINGS

¾ lb. sliced hard salami, cut
   into strips
4 cups chopped cooked
   potatoes
3 hard cooked eggs, chopped
1 package (10 ozs.) frozen
   peas, cooked and drained

½ cup sliced celery
¾ teaspoon salt
⅛ teaspoon freshly ground
   black pepper
¾ cup mayonnaise
   Crisp lettuce leaves, celery
   leaves

1. Combine salami, potatoes, eggs, peas, celery, salt and pepper.
2. Add mayonnaise; toss lightly. Chill.
3. To serve, arrange lettuce leaves on serving plate. Pile potato salad in center. Garnish with celery leaves.

HOT GERMAN POTATO SALAD

MAKES 4 TO 6 SERVINGS

6 medium-size (2 lbs.)
   potatoes
¼ lb. bacon, diced
2 tablespoons finely chopped
   onion
¼ cup beef bouillon
¼ cup vinegar

1 teaspoon salt
2 teaspoons sugar
¼ teaspoon freshly ground
   black pepper
1 tablespoon finely chopped
   parsley

240

1. Boil potatoes in skins until fork tender. Peel and slice while hot; keep warm.

2. Fry bacon until golden; add onion and cook, stirring 3 minutes. Do not drain.

3. Add bouillon, vinegar, salt, sugar and pepper to bacon mixture; heat to boiling. Pour over hot sliced potatoes; toss gently.

4. Serve salad warm or hot; garnish with parsley.

CHEESE SCALLOPED POTATOES

MAKES 8 SERVINGS

1½ cups chicken or beef broth
6 medium potatoes (about 2 lbs.), peeled and sliced
¼ teaspoon freshly ground black pepper

1 teaspoon seasoned salt
1 cup grated Swiss cheese, lightly packed
3 tablespoons grated Parmesan cheese

1. Heat broth in large saucepan. Add potatoes, pepper and seasoned salt. Heat to boiling; simmer 5 minutes. Do not drain.

2. Layer potato mixture and Swiss cheese in 1½-qt. baking dish. Bake, covered, at 350°F. for 1 hour.

3. Uncover, sprinkle with Parmesan cheese and continue baking until top is golden and potatoes are tender.

OVEN-ROASTED POTATO WEDGES

MAKES 4 TO 6 SERVINGS

4 to 6 russet baking potatoes or long white potatoes
2 tablespoons vegetable oil
½ teaspoon salt

⅛ teaspoon freshly ground black pepper
¼ teaspoon paprika

1. Preheat oven to 450°F. Leaving skins on, scrub potatoes and cut lengthwise into ½-inch strips.

2. In small bowl, combine oil, salt, pepper and paprika. Toss potato wedges in seasoned oil.

3. Place potatoes on foil-lined baking sheet and bake for about 20 minutes, or until tender. Turn potatoes once while baking.

CANDIED-YAM CASSEROLE

MAKES 10 TO 12 SERVINGS

3 lbs. yams, scrubbed
Boiling water
1 teaspoon salt
1/4 teaspoon ground white
pepper

1/4 cup butter or margarine
3/4 cup milk
16 whole regular-size
marshmallows

1. In large saucepan or Dutch oven, cook yams in boiling water to cover, to which one teaspoon salt has been added. Boil, covered, about 25 to 30 minutes, until fork-tender; drain.
2. Peel yams, mash with fork on wooden board. Scoop into large bowl, add 1 teaspoon salt and the pepper.
3. Preheat oven to 350°F. Grease a 2½-qt. casserole. Heat butter with milk until rim of bubbles forms around edge of pan. Slowly pour hot milk and butter into mashed yams, beating at low speed of electric mixer as you add. (Or use potato masher.) Continue beating at high speed until very smooth.
4. Spoon yam mixture into prepared casserole. Place marshmallows ½ inch into yam mixture, about 1 inch apart. Bake 35 to 40 minutes, or until tops of marshmallows are golden brown.

BAKED YAMS AMALIE

MAKES 8 TO 10 SERVINGS

8 to 10 medium yams, washed
½ cup butter or margarine,
softened

1/4 cup molasses
1 teaspoon ground cinnamon
1/4 teaspoon salt

1. Wrap yams individually in heavy-duty foil. Place yams on grill over moderate-hot coals, 1 hour to 1 hour 20 minutes, turning frequently. (Or bake in preheated 350°F. oven, 1 hour to 1 hour and 20 minutes.)
2. In medium bowl, combine butter, molasses, cinnamon and salt; beat until creamy.
3. When yams are fork-tender, open foil, make a lengthwise slit in the top of each; push ends toward center to open. Fluff yam with fork. Spoon some molasses butter into center of each yam. Serve hot in foil, or remove foil before serving.

POTATO-YEAST ROLLS

MAKES 24 ROLLS

1 package active dry yeast
¼ cup very warm water (110°F.-115°F.)
½ cup boiling hot milk
⅓ cup shortening or margarine
¼ cup sugar
1½ teaspoons salt

1 cup unseasoned mashed potatoes
2 eggs, beaten
3½ to 3¾ cups unsifted all-purpose flour
Additional flour, as needed
¼ cup butter or margarine, melted
½ cup yellow cornmeal

1. Soften yeast in very warm water, set aside.
2. Pour boiling hot milk into a large mixing bowl over shortening, sugar and salt. Stir until shortening melts. Stir in potatoes and eggs, and cool to lukewarm.
3. Stir in yeast, then stir in half the flour. Beat until batter is smooth and thick. Gradually blend in remaining flour, adding enough to make a moderately stiff dough.
4. Turn dough out onto heavily floured board and knead about 5 minutes until dough is smooth and elastic. Add flour as needed to keep dough from sticking.
5. Place in greased bowl, turn dough over so that top is greased, and cover. Let rise in warm place until doubled in bulk, about 1½ hours.
6. Punch down dough and divide in half. Cut each half into 12 even-size pieces and shape into small balls.
7. Roll each ball in melted butter, then in cornmeal, and place 1½ inches apart in 3 greased 8- or 9-inch cake pans. Cover loosely with a dish towel. Let rise in warm place until doubled, about 40 to 45 minutes.
8. Preheat oven to 400°F. Bake rolls 15 to 20 minutes or until golden brown. Serve warm in napkin-lined basket.

CHOCOLATE POTATO TORTE

MAKES 1 (9-INCH) TORTE,
12 SERVINGS

1 cup butter or margarine	4 squares (1 oz. each) baking
2 cups sugar	chocolate, melted
4 large eggs, separated	1½ cups sifted all-purpose
½ cup cream or evaporated	flour
milk	¼ teaspoon salt
1½ teaspoons pure vanilla	⅛ teaspoon ground cloves
extract	1 teaspoon ground
1 cup freshly cooked riced	cinnamon
potatoes	2 teaspoons baking powder
1 cup finely chopped	Chocolate Butter Cream
walnuts	Frosting (recipe below)

1. In medium bowl with electric mixer, beat butter until creamy; gradually add sugar, beating until fluffy.
2. Beat in egg yolks, one at a time.
3. Add cream, vanilla, potatoes and walnuts. Blend in chocolate, mixing well.
4. Sift together flour, salt, cloves, cinnamon and baking powder. Add dry ingredients to beaten mixture, blending well.
5. Beat egg whites until stiff peaks form. Fold whites into beaten mixture.
6. Turn batter into 9-inch spring-form pan and bake in a preheated 350°F. oven for 1½ hours or until a cake tester poked in center comes out clean. Cool on rack.
7. Spread top and sides with Chocolate Butter Cream Frosting.

CHOCOLATE BUTTER
CREAM FROSTING

MAKES 2 CUPS

¾ cup cocoa powder	1 teaspoon pure vanilla
2⅔ cups confectioners' sugar	extract
6 tablespoons butter or	1 tablespoon light or dark
margarine	corn syrup
6 tablespoons milk or water	

1. Combine cocoa and confectioners' sugar. In medium bowl with electric mixer, beat butter with ½ cup cocoa mixture.
2. Add remaining cocoa mixture alternately with milk, beating to spreading consistency. Blend in vanilla and corn syrup.

November

November is a fickle month, at times bright blue and benign and at other times clouded with dark skies and torrents of rain. It is our traditional month for celebrating the harvest and Thanksgiving, and we feature a guide to varied herb and spice stuffings for the favored birds of the season. When you have chosen your stuffing, we explain how to roast your turkey, chicken, duck or goose to perfection.

In "After the Feast," there is a great variety of ways to use the leftovers. It seems to us that just about everyone loves leftovers.

"Oh, those Thanksgiving pies—weren't they good!" With Old-Fashioned Pumpkin, Fresh Cranberry Chiffon and Quick Deep-Dish Apple to choose from, we agree.

The Vegetables of the Month are squash and pumpkin which lend their goodness to soups, soufflés and breads.

Herb and Spice Stuffings

TO MAKE	SEASONINGS	ADD	USE FOR
Traditional Sage Stuffing To 8 cups day-old bread cubes	1 tablespoon sage leaves, 1 teaspoon poultry seasoning, 1 cup chopped onion, 1 cup chopped celery	optional 1 cup chopped apple and/or 1 cup sliced mushrooms	Turkey, Duck or Goose
Hawaiian Bread Stuffing To 12 cups dry bread cubes	⅛ teaspoon ground red pepper, ½ cup sesame seed, toasted, 2 cups chopped green onion, 2 teaspoons ground ginger	2 cups sliced water chestnuts 2 cans (17 ozs.) pineapple chunks, drained	Turkey, Duck or Whole Fish
Herbed Mushroom Stuffing To 12 cups dry bread cubes	½ cup chopped parsley, 1 cup chopped onion, 2 tsp. poultry seasoning or marjoram leaves	2 cup sauteed sliced mushrooms	Chicken, Turkey or Goose
Apricot Rice Stuffing To 6 cups cooked rice	1 tsp. ground cinnamon, ¼ tsp. ground allspice	1 cup chopped dried apricots 1 cup chopped walnuts	Chicken Breasts, Cornish Hen, or Sliced Turkey
Herbed Rice Stuffing To 8 cups cooked rice & 2 cups soft bread crumbs	1 chopped onion, ¼ cup chopped parsley, 1 teaspoon sage leaves, 1 teaspoon thyme leaves	optional 1 lb. crumbled cooked sausage meat or 1 lb. chopped cooked shrimp	Turkey or Whole Fish

GENERAL RULES FOR STUFFING

- Season stuffing with about 1 teaspoon salt and $\frac{1}{8}$ teaspoon freshly ground black pepper to 4 cups bread cubes, rice or bulgur
- Use about 4 tablespoons melted butter, margarine or oil to 4 cups bread cubes, rice or bulgur
- For a firmer stuffing add 1 well-beaten egg to about 4 cups bread cubes or rice
- Use about 1 cup of stuffing to a pound of turkey, chicken, duck, Cornish hen or fish

TO MAKE	SEASONINGS	ADD	USE FOR
Corn Bread Stuffing To 4 cups corn bread cubes & 7 cups dry bread cubes	1 cup chopped celery, 1 cup chopped onion, $\frac{1}{4}$ cup parsley, $1\frac{1}{2}$ tablespoons poultry seasoning	optional 1 lb. crumbled cooked sausage meat	Turkey, Chicken or Pork Chops
Bulgur Stuffing To 4 cups cooked bulgur	1 cup chopped celery, 1 teaspoon mint flakes	$\frac{1}{2}$ cup chopped dried apricots $\frac{1}{2}$ cup chopped dried prunes	Rock Cornish Hens or Chicken
Liver Stuffing To 5 cups day-old bread cubes	1 cup chopped celery, $\frac{1}{2}$ cup chopped onion, 1 tsp. paprika, 1 tsp. poultry seasoning, $\frac{1}{4}$ tsp. garlic powder	$\frac{1}{4}$ lb. coarsely chopped sauteed chicken livers	Chicken
Sweet Potato and Sausage Stuffing To 4 cups mashed sweet potatoes & 12 cups dry bread crumbs	4 tsps. poultry seasoning, $1\frac{1}{2}$ tsp. ground nutmeg	1 lb. crumbled cooked sausage meat	Chicken, Turkey

The Birds

BUYING THE BIRD

Whole, ready-to-cook turkeys are available fresh-frozen or fresh-chilled. The majority are sold frozen, which makes turkey a year-round meat. Sizes of the bird, ready-to-cook, can range from 4 to more than 24 pounds.

Practically all turkeys are retailed young, 3 to 6 months, and are suited to dry-heat methods of cooking: broiling, frying, roasting.

HOW MUCH TO BUY

When buying whole ready-to-cook turkeys under 12 pounds, allow ¾ to 1 pound per serving. For larger birds, allow ½ to ¾ pound. In most cases, large turkeys are more economical than the smaller birds and are excellent for use in future meals.

THAWING AND STORAGE

Turkeys frozen with neck and giblets inside the body and neck cavities need to be thawed before cooking. If thawing in your refrigerator, place turkey, still in its original wrap, on tray or drip pan. If you want to quick-thaw, place turkey, again in its original wrap, in sink covered with cool or cold water. Change water often to hasten thawing. If you thaw at room temperature, leave turkey in original wrap and place in brown paper bag, or wrap in 2 or 3 layers of newspaper. Place on tray or in baking pan and allow to thaw until turkey is pliable and neck and giblets can be removed easily. Cook turkey immediately.

248

TIMETABLE FOR ROASTING

Based on stuffed whole turkeys, chilled or completely thawed at a temperature of about 40°F. The times are for stuffed birds placed into 325°F. preheated ovens. Time will be slightly less (1 to 3 minutes per pound) for unstuffed birds.

READY-TO-COOK (Pounds)	APPROXIMATE TIME AT 325°F. (Hours)
4 to 8	2½ to 3½
8 to 12	3½ to 4½
12 to 16	4½ to 5½
16 to 20	5½ to 6½
20 to 24	6½ to 7

TEST FOR DONENESS

There is nothing as accurate as a meat thermometer placed in the center of the inside thigh muscle. When it registers 180° to 185°F., the turkey is done.

If the bird is stuffed, the point of the thermometer should be in the center of the stuffing and register 165°F.

TIPS ON "DOING" A GOOSE

How much to buy: Allow ½ lb. ready-to-cook weight per 3-ounce serving.

Thawing and storage: You can thaw a goose three ways—in your refrigerator, by leaving it in your sink under running cold water, or by placing it in a paper bag and letting it thaw at room temperature. *Always leave the bird in its original wrap.* A 10- to 14-lb. goose will take 1½ to 2 days in a refrigerator; 5 to 6 hours in cool water; or 10 to 12 hours at room temperature. *Refrigerate or cook goose immediately after thawing.*

Roasting time: A 10 to 12-lb. goose takes 1 hour at 400°F., plus another 2 to 2½ hours at 325°F.

SPIT-ROASTED TURKEY

MAKES 6 TO 8 SERVINGS

1 (8 to 12 lb.) turkey, frozen
and thawed or fresh
Salt
Freshly ground black
pepper

1 teaspoon thyme leaves
½ cup melted butter or
margarine

1. Remove giblets from thawed turkey. (Reserve giblets for giblet gravy.) Wash turkey. Drain and wipe dry with paper towel. Fasten neck skin to back of turkey with small skewers.
2. Sprinkle inside of turkey with salt, pepper and thyme leaves.
3. Using heavy cord, truss the turkey in four places: (1) tie the legs and tail together; (2) tie the legs and thighs tightly to the body of the turkey; (3) and (4) tie the wings to the body in 2 places.
4. Thread one spit prong or fork onto spit so that points are away from handle. Insert spit in turkey just below the breastbone and bring out above the tail. Center turkey on spit.
5. Thread second prong onto spit. Push prongs into breast and thigh sections of turkey; fasten securely.
6. Tie another cord lengthwise around the turkey, wrapping the lengthwise cord around each of the crosswise cords.
7. When preparing coals for lighting, arrange them in back half of barbecue. Place a drip pan about 4 inches longer than the turkey in front half of barbecue. If desired, shape a drip pan from heavy-duty foil.
8. When coals have reached a medium temperature, attach spit to motor. Grill, brushing occasionally with butter, until turkey reaches 185°F. internal temperature. (Either insert a meat thermometer in the thickest part of the thigh before starting to grill or use a thermometer that can be inserted periodically for a reading.)
9. The following chart can be used as a guide for barbecuing time:

APPROXIMATE TIMETABLE FOR BARBECUING WHOLE TURKEY

READY-TO-COOK WEIGHT	APPROXIMATE COOKING TIME
6 to 8 pounds	3 to 3½ hours
8 to 10 pounds	3½ to 4 hours
10 to 12 pounds	4 to 5 hours

10. About 1 hour before turkey is done, wrap stuffing in heavy-duty-foil packet and place on coals. Turn occasionally and cook until heated throughout.

11. Remove turkey from spit and allow to rest 15 minutes before carving.

GIBLET GRAVY

MAKES 2 CUPS

Giblets and neck from turkey
1 onion
2 stalks celery and leaves
1 carrot cut in chunks
1 teaspoon salt
⅛ teaspoon freshly ground black pepper

3 cups water
⅓ cup turkey drippings
⅓ cup all-purpose flour
2 cups giblet broth
Salt
Freshly ground black pepper

1. In medium saucepan, combine turkey giblets and neck, onion, celery, carrot, 1 teaspoon salt, ⅛ teaspoon pepper and water.

2. Bring to boiling. Reduce heat and simmer covered about 1 hour, until giblets are fork-tender.

3. Drain giblets, discard vegetables and neck, reserve broth. Chop giblets fine.

4. Blend turkey drippings and flour smoothly. Gradually add reserved giblet broth. Heat to boiling, stirring. Season to taste with salt and pepper. Add chopped giblets.

ROAST TURKEY AND GRAVY

MAKES 10 TO 12 SERVINGS

1 (12 lb.) turkey	Fresh Fruit Stuffing (recipe
1 qt. water	below)
Onion stuck with 2 cloves	2 tablespoons butter or
1 bay leaf	margarine
1 celery stalk	1/4 teaspoon salt
1/2 teaspoon salt	1/4 teaspoon paprika
1/4 teaspoon black peppercorns	Fresh cranberries
	Grapes

1. Preheat oven to 350°F. Remove neck and giblets, rinse. Wash turkey inside and out. Pat dry.

2. Place turkey neck, heart and gizzard in saucepan; cover with 1 qt. water. Add onion, bay leaf, celery stalk, 1/2 teaspoon salt and peppers. Heat to boiling, reduce heat and simmer, covered, 30 to 45 minutes, until tender. Save stock for gravy.

3. Spoon Fresh Fruit Stuffing into body and neck cavity. Skewer neck skin to back. Truss turkey and tie drumsticks together.

4. Place turkey, breast side up, on rack in shallow, open roasting pan. Insert meat thermometer in thick part of thigh.

5. Melt butter. Add 1/4 teaspoon salt and paprika. Brush turkey with seasoned butter. Place a loose covering of aluminum foil over turkey.

6. Place bird in preheated oven. Allow 2 1/2 to 3 hours for 8- to 12-pound bird.

7. Remove foil during last 45 minutes to brown. Turkey is done when thermometer reads 185°F. or leg moves easily.

8. Remove turkey from oven and allow to stand 20 to 30 minutes before serving. Make gravy. Remove turkey to serving platter. Garnish with fresh cranberries and grapes.

FRESH FRUIT STUFFING

MAKES ENOUGH STUFFING FOR
A 12-POUND TURKEY

2 tablespoons butter or margarine
1 cup chopped, fresh celery
1 cup chopped onion
1¾ teaspoons salt
¼ teaspoon freshly ground black pepper
½ teaspoon powdered sage
½ teaspoon thyme leaves, crumbled

6 cups dry bread cubes, (about 10 slices)
2 medium apples, cored and chopped
1 cup seedless grapes, halved
½ cup coarsely chopped walnuts or pecans
2 eggs, slightly beaten

1. Melt butter in large skillet over medium heat. Sauté celery and onions until tender, about 8 minutes.
2. Stir in salt, pepper, sage and thyme. In large bowl, mix bread cubes, apples, grapes and nuts.
3. Stir in onion mixture and eggs; toss lightly. Stuff lightly into body and neck cavity of prepared turkey.

TURKEY GRAVY

MAKES 2½ CUPS

4 tablespoons pan drippings from turkey
3 tablespoons all-purpose flour

2½ cups turkey stock
¼ teaspoon salt
⅛ teaspoon freshly ground black pepper

1. Combine pan drippings and flour smoothly. Cook over low heat, stirring constantly, until bubbly. Add stock all at once and cook, stirring briskly with wire whisk until mixture boils.
2. Add salt and pepper to taste.

ROAST GOOSE BURGUNDY

MAKES 5½ CUPS GRAVY,
6 TO 8 SERVINGS

1 (10 to 12 lb.) ready-to-cook goose, thawed
4 cups water
1 onion studded with 2 whole cloves
1 bay leaf
¼ teaspoon whole black peppercorns
½ teaspoon salt

Stuffing:
¼ cup butter or margarine
1 cup chopped onion
1 cup chopped celery
½ cup chopped parsley
1 large clove garlic, chopped
1 teaspoon thyme leaves
1 teaspoon sage leaves
1 teaspoon savory leaves
1 teaspoon salt
¼ teaspoon freshly ground black pepper
1 package (7 ozs.) herb-seasoned croutons
1 can (6 ozs.) frozen orange juice concentrate, thawed, undiluted
2 tablespoons honey
½ cup chopped fresh cranberries
⅓ cup water
⅓ cup Burgundy

Burgundy Glaze:
2 tablespoons butter or margarine, melted
2 tablespoons honey
½ cup Burgundy or dry red wine
½ teaspoon liquid gravy seasoning

Burgundy Sauce:
½ cup goose drippings
6 tablespoons all-purpose flour
3 cups goose broth
1 cup Burgundy or dry red wine
1 teaspoon salt
Few twists freshly ground black pepper
2 teaspoons liquid gravy seasoning
2 tablespoons frozen orange juice concentrate, thawed

Garnish:
Parsley
2 cups fresh cranberries
6 orange-slice twists
2 packages (1-lb. size) frozen bacon-flavored potato rounds

1. Preheat oven to 400°F.

2. Remove neck and giblets from body cavity; rinse. Place neck, heart and gizzard in 2-qt. saucepan with 4 cups water, clove-studded onion, bay leaf, peppercorns and ½ teaspoon salt. Bring to boiling. Cover, boil gently about 1½ to 2 hours, until very tender. Add goose liver last 20 minutes of cooking.

3. Remove heart, gizzard and liver and chop finely. Use neck meat for sandwiches; discard onion and cloves. Save broth (you should have 3 cups).

4. Remove excess fat from body cavity and excess neck skin. (Reserve fat and render for use in other cooking if desired.) Rinse bird and drain.

5. Tie wings flat against body with cord around each wing and across back.

6. Make stuffing: In large skillet, heat butter until melted. Add onion, celery, parsley and garlic and sauté, stirring frequently, for 5 minutes. Stir in thyme, sage, savory, salt and pepper.

7. Turn vegetable-herb mixture into large bowl. Add croutons, orange juice concentrate, honey, cranberries, water and the Burgundy. Mix well with large spoon.

8. To stuff: Fill neck and body cavity loosely. Fasten neck skin to back with skewer. Close body cavity with skewers, poultry pins or stitching. Tie legs together tightly with cord.

9. Place goose, breast side up, on rack in shallow foil-lined roasting pan. Insert meat thermometer deep into side thigh muscle.

10. Prepare Burgundy Glaze: Combine all glaze ingredients in small saucepan, heat to boiling point.

11. Brush goose liberally with glaze. Roast goose breast side up, 30 minutes. Remove from oven, turn goose, breast side down and baste again with glaze. Return to oven and roast 30 minutes longer.

12. During roasting, spoon, pour or siphon off accumulated fat. This should be done at ½-hour intervals so that the fat doesn't brown excessively.

13. After roasting for 1 hour, reduce the oven temperature to 325°F. Turn the goose breast side up again, and continue roasting.

14. Roast until thermometer in thigh registers 180°-185°F. Stuffing temperature should also be checked and it should register 165°F.

15. If a thermometer is not used, press meaty part of leg between protected fingers. It should feel very soft. Also prick thigh with a fork. The juices running out of thigh should be beige in color, not pink. The skin should be deep mahogany brown and crisp.

16. Place goose on heated serving platter. Cover loosely with foil to keep warm.

17. Make Burgundy Sauce: Pour ½ cup drippings into 2-qt. saucepan, blend in flour smoothly. Add reserved goose broth and Burgundy. Bring to boiling, stirring. Season with salt, pepper, liquid gravy seasoning and orange juice concentrate.

18. To serve: Garnish goose platter with parsley, frosted cranberry garland and orange twists. Spoon hot potato rounds (prepared as package label directs) on the side of goose.

HERB ROAST CHICKEN

MAKES 4 TO 6 SERVINGS

1 (5½ to 6 lb.) roasting
chicken
1 onion, quartered
½ cup (1 stick) butter or
margarine, melted
1 teaspoon salt

¼ teaspoon freshly ground
black pepper
1 teaspoon rosemary leaves
1 teaspoon savory leaves
1 teaspoon thyme leaves

1. Rinse chicken, pat dry with paper towels. Place onion inside chicken, truss for roasting or secure on spit.
2. Preheat oven to 325°F. or prepare rotisserie.
3. Combine remaining ingredients. Brush chicken with mixture. Roast about 2½ to 3 hours, until done, or grill on rotisserie, basting frequently with butter-herb mixture.

ROAST CHICKEN WITH RICE-AND-SAUSAGE STUFFING

MAKES 4 TO 6 SERVINGS

1 (4½ to 5 lb.) roasting
chicken
2 tablespoons lemon juice
¼ teaspoon salt
¼ teaspoon freshly ground
black pepper
4 cups Rice-and-Sausage
Stuffing (recipe below)
¼ cup melted butter or
margarine
3½ cups water
½ teaspoon salt
Dash freshly ground black
pepper

½ teaspoon thyme leaves
1 bay leaf
1 onion stuck with 2 whole
cloves
1 stalk celery with leaves
1 carrot, peeled
3 tablespoons all-purpose
flour
¼ teaspoon liquid gravy
seasoning
Salt
Freshly ground black
pepper

1. Preheat oven to 350°F. Remove giblets and neck from chicken. Rinse under cold running water, pat dry with paper towels.

2. Sprinkle inside of chicken with lemon juice, ¼ teaspoon salt and ¼ teaspoon pepper.

3. Spoon Rice-and-Sausage Stuffing into wishbone area first. Fasten neck skin to back with skewer or hibachi stick.

4. Fill body cavity of chicken with remaining stuffing, do not pack. (Bake any leftover stuffing in shallow greased casserole, along with chicken, the last 30 minutes of roasting.)

5. Truss chicken: Fold wings under chicken across back with wing tips touching. Close body cavity with poultry pins or wooden picks. Tie legs together at ends with soft cord.

6. Place chicken, breast side up, on rack in shallow open roasting pan. Cover with cheesecloth dipped in ¼ cup melted butter, reserve remaining butter; roast the chicken uncovered, 1½ hours.

7. Remove cheesecloth. Brush chicken with rest of melted butter; roast 40 to 45 minutes longer. Remove chicken to heated serving platter, keep warm.

8. Meanwhile, while chicken is roasting, cook giblets and neck. In 2 qt. saucepan combine giblets, neck, 3½ cups water, ½ teaspoon salt, dash pepper, thyme, bay leaf, onion, broken celery stalk and leaves, and carrot.

9. Bring to boiling, reduce heat and simmer covered 1 hour, until giblets are fork-tender. Strain, reserve 2¼ cups broth, chop giblets. Discard neck and vegetables.

10. Make gravy: When chicken has finished roasting, pour off drippings from roasting pan. Measure 3 tablespoons of liquid and return to pan, stir in flour until smooth.

11. Gradually add reserved 2¼ cups broth, stirring until smooth; bring to boiling, stirring constantly.

12. Reduce heat, add reserved chopped giblets, liquid gravy seasoning, season to taste with salt and pepper.

13. Pour hot gravy into heated gravy boat. Serve with chicken and stuffing.

RICE-AND-SAUSAGE STUFFING

MAKES ABOUT 4 CUPS

½ lb. pork sausage
1 cup sliced celery
½ cup finely chopped onion
1½ cups cooked rice
¼ cup raisins or currants

½ teaspoon salt
½ teaspoon thyme leaves
⅛ teaspoon freshly ground
   black pepper

1. In large skillet, combine sausage meat, celery and onion. Cook over medium heat, stirring occasionally, about 10 minutes, or until sausage is cooked.
2. Stir in rice, raisins, salt, thyme and pepper; mix well.

ROAST DUCKLING WITH APRICOTS

MAKES 4 SERVINGS

1 (4 to 5 lb.) duckling,
   quartered
1 teaspoon salt
   Few twists freshly ground
   black pepper
¼ teaspoon thyme leaves
⅛ teaspoon ground nutmeg
1 can (17 ozs.) apricots,
   drained, liquid reserved*

½ cup apricot liquid
½ cup dry sherry
2 tablespoons apricot jam
¼ cup apricot liquid
¼ cup water
1 tablespoon cornstarch
   Dash freshly ground black
   pepper
   Watercress or parsley

1. Preheat oven to 325°F. Place duckling skin side up on rack on roasting pan. Sprinkle with salt, pepper, thyme and nutmeg.
2. Roast duckling uncovered 2 to 2½ hours or until tender, cover loosely with foil, keep warm.
3. Make sauce: pour off all fat from roasting pan. Deglaze pan with ½ cup liquid from apricots.
4. Pour pan liquid into small saucepan, add sherry and apricot jam.
5. Blend ¼ cup apricot liquid and water with cornstarch smoothly. Stir into apricot pan mixture. Heat to boiling, stirring constantly. Add pepper and apricots, heat until butter melts. Taste for seasoning.
6. Ladle some sauce and apricots over duck. Serve remaining sauce separately. Garnish platter with watercress.

*Editor's Note: 1 can (17 ozs.) plums or 1 can (20 ozs.) pineapple chunks may also be used. Also 2 cups halved, pitted plums, prunes or peaches plus ¾ cup fruit juice substituted for apricot liquid.

After the Feast

TURKEY CURRY WITH ALMOND RAISIN RICE

MAKES 6 SERVINGS

1½ cups chopped unpeeled
  apples
⅔ cup minced onion
1 clove garlic, minced
2 tablespoons butter or
  margarine
2 tablespoons all-purpose
  flour

1 teaspoon curry powder
1½ teaspoons salt
¼ teaspoon ground ginger
1½ cups turkey or chicken
  broth
2½ cups cooked turkey, cut-up
  Almond Raisin Rice
  (recipe below)

1. Sauté apples, onion and garlic in butter until tender-crisp. Stir in
flour, seasoning and turkey broth.
2. Cook and stir over medium heat until thickened. Add turkey; heat
thoroughly. Serve with Almond Raisin Rice.

ALMOND RAISIN RICE

MAKES 6 SERVINGS

½ cup slivered almonds
2 tablespoons butter or
  margarine

¾ cup light raisins
3 cups cooked rice

1. Sauté ½ cup slivered almonds in 2 tablespoons butter until golden
brown. Stir in raisins and rice, tossing lightly to combine. Heat thoroughly.

TURKEY CANTONESE

MAKES 8 SERVINGS

3 cups thinly sliced celery
2 cups sliced onion
2 cups green pepper pieces,
   cut into 1-inch squares
1 qt. turkey or chicken broth
1 can (4 ozs.) water chestnuts,
   drained and sliced
1 can (4 ozs.) sliced

mushrooms, drained, or ½
lb. fresh mushrooms, sliced
½ cup soy sauce
¼ cup cornstarch
¼ cup cold water
3 cups cooked turkey pieces
6 cups hot cooked rice

1. Parboil celery, onion and green pepper in broth about 5 minutes.
2. Add water chestnuts, mushrooms and soy sauce. Dissolve cornstarch in ¼ cup cold water; stir into vegetable mixture. Cook 10 minutes longer.
3. Add turkey and heat thoroughly. Serve over hot rice. If desired, garnish with additional turkey, cut in strips.

TURKEY NOODLE SOUP

MAKES 5 QUARTS

Leftover cooked carcass
from a 15- to 20-lb. turkey
5 qts. water
1 cup chopped celery
½ cup chopped celery leaves
1 cup chopped onion
7 chicken bouillon cubes
1 tablespoon salt
¼ teaspoon freshly ground
   black pepper

1 bay leaf
½ cup chopped parsley
1 cup fresh, frozen or canned
   peas
1 cup sliced carrots
1 cup cut green beans
4 cups (8 ozs.) fine egg
   noodles
¼ cup butter or margarine
¼ cup all-purpose flour

1. In 8-qt. kettle or Dutch oven, place turkey carcass, water, celery, celery leaves, onion, bouillon cubes, salt, pepper and bay leaf. Heat to boiling; lower heat; cover and simmer 1 hour. Remove carcass and let cool.
2. Add parsley, peas, carrots and green beans to soup; heat to boiling; reduce heat and simmer 10 minutes until vegetables are just tender.
3. Remove meat from carcass, return pieces to soup. Discard bones.
4. Heat soup to boiling, add noodles, cook, uncovered, 10 minutes.
5. Melt butter in small frying pan; stir in flour. Cook over low heat, stirring constantly until flour is browned. Stir into boiling soup. Return to boiling and stir. Reduce heat and simmer 5 minutes.

TURKEY AND OLIVE MANICOTTI

MAKES 4 SERVINGS

8 pieces packaged manicotti tubes
1 package (10 ozs.) frozen chopped spinach
1 cup pitted ripe olives, drained
1 tablespoon oil
1 teaspoon finely chopped garlic
1 cup finely chopped onion
1 cup finely chopped cooked turkey
1 teaspoon salt
½ teaspoon freshly ground black pepper
½ teaspoon oregano leaves, crumbled
1 large egg, beaten

½ cup grated Parmesan cheese
1 can (15 ozs.) tomato sauce with tomato bits
½ cup water
1 chicken bouillon cube, crushed
½ teaspoon basil leaves, crumbled
¼ cup grated Parmesan cheese
½ cup whole pitted ripe olives, drained
¼ cup grated Parmesan cheese
½ cup sliced Monterey Jack or Muenster cheese

1. Cook manicotti as package label directs; drain and cool. Defrost spinach and press out all excess liquids.
2. Finely chop 1 cup pitted ripe olives.
3. Heat oil. Add garlic and onion and cook until onion is soft. Add turkey, spinach, salt, pepper, oregano, beaten egg and ½ cup Parmesan cheese to onion.
4. Fill manicotti with this mixture. (If any filling is left over, stir into the tomato sauce.)
5. In medium saucepan, combine tomato sauce, water, chicken bouillon cube and basil. Heat to boiling. Simmer for one minute. Stir in ¼ cup Parmesan cheese and ½ cup whole pitted ripe olives.
6. Preheat oven to 375°F. Pour ½ cup sauce in bottom of a 1½-qt. shallow baking dish. Arrange filled manicotti in sauce. Pour remaining sauce over top. Sprinkle with remaining ¼ cup Parmesan and sliced Monterey cheese.
7. Bake 25 to 30 minutes until bubbly throughout.

Thanksgiving Pies

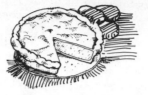

FRESH SWEET POTATO PIE

MAKES 1 (9-INCH) PIE, 8 SERVINGS

2 cups mashed, cooked sweet potatoes (4 medium)
3 eggs
1 cup packed brown sugar
1 teaspoon salt
½ teaspoon ground cinnamon
½ teaspoon ground nutmeg

¼ teaspoon ground ginger
⅛ teaspoon ground cloves
1 cup evaporated milk or light cream
1 unbaked 9-inch pastry shell
Pecans for garnish

1. Cook sweet potatoes: bake in preheated 350°F. oven 40 minutes or boil in water to cover for 20 minutes, until soft. Cool, peel and mash until smooth.
2. In large bowl, beat eggs with sugar, salt and spices. Add mashed sweet potatoes and evaporated milk; mix well.
3. Turn into unbaked pastry shell. Bake in preheated 350°F. oven 1 hour and 15 minutes or until the tip of a silver knife inserted in center comes out clean. Garnish with pecans. Serve with whipped cream or ice cream, if desired.

OLD-FASHIONED PUMPKIN PIE

MAKES 1 (9-INCH) PIE, 8 SERVINGS

1 9-inch unbaked pie shell
1 can (16 ozs.) mashed pumpkin (2 cups)
1 can (13 ozs.) evaporated milk
2 eggs
1 cup packed dark brown sugar

1¼ teaspoons ground cinnamon
½ teaspoon ground ginger
½ teaspoon ground nutmeg
¼ teaspoon ground allspice
¼ teaspoon ground cloves
¼ teaspoon salt
Whipped cream

1. Prepare pie crust pastry and line 9-inch pie pan, flute edges.

2. Preheat oven to 425°F.

3. In large bowl with electric mixer or in food processor with mixing blade, combine pumpkin, evaporated milk, eggs, brown sugar, cinnamon, ginger, nutmeg, allspice, cloves and salt. Beat at low speed until blended.

4. Pour pumpkin mixture into prepared pie shell. Bake for 12 to 15 minutes to set crust, reduce heat to 350° and continue baking 35 to 40 minutes longer or until tip of silver knife inserted in center comes out clean. Remove from oven and cool.

5. Serve slightly warm with whipped cream.

FRESH CRANBERRY CHIFFON PIE

MAKES 1 (9-INCH) PIE, 8 SERVINGS

2 envelopes unflavored gelatin	2 teaspoons grated orange rind
½ cup cold water	3 egg whites
1½ cups fresh cranberries, rinsed	½ cup sugar
¼ cup water	1 baked 9-inch pastry shell
½ cup sugar	Sweetened whipped cream, optional
½ teaspoon salt	Orange rind, optional
¼ cup orange juice	8 cranberries, optional

1. Soften gelatin in ½ cup cold water and set aside.

2. Place cranberries in saucepan with ¼ cup water. Cover and cook only until skins pop, about 10 minutes.

3. Add ½ cup sugar, salt and softened gelatin. Mix well. Stir in orange juice and rind.

4. Chill until mixture is completely cooled and begins to thicken. Beat egg whites until they stand in soft peaks. Gradually beat in ½ cup sugar and beat until stiff.

5. Fold meringue into cranberry mixture. Spoon into baked pie shell. Chill until ready to serve.

6. Garnish with whipped cream, orange rind and cranberries, if desired.

QUICK DEEP-DISH APPLE PIE

MAKES 1 (9-INCH) PIE, 6 SERVINGS

2 cans (21-oz. size) apple-pie filling
4 tablespoons bourbon or rum
2 tablespoons maple-blended syrup
1 tablespoon butter or margarine
Pastry for 9-inch pie crust, your own or a mix
Vanilla ice cream, optional

1. Preheat oven to 425°F.
2. Turn pie filling into 7 x 11-inch glass pan; stir in bourbon and syrup. Dot surface of filling with butter.
3. Roll out pie crust to a rectangle 9 x 12 inches and cover filling. Turn edges under and crimp with fork. Pierce surface of crust in several places.
4. Bake 25 to 30 minutes, until crust is golden brown. Serve warm with vanilla ice cream if desired.

PURPLE PLUM MINCEMEAT PIE

MAKES 1 (9-INCH) PIE, 8 SERVINGS

Pastry for 2-crust, 9-inch pie, your own or a mix
3 cups Purple Plum Mincemeat (recipe below)
2 cups sliced tart apples
2 tablespoons flour
2 tablespoons sugar
2 tablespoons butter or margarine
Hard Sauce (recipe below) or vanilla ice cream

1. Preheat oven to 425°F. Line pie plate with pastry.
2. In large bowl combine Purple Plum Mincemeat and apples. Mix flour and sugar, add to mincemeat-apple mixture.
3. Pour filling into pie crust, dot top with butter. Place top crust on filling. Cut steam vents in top crust and flute edges.
4. Bake about 40 minutes, until crust is golden and filling is bubbly. If crust gets too brown, cover edges with foil during last 10 minutes of baking.
5. Serve warm with Hard Sauce or soft vanilla ice cream.

PURPLE PLUM MINCEMEAT

MAKES 6 PINTS

4 lbs. purple prune plums
2 lbs. Bartlett pears
1 lb. seedless raisins
1 tablespoon grated lemon rind
¼ cup lemon juice
2½ tablespoons grated orange rind

½ cup orange juice
1½ lbs. light brown sugar
½ cup cider vinegar
1 teaspoon salt
1 tablespoon ground cinnamon
2 teaspoons ground cloves
1 teaspoon ground nutmeg
½ teaspoon ground allspice

1. Quarter and pit purple prune plums. Core and dice unpeeled pears.
2. Combine fruits with remaining ingredients in large kettle. Bring to boiling. Reduce heat, cover and simmer 30 minutes. Remove cover and simmer 1 hour until slightly thickened, stirring from time to time.
3. Ladle hot mixture to within ⅛ inch of top of hot sterilized jars; wipe off anything spilled on tops or threads of jars with clean, damp cloth.
4. Put sterilized lids on jars, screw sterilized bands tight. As each jar is filled, stand it on rack in a canner full of hot, not boiling, water. Water should cover jars 1 to 2 inches.
5. Put cover on canner, bring water to a boil. Process jars in boiling-water bath 25 minutes.
6. Remove jars from canner. Let cool for about 12 hours. Remove bands, test for seal: If dome of lid is down or stays down when pressed, the jar is properly sealed. Label. Store in cool, dark, dry place.

HARD SAUCE

MAKES ABOUT 1 CUP

½ cup butter or margarine, softened
1 cup confectioners' sugar

2 teaspoons pure vanilla extract

1. In medium bowl, beat butter and sugar together until fluffy. Add vanilla extract.

Vegetables of the Month: Squash and Pumpkin

JAMAICAN SQUASH SOUP

MAKES ABOUT 3 QUARTS

2 lbs. peeled, cubed winter squash: turk's turban, butternut, Hubbard or acorn
1 lb. tomatoes, peeled and diced
½ cup rice
1 large clove garlic, crushed
2 bay leaves
¼ teaspoon marjoram leaves
¼ teaspoon thyme leaves
1 cup chopped scallions
1 tablespoon bottled steak sauce
Dash ground allspice
1 teaspoon sugar
2 teaspoons salt
½ teaspoon freshly ground black pepper
3 cans (10½-oz. size) beef consommé
5 cups water
4 tablespoons chopped parsley

1. Place squash, tomatoes, rice, garlic, bay leaves, marjoram, thyme, scallions, steak sauce, allspice, sugar, salt, pepper, consommé and water into large kettle or Dutch oven.
2. Heat to boiling, stir, reduce heat and let boil gently 45 to 60 minutes until vegetables and rice are very tender.
3. Ladle into soup bowls; sprinkle each serving with a little parsley.

GLAZED ACORN RINGS

MAKES 6 SERVINGS

2 acorn squash
⅓ cup fresh orange juice
½ cup packed dark brown sugar
¼ cup light corn syrup
¼ cup butter or margarine
2 teaspoons grated fresh lemon rind
⅛ teaspoon salt

1. Cut off ends of squash. Slice crosswise into 1-inch rings and remove seeds.
2. Place in a single layer in a large, shallow baking dish and add orange juice.
3. Cover and bake in preheated 350°F. oven 30 minutes. Combine remaining ingredients; simmer 5 minutes. Pour over squash rings and bake, uncovered, 15 minutes longer, basting occasionally.

GOLDEN SQUASH SOUFFLÉ

MAKES 4 TO 6 SERVINGS

1½ cups mashed, cooked winter squash: turk's turban, Hubbard, acorn or spaghetti	½ teaspoon salt
	⅛ teaspoon freshly ground black pepper
6 eggs, separated	⅛ teaspoon ground nutmeg
1 cup grated natural Swiss cheese	⅛ teaspoon cream of tartar
	2 tablespoons grated Parmesan cheese

1. Preheat oven to 350°F. and grease a 2-qt. casserole.
2. Beat squash until fluffy. Add egg yolks, one at a time, beating well after each addition. Stir in cheese, salt, pepper and nutmeg.
3. In medium bowl, with clean beaters, beat egg whites with cream of tartar until stiff peaks form.
4. Fold whites into squash mixture, turn into soufflé dish and sprinkle surface with Parmesan cheese. Bake 1 hour until puffy.

MACE SQUASH CUBES

MAKES 8 SERVINGS

3 lbs. butternut squash	¼ teaspoon ground mace
Boiling water	Dash ground white pepper
¾ teaspoon salt	

1. Peel, remove seeds and stringy portion from squash. Cut into 1-inch cubes (makes about 8 cups).
2. Cook, covered, in 1-inch boiling salted water, until just tender, about 15 minutes. Drain well.
3. Sprinkle with mace and pepper, toss gently. Pile into heated serving dish.

PUMPKIN TORTE

MAKES 12 SERVINGS

24 graham crackers, crushed
⅓ cup sugar
½ cup butter or margarine, softened
2 eggs
¾ cup sugar
1 package (8 ozs.) cream cheese, room temperature
1 envelope unflavored gelatin
¼ cup cold water
2 cups canned pumpkin
3 eggs, separated
½ cup sugar
½ cup milk
½ teaspoon salt
1 tablespoon ground cinnamon
¼ cup sugar

1. Preheat oven to 350°F. Blend graham cracker crumbs, ⅓ cup sugar and ½ cup butter. Spread in bottom of 9 x 13 x 2-inch pan, pressing firmly to make a crust.

2. In medium bowl, combine 2 eggs, ¾ cup sugar and cream cheese; blend until mixed, then beat until very smooth. Pour over crust and bake for 20 minutes. Cool.

3. Soften gelatin in water and set aside.

4. In 2-qt. saucepan, combine pumpkin, egg yolks, ½ cup sugar, milk, salt and cinnamon. Heat to boiling, stirring constantly until thickened.

5. Add softened gelatin to pumpkin mixture, stirring until dissolved. Cool.

6. In large bowl, beat egg whites with electric mixer until soft peaks form; gradually add ¼ cup sugar and beat until stiff peaks form and mixture is shiny.

7. Fold egg whites into cooled pumpkin mixture. Pour over cooled cream cheese crust. Refrigerate several hours before serving, then cut into 3 x 3-inch squares.

8. To serve, garnish with a little sweetened whipped cream and grated orange rind.

December

December's days are shorter with long nights. We tend to stay at home now and burn the lights longer in the evening. Preparations for Christmas, Chanukah and the holiday season bring urgency and anticipation to the whole month.

Our feature this month is the Winter Party Planner, a guide to help you choose what, when and how to serve your guests from early December through New Year's Eve.

There's no time to lose in making gifts from the kitchen. We want to make them early, so we have time to present them prettily.

A convivial cup is in order on these festive days. Punches, eggnog and hot drinks of all manner will help the celebrations.

Polish the silver and put it out with your best china to serve up the spectacular dishes in our "Holiday Entertaining" section.

The unique mushroom is our Vegetable of the Month. It lends itself to soups, salads and stuffing.

Winter Party Planner: Christmas to New Year's Eve

BUFFETS	APPETIZER	SALAD	SOUP	MAIN DISH
Brunch	Crabmeat Mold Crackers	Tomato Aspic Carib		Florentine Rice Quiche
Skating Party	Assorted Cheese Tray Crackers			Chili Dogs for a Crowd
Apres Ski	Liptauer and Crackers Sweet 'n' Simple Coleslaw	Cold Sauerkraut Salad	Canadian Cheese Soup	Grilled Wursts & Sausages
Open House	Holiday Sandwich Tree	Good Earth Salad		Baked Ham Apricot Glaze
Formal	Coppermine Country Pate Melba Toast	Mixed Green Salad With Walnut Dressing	Claret Consomme	Beef Stroganoff

VEGETABLE	ACCOM-PANI-MENT	BREAD	DESSERT	BEVERAGE
Coleslaw	Baked Stuffed Clams	Stollen	Baked Fruit Compote	Cranberry Wine Punch Coffee
Fresh Vegetable Sticks	Baked Beans		Frosted Carrot Bars	Hot Spiced Cider with Roasted Apples
Texas Ranch Beans	Assorted Mustards	Black Raisin Bread	Chocolate Potato Torte	Glogg
Cheese Grits Casserole	Seafood Stuffed Mushrooms	Basket Assorted Crusty Bread: Rye Anadama Pumper- nickel	Cranberry Mousse Raspberry Sauce	Beaujolais Hot Spiced Fruit Punch
Wild 'n' White Rice	Savory Green Beans and Red Peppers	Crusty Rolls	Eggnog Chiffon Pie	Burgundy

Gifts from the Kitchen

LIPTAUER

MAKES 2 CUPS

1 teaspoon ground mustard
2 tablespoons warm water
½ cup butter or margarine, softened
1 package (8 ozs.) cream cheese, softened
1 tablespoon minced onion
3 anchovy fillets, minced
1 tablespoon capers, minced
1 tablespoon caraway seed
Few twists freshly ground black pepper

1. In a cup, combine mustard and warm water. Let stand 10 minutes to develop flavor.
2. In a small mixing bowl, beat butter with electric mixer until soft. Add cream cheese, blending well.
3. Add mustard mixture along with remaining ingredients. Mix thoroughly. Serve as a spread with crackers.

WINE JELLY

MAKES 4 (6-OUNCE)
GLASSES

3 cups (1¼ lbs.) sugar
2 cups wine (sherry, port, Burgundy, muscatel, claret, Tokay or fruit wines:
loganberry, currant or blackberry)
½ bottle (6-oz. size) liquid fruit pectin
Paraffin

1. Measure sugar and wine into a large saucepan. Stir over medium heat, bringing mixture to just below the boiling point.
2. Continue stirring until the sugar is dissolved, about 5 minutes. Remove from heat. Stir in fruit pectin at once and mix well.

3. Skim off foam, if necessary. Pour quickly into sterilized glasses. Cover at once with ⅛-inch hot paraffin. Cool.
4. Label and date glasses.

Editor's Note: Recipe may be doubled.

CHOCOLATE FUDGE

ABOUT 2¼ POUNDS FUDGE

1 can (6 ozs.) evaporated milk
⅔ cup water
4 sq. (4 oz.) unsweetened chocolate
4 cups sugar
½ teaspoon salt

2 tablespoons light corn syrup
¼ cup butter or margarine
4 teaspoons pure vanilla extract
¾ cup walnut halves

1. Combine first six ingredients in a heavy 3-qt. saucepan. Stir over low heat until sugar is dissolved and chocolate melted, washing down crystals occasionally.
2. Increase heat to medium and bring mixture to boiling. Cook, stirring occasionally, until candy thermometer registers 234°F. (soft ball stage: forms soft ball in very cold water).
3. Remove mixture from heat and cool to lukewarm (about 110°F.) without stirring or jarring saucepan.
4. Add butter and extract; beat until mixture is dull in color and begins to thicken. Quickly turn into buttered 9-in. square pan and spread evenly. Lightly mark into 64 squares and press a walnut half into center of each piece. Set aside to cool completely.
5. When firm, cut into squares.

Editor's Note: If desired, vary the toppings on batches of fudge, using flaked coconut on some and toasted almonds on others.

Variations:

ALMOND FUDGE—Stir ½ cup chopped toasted almonds into cooled fudge along with butter and extract.

PEANUT BUTTER FUDGE—Stir ½ cup creamy peanut butter into the cooled fudge along with the butter and extract.

MARSHMALLOW FUDGE—Stir 32 (½ lb.) marshmallows, quartered, into cooled fudge along with butter and extract.

TUTTI-FRUTTI FUDGE—Sir ⅓ cup each candied cherries, candied pineapple, and raisins into cooled fudge along with butter and extract.

PECAN CRUNCH

ABOUT 2 POUNDS CANDY

2 cups (about 8 oz.) pecans
1 teaspoon baking soda
2¼ cups sugar
1½ cups butter or margarine

½ cup water
1 tablespoon cider vinegar
1 teaspoon salt
4 oz. milk chocolate

1. Very coarsely chop 1 cup of the pecans; finely chop the other pecans and reserve ½ cup for topping. Mix the 1 cup coarsely chopped and ½ cup finely chopped pecans with the baking soda. Set aside.
2. In a heavy 2-qt. saucepan, combine the next five ingredients. Set over low heat and stir until sugar is dissolved. Continue cooking without stirring, until candy thermometer registers 290°F. (crack stage—forms threads which are hard but not brittle in very cold water).
3. Remove from heat and remove thermometer; add nut-soda mixture and stir until just blended. Pour into a buttered 10-inch square pan. Cool completely on cooling rack.
4. When candy is cooled, melt chocolate over simmering water, cool slightly, and spread evenly over candy. Sprinkle the remaining ½ cup finely chopped nuts over the melted chocolate.
5. When chocolate is set, turn candy out of pan and break into pieces. Store between pieces of plastic wrap in a tightly covered container.

WINTER STRAWBERRIES

MAKES 45 CANDIES

1½ cups grated walnuts
1½ cups grated coconut
3 packages (3-oz. size) strawberry gelatin
1 can (14 ozs.) sweetened condensed milk

1 teaspoon pure vanilla extract
⅓ cup red-colored sugar
Green spearmint leaves

1. Combine walnuts, coconut, gelatin, condensed milk and vanilla in medium bowl. Work until smoothly mixed. Form into a ball and chill for at least 1 hour.
2. Shape chilled mixture into strawberries, using 1 tablespoon of mixture for each strawberry. Chill again.
3. Roll strawberries in red sugar. Cut stems from spearmint leaves; insert stem in each strawberry. Refrigerate in airtight container until ready to serve.

FLORENTINES

MAKES 24 COOKIES

½ cup sugar
⅓ cup heavy cream
⅓ cup honey
Dash of salt
1½ cups sliced, unblanched almonds

⅓ cup finely chopped candied orange peel
6 tablespoons all-purpose flour
1 package (6 ozs.) semisweet chocolate bits
1 teaspoon shortening

1. Combine sugar, cream and honey in saucepan. Bring to boil, stirring, then gently boil to 238°F. (soft-ball stage.) Remove from heat.
2. Stir in salt, almonds, orange peel and flour.
3. Drop by level tablespoonfuls onto foil placed on cookie sheet. Flatten cookies slightly.
4. Bake at 325°F. for 10 to 13 minutes or until golden brown around the edges and done in center. Cool thoroughly on foil, then peel off and invert on wire rack.
5. Melt chocolate in top of double boiler. Stir in shortening. Spread mixture over flat bottoms of cookies.

VANILLA-COFFEE LIQUEUR

MAKES ABOUT 1½ QUARTS

1 pt. light corn syrup
1 cup sugar
½ cup water
½ cup instant coffee powder

1 bottle (⅘ qt.) vodka
1 vanilla bean, split lengthwise, or 2 tablespoons pure vanilla extract

1. In a large saucepan combine syrup, sugar and water. Heat to boiling point, stirring constantly. Reduce heat; simmer and stir just until sugar dissolves (about 2 minutes).
2. With a wire whisk, gradually beat in coffee powder. Beat until thoroughly dissolved over very low heat.
3. Remove from heat, add vodka and vanilla bean. Pour into jars or bottles, dropping a piece of vanilla bean in each jar. Cover, label and let age for at least 2 weeks. (This allows flavors to mellow.)
4. At holiday time pour into attractive, dark decanter type bottles, cork. Tie with yarn or ribbon.
5. It is a nice idea to write the recipe and give it along with the liqueur. Serve in cordial glasses or pour a little over vanilla, coffee or chocolate ice cream.

ORANGE-VANILLA LIQUEUR

MAKES 1 QUART

1 cup water
1 cup light corn syrup
2 tablespoons dark corn syrup
⅓ cup sugar
  Peel from 2 large oranges

1 vanilla bean, split
  lengthwise
¼ cup pure orange extract
2 cups vodka

1. In small saucepan combine water, corn syrup, sugar, orange peel and vanilla bean. Bring to boiling, stirring to dissolve sugar. Boil 8 to 10 minutes, stirring occasionally.
2. Remove from heat, stir in orange extract. Cool. Add vodka. Pour into a jar or decanter with tight-fitting top. Let stand at room temperature 2 weeks to mellow before serving.

OLD-TIME MOLASSES FRUITCAKE

MAKES 4 (3-POUND) FRUITCAKES

3 cups (one 15-oz. package) dark raisins or 3 cups chopped dates or pitted prunes
3 cups (one 15-oz. package) golden raisins or 3 cups dried apricots, chopped
2 packages (16-oz. size) mixed candied fruit
¾ cup brandy or rum or apple juice
3 cups butter, margarine or shortening
2½ cups sugar
12 eggs
1 tablespoon pure vanilla extract
1 bottle (12 ozs.) dark molasses
1 tablespoon grated orange rind

1 tablespoon grated lemon rind
1 package (2 lbs.) all-purpose flour or 7 cups unsifted all-purpose flour
2 teaspoons baking soda
2 teaspoons salt
2 tablespoons ground cinnamon
2 tablespoons ground nutmeg
1 tablespoon ground cloves
2 cans (8-oz. size) or 4 cups walnuts, coarsely chopped
½ to 1 cup brandy or apple juice
½ cup light corn syrup
2 tablespoons water
  Candied cherry halves
  Citron bits
  Walnut halves

1. In large bowl combine dark raisins, golden raisins and mixed candied fruit. Toss with brandy. Cover with plastic wrap and allow to soak overnight at room temperature.

2. Next day, preheat oven to 300°F. Tear off four 13 x 18-inch sheets of heavy-duty foil and line four 9 x 5 x 3-inch loaf pans. Carefully press foil into corners and smooth out folds; allow some of foil to hang over edges of the pans. Do not grease.

3. In large bowl with electric mixer at medium-high speed, beat butter until light and fluffy. Gradually beat in sugar. Clean side of bowl and beaters.

4. Beat in eggs one at a time; add vanilla extract. Gradually beat in molasses until well-blended. Stir in orange and lemon rinds. Turn into large pot.

5. Sift together flour, baking soda, salt and spices. Add to creamed mixture and beat until well-blended and smooth.

6. Stir in brandy-soaked fruits and walnuts. Spoon batter into foil-lined pans and spread evenly into corners.

7. Bake for 2 to 2½ hours, or until cake tester poked in center of cakes comes out clean.

8. Remove from oven and cool 10 minutes. Using foil overhang, lift loaves from pans; place on wire racks, cool completely. Remove foil.

9. Cut 4 lengths of cheesecloth to wrap around each cake. Soak cheesecloths in ½ cup brandy and wrap each cake. Overwrap completely and securely with foil or plastic wrap. Store in tightly covered container in cool, approximately 50°F., atmosphere.

10. If stored more than 2 weeks, unwrap and resoak cheesecloth and wrap again. Repeat every 2 weeks. Store fruitcakes up to 4 to 6 weeks. The fruitcakes may be served immediately after making, but the soaking and storing process gives a mellow, rich flavor to the cakes.

11. After storing time is up, make glaze: Combine corn syrup and water in small saucepan. Bring to rolling boil, cool slightly.

12. Unwrap fruitcakes, brush off surface crumbs, brush with glaze. Decorate with candied cherry halves, bits of citron and walnut halves. Brush with glaze again, allow glaze to set 15 minutes. Cut in thin slices to serve.

13. To present fruitcakes as gifts: Wrap each decorated, glazed fruitcake in plastic wrap. Tie with ribbon, label and decorate with holiday stickers. Place in appropriate tissue-lined box (a decorated shoe box is good). Wrap entire box with gift paper and tie with ribbon, finishing off with a sprig of holly or Christmas evergreens.

STOLLEN

MAKES 3
STOLLEN

2 cups unsifted all-purpose flour or unbleached all-purpose flour
½ cup sugar
1¼ teaspoons salt
2 packages active dry yeast
¾ cup milk
½ cup water
⅔ cup margarine
3 eggs, room temperature
½ cup unsifted all-purpose flour

3 to 4 cups unsifted all-purpose flour
¾ cup chopped blanched almonds
¾ cup mixed candied fruits
⅓ cup golden raisins
1½ cups confectioners' sugar
2 tablespoons milk
Blanched almonds, optional
Candied cherries, optional
Candied citron, optional

1. In a large bowl, thoroughly mix 2 cups flour, sugar, salt and undissolved dry yeast.

2. Combine milk, water and margarine in a saucepan. Heat over low heat until liquids are warm. (Margarine does not need to melt.)

3. Gradually add warm liquid to dry ingredients and beat 2 minutes at medium speed of electric mixer, scraping bowl occasionally.

4. Add eggs and ½ cup flour, or enough flour to make a thick batter. Beat at high speed 2 minutes, scraping bowl occasionally.

5. With large spoon stir in enough additional flour to make a soft dough.

6. Turn out onto lightly floured board; knead until smooth and elastic, about 8 to 10 minutes. Place in greased bowl, turning to grease top.

7. Cover; let rise in warm place, free from draft, until double in bulk, about 1½ hours.

8. Combine almonds, candied fruits and raisins.

9. Punch down dough; turn out onto lightly floured board. Knead in nut-and-fruit mixture. Divide dough into three equal pieces. Roll each piece of dough into a 12 x 7-inch oval. Fold in half lengthwise.

10. Place on greased baking sheets. Cover; let rise in warm place, free from draft, until double in bulk, about 45 minutes.

11. About 15 minutes before rising time is up, preheat oven to 350°F.

12. Bake stollen 20 to 25 minutes until done, or until they sound hollow when rapped with knuckle.

13. Remove from baking sheets immediately and cool on wire racks. Combine confectioners' sugar and milk smoothly. Pour on top of slightly warm stollen. If desired decorate with blanched almonds, candied cherries and citron.

Holiday Drinks

OLD-FASHIONED EGGNOG

MAKES 20 (½ CUP) SERVINGS

4½ cups milk
¼ cup sugar
6 eggs, separated
1 pt. vanilla ice cream
2 teaspoons brandy or rum extract

½ teaspoon pure vanilla extract
¼ teaspoon salt
¼ cup sugar
Ground nutmeg

1. Combine milk and ¼ cup sugar in a medium saucepan. Heat over medium heat, stirring to dissolve sugar until a rim of fine bubbles appears around edge of pan.
2. Beat egg yolks until thick and lemon-colored. Add a small amount of hot milk and egg yolks; return all to saucepan.
3. Cook over medium heat for 5 minutes, stirring constantly. Pour into a bowl. Add ice cream by spoonfuls, stirring until melted. Add brandy and vanilla extracts. Cover and refrigerate.
4. Refrigerate unbeaten egg whites, covered, in a separate container.
5. Just before filling punch bowl, let egg whites stand at room temperature in large bowl for 15 minutes.
6. Beat whites until foamy; add salt and continue beating until soft peaks form. Add ¼ cup sugar, 1 tablespoon at a time, beating constantly.
7. Continue beating until sugar is dissolved and whites are glossy and again stand in soft peaks.
8. Fold custard mixture into whites, using a large wire whisk.
9. Pour eggnog into chilled punch bowl. Ladle into punch cups and sprinkle with nutmeg.

Editor's Note: If desired, ¾ to 1 cup brandy or rum may be substituted for the extracts. Reduce milk by ⅔ cup.

GLOGG

MAKES 20 TO
25 SERVINGS

2 qts. dry red wine	1 tablespoon whole
2 qts. muscatel	cardamom seeds, crushed
1 pt. sweet vermouth	2 teaspoons whole cloves
1 tablespoon bitters,	2 cinnamon sticks
optional	1½ cups aquavit or vodka
2 cups raisins	1½ cups sugar
Peel from 1 orange	2 cups whole blanched
	almonds

1. In 6- to 8-qt. enameled or stainless steel pot, combine red wine, muscatel, sweet vermouth, bitters, raisins, orange peel and the spices: crushed cardamoms, cloves, and cinnamon sticks.
2. Cover and let stand several hours to develop flavor.
3. Just before serving, add aquavit and sugar. Stir well and bring to a full boil over high heat. Remove at once from the heat; stir in almonds and ladle hot glogg into mugs.

Editor's Note: For a simpler version leave out bitters, cardamom and aquavit.

HOT SPICED FRUIT PUNCH

MAKES 12 SERVINGS

½ cup sugar	½ cup fresh lemon juice
1 cup water	2½ cups pineapple juice
2 cinnamon sticks	2 cups grapefruit juice
¼ teaspoon ground ginger	1½ cups apricot nectar
½ teaspoon whole cloves	12 fresh orange slices, cut in
½ teaspoon whole allspice	half

1. Place sugar, water and spices into saucepan; heat to boiling, stirring to dissolve sugar. Boil 5 minutes, uncovered.
2. Add lemon juice, pineapple juice, grapefruit juice and apricot nectar. Heat just to boiling.
3. Serve in mugs or punch cups. Garnish with a fresh orange slice.

RUSSIAN TEA

MAKES 2 CUPS MIX,
ENOUGH FOR 4 QUARTS
OR 24 (5-OUNCE) CUPS

1¼ cups (or one 9-oz. jar) orange-flavored instant breakfast drink
½ cup sugar
⅓ cup instant tea
½ teaspoon ground cinnamon
¼ teaspoon ground cloves
Dash salt
Boiling water
Cinnamon sticks, optional

1. To prepare Russian Tea Mix, combine instant breakfast drink, sugar, instant tea, spices and salt. Stir well. Store in tightly covered labeled jar.
2. For each serving of hot Russian Tea, place 2 well-rounded teaspoons of mix in a cup. Add boiling water; stir until dissolved. Serve immediately, garnished with cinnamon-stick stirrers, if desired.
3. For 1 qt. of hot Russian Tea, combine ½ cup of the mix with 1 qt. boiling water in a heat-proof pitcher or serving bowl.

HOT MULLED PORT

MAKES 1¾ QUARTS

3 cups clear apple juice or cider
⅓ cup light corn syrup
3 cinnamon sticks
6 whole allspice
1 small orange, thinly sliced
Whole cloves
1 bottle (⅘ qt.) Cream Port
¾ cup brandy
Cinnamon-stick stirrers, optional

1. In large saucepan combine apple juice, corn syrup, 3 cinnamon sticks and allspice. Heat to boiling, stirring. Reduce heat and simmer covered 5 minutes.
2. Stud orange slices with cloves. Add orange slices, port and brandy to apple-juice mixture and heat to simmering.
3. Serve hot in heat-proof glasses or mugs with cinnamon sticks for stirrers, if desired.

CITRUS-SPARKLE PUNCH

MAKES 2 QUARTS, 16 (½-CUP) SERVINGS

⅔ cup orange-flavored instant breakfast drink
1 qt. cold water

2 cups ginger ale, chilled
Strawberry Sherbet (recipe below)

1. In pitcher, stir instant breakfast drink into water; stir to dissolve. Cover, refrigerate.
2. Just before serving, pour into chilled punch bowl, mix in ginger ale. Float small scoops of Strawberry Sherbet on punch.
3. Ladle into punch cups and top with scoops of sherbet.

STRAWBERRY SHERBET

MAKES ABOUT 4¾ CUPS,
8 TO 10 SERVINGS

1 pt. strawberries, washed and hulled
2 tablespoons lemon juice
½ cup sugar
¼ cup light corn syrup

⅛ teaspoon salt
2 egg whites
1 cup frozen whipped topping, thawed

1. Place strawberries and lemon juice in an electric blender container. Cover and blend until smooth.
2. Pour into bowl; stir in sugar, corn syrup and salt.
3. In medium bowl, beat egg whites till stiff. Fold into strawberry mixture, smoothly. Fold in whipped topping thoroughly.
4. Pour into 1½-qt. freezer container. Cover, freeze until firm, about 3 hours. Remove from freezer 10 minutes before serving.

SANGRIA

MAKES 6
SERVINGS

1½ lbs. seedless grapes
½ lemon
½ orange
2 tablespoons sugar

1½ quarts red wine
¼ cup brandy
6 cinnamon sticks
Ice cubes

1. Rinse and drain grapes; remove from stems. Chill.
2. Cut lemon and orange into thin slices. Place in pitcher along with sugar, wine and brandy. Chill to blend flavors, about 1 hour or longer.
3. To serve: Place about ½ cup grapes into stemmed glasses. Add ⅓ cup wine mixture and a lemon and orange slice to each. Garnish each with a cinnamon stick and ice as desired.

CRANBERRY-WINE PUNCH

MAKES ABOUT 3 QUARTS

2 qts. cranberry-juice cocktail, chilled
1 bottle (⅘ qt.) port wine, chilled

½ cup brandy
1 bottle (12 ozs.) club soda, chilled

1. Prepare cranberry rocks: Pour 1 qt. cranberry juice into 2 ice-cube trays. Freeze until solid.
2. In a large (4 qt.) punch bowl, combine remaining 1 qt. cranberry-juice cocktail, port wine, brandy and club soda. Add cranberry rocks and stir until very cold. Serve in punch cups.

MALIKIHIKI MAI TAI PUNCH

MAKES 12 (6-OUNCE) SERVINGS

1 cup light rum
1 cup dark rum
½ cup Cointreau
⅓ cup lime juice

1 can (46 ozs.) pineapple juice
Ice cubes
Fresh pineapple spears
Mint sprigs

1. Combine all ingredients except ice cubes, pineapple and mint; chill well.
2. Just before serving fill 12 large glasses with ice (or use large punch bowl). Add punch.
3. Garnish each serving with a pineapple spear and a mint sprig. Serve at once.

Holiday Entertaining

CLARET CONSOMMÉ

MAKES 5 CUPS, 8 SERVINGS

2 cans (10¾-ozs. size)
consommé, undiluted
1 soup-can water

1 soup-can claret
2 cinnamon sticks
8 lemon slices

1. In medium saucepan combine consommé, water, claret and cinnamon. Bring to boiling, reduce heat and simmer, covered, 15 minutes.
2. Remove cinnamon sticks, pour soup into a heated tureen or ladle into soup cups. Float lemon slices on top.

GOLDEN CHEESE SPREAD

MAKES 2½ CUPS

8 ozs. natural sharp Cheddar
cheese, finely grated (about
2¼ cups)
4 ozs. Gouda or Edam cheese,
finely grated (about 1 cup)
¼ cup grated Parmesan cheese
2 tablespoons butter or
margarine, softened

⅛ teaspoon garlic salt
1 teaspoon ground mustard
¼ cup dry white wine or apple
juice
¼ cup chopped ripe olives
Assorted crackers

1. Using electric mixer, beat together cheddar cheese, Gouda, Parmesan and butter until blended.
2. Add garlic salt, mustard and wine. Beat until blended, clean beaters. Stir in ripe olives.
3. Cover; chill overnight. Allow to stand at room temperature 1 hour before serving.
4. Serve in attractive bowl with assorted crackers in basket.

Editor's Note: Should be made day before.

HOLIDAY SANDWICH TREE

MAKES 32 PARTY-SIZE SANDWICHES

1 can (4½ ozs.) corned-beef spread
¼ cup small-curd creamed cottage cheese
2 teaspoons chopped chives or freeze-dried chives
½ teaspoon prepared horseradish
3 drops liquid hot pepper sauce

1 can (4¾ ozs.) chicken spread
2 tablespoons finely chopped water chestnuts, celery or cucumber
Dash ground ginger
1 loaf (16 ozs.) thinly sliced white bread (17 slices)
2 tablespoons mayonnaise
½ cup finely chopped parsley

1. Make fillings first: In small bowl combine corned-beef spread, cottage cheese, chives, horseradish and hot pepper sauce.
2. In another bowl combine chicken spread, water chestnuts and ginger.
3. Trim crusts from bread slices. (Keep bread slices under damp dish towel to keep them from drying out as you work.)
4. Spread corned-beef filling on four slices of bread, cover with four additional slices of bread. Repeat with chicken filling.
5. Cut each sandwich in quarters, making four squares. Dip one corner of each square into mayonnaise and then into parsley.
6. Arrange sandwiches into tree shape on serving plate, beginning with 9 squares in bottom layer: 7 on the outside and 2 in middle, so that the parsleyed points project.
7. In shaping the remaining four layers, use 7 squares outside and 1 in the middle; 6 squares outside and 1 in the middle; 5 squares and 4 squares.
8. Top tree with remaining slice of bread cut into star shape. (Use a star-shaped cookie cutter if you have one.) Points of star should also be dipped in mayonnaise and parsley; secure star on top with a toothpick.
9. Cover with foil or plastic film and refrigerate if not serving at once.

Editor's Note: If you are short on time, arrange sandwiches in tree shape and sprinkle all over with chopped parsley.

DORIS' CRABMEAT MOLD

MAKES ABOUT 48 APPETIZER SERVINGS

1 can (10¾ ozs.) cream of
   shrimp soup, undiluted, or
   1 can (10¾ ozs.) cream of
   mushroom soup, undiluted
2 packages (3-oz. size) cream
   cheese
¼ cup finely chopped onion
1 cup mayonnaise
2 envelopes unflavored
   gelatin

1 cup cold water
1 can (about 7½ ozs.) crab-
   meat, drained and flaked
1 cup finely chopped celery
Salad greens
Lemon wedges
Sliced pitted black olive
Pimiento strips
Assorted crackers

1. In medium saucepan, combine soup, cheese and onion. Heat until cheese is melted; stirring. Blend in mayonnaise, remove from heat.

2. In another saucepan, sprinkle gelatin over water. Over low heat, stir until gelatin dissolves. Stir into soup mixture. Add crabmeat and celery.

3. Pour mixture into 6-cup mold. Refrigerate 6 hours, or until firm.

4. Unmold on serving plate,* garnish with salad greens and lemon wedges. Use olive slices for eyes, pimiento strips for scales. Serve as a spread with crackers.

* Follow unmolding directions at end of Ardeth's Cranberry Mold.

CHRISTMAS RIBBON SALAD

MAKES 8 TO 10 SERVINGS

Layer One:
1 package (3 ozs.) lime-
   flavored gelatin
1 cup hot water
¾ cup ginger ale
2 tablespoons fresh lemon or
   lime juice

1 can (8 ozs.) crushed
   pineapple, drained
1 red apple, unpeeled and
   diced
1 cup mandarin oranges, well
   drained

Dissolve gelatin in hot water. Add ginger ale and juice. Pour into 4-qt. glass baking dish or mold. Chill until slightly thickened. Stir in remaining ingredients. Cover, chill until almost firm.

Layer Two:
1 package (3 ozs.) lime-flavored gelatin
½ cup boiling water
1 cup chopped walnuts

2 cups cottage cheese (cream-style)
2 tablespoons mayonnaise
1 cup heavy cream, whipped

Dissolve gelatin in hot water. Let cool. Chill in refrigerator until thickened. Stir in remaining ingredients. Pour over first layer and chill until almost firm.

Layer Three:
1 package (3 ozs.) lime-flavored gelatin
1 cup hot water
¾ cup ginger ale
2 tablespoons fresh lemon or lime juice

1 red apple unpeeled and diced
1 cup mandarin oranges, well drained
½ ripe avocado, sliced

Proceed as directed in Layer One. Wait until gelatin has thickened before adding apple and oranges. Pour over top two layers. Chill until very firm. Unmold. Garnish with avocado slices and lettuce. Lovely for a Christmas buffet!

ARDETH'S CRANBERRY MOLD

MAKES 16 (¼-CUP) SERVINGS

1 lb. (4 cups) fresh cranberries, rinsed and drained
1 package (3 ozs.) orange-flavored gelatin

1 package (3 ozs.) raspberry-flavored gelatin
¼ cup sugar
1½ cups boiling water
1 thin orange slice

1. Grind cranberries in grinder, saving all juice. (You may also grind cranberries, about ¼ cup at a time, in electric blender.)
2. In medium bowl dissolve orange gelatin, raspberry gelatin and sugar in boiling water. Stir in cranberries. Pour into 4-cup mold.
3. Cover and refrigerate 4 hours, or until firm. Unmold on attractive serving plate. Garnish with orange twist.

Editor's Note: The best way to unmold a gelatin mold is to run a knife around edge of mold to a depth of ½ inch. Invert mold on serving plate. Place hot, wet, wrung-out dish towel on top of mold, repeat if necessary. Mold should slip out easily.

HERBED STANDING RIB ROAST WITH YORKSHIRE PUDDING PUFFS AND TOMATO CUPS WITH MUSHROOMS AND PEAS

MAKES 12 SERVINGS

1 tablespoon onion powder
1 teaspoon garlic powder
½ teaspoon thyme leaves, crumbled
11 to 12 lb. standing rib roast, about 8 inches
2 cups grated carrots
2 tablespoons chopped parsley
1 teaspoon salt
¼ teaspoon ground black pepper
Yorkshire Pudding Puffs (recipe below)
Tomato Cups With Mushrooms and Peas (recipe below)

1. Preheat oven to 325°F. In small bowl, combine onion and garlic powders with thyme; rub over entire roast. Stand roast fat side up in a large roasting pan. Insert meat thermometer in center of meat.
2. Roast until meat thermometer registers 120°F., about 2½ to 3 hours. Meanwhile combine carrots with parsley, salt and black pepper. Spoon on fat side of roast. Return meat to oven; roast until meat thermometer registers 130°F. for rare, about 30 minutes, or 140°F. for medium, about 1 hour.
3. Place roast on cutting board; let stand for 20 minutes. Meanwhile turn oven to 400°F. for Yorkshire Pudding Puffs. Remove drippings from roasting pan; skim off fat and discard. Use 6 tablespoons of drippings in preparing Yorkshire Pudding Puffs; use rest for gravy. Serve roast with Tomato Cups With Mushrooms and Peas.

YORKSHIRE PUDDING PUFFS

MAKES 24 PUDDING PUFFS

2½ cups unsifted all-purpose flour
2 teaspoons onion powder
1 teaspoon salt
4 eggs, lightly beaten
2½ cups milk
6 tablespoons rib-roast pan drippings

1. Preheat oven to 400°F. In large bowl combine flour, onion powder and salt. Make a well in center; add eggs and milk. Beat with wire whisk until smooth.

2. Spoon some drippings into each of 24 3-inch muffin-pan cups; tilt pans to coat bottoms.

3. Heat pans 1 minute in hot oven. Remove from oven. Pour ¼ cup batter into each cup. Bake until puffed and golden, about 30 minutes; loosen with spatula and serve with Herbed Standing Rib Roast.

TOMATO CUPS WITH MUSHROOMS AND PEAS

MAKES 12 SERVINGS

12 medium-size tomatoes
 3 tablespoons instant minced onion
 3 tablespoons water
 8 tablespoons butter or margarine
 1 lb. fresh mushrooms, rinsed and sliced, or 2 cans (6- to 8-ozs. each) sliced mushrooms, drained

 2 packages (10-oz. size) frozen tiny peas
 2 tablespoons chopped parsley
 ½ teaspoon salt
 1 teaspoon Worcestershire sauce
 1 cup soft bread crumbs

1. Preheat oven to 325°F. Cut a slice from top of each tomato; scoop out centers. Set tomato cups aside.

2. Rehydrate minced onion in water for 10 minutes. In large skillet heat 7 tablespoons butter until melted. Add rehydrated onion; sauté for 2 minutes. Add mushrooms; sauté for 3 minutes.

3. Cook peas as package directs. Stir into mushroom mixture along with parsley, salt and Worcestershire sauce.

4. Use about ⅓ cup of mushroom mixture to fill each tomato cup. Place cups in baking pan. Melt remaining 1 tablespoon butter, stir in bread crumbs. Sprinkle lightly on top of filled tomato cups. Bake about 15 minutes, until crumbs are golden and tomatoes are hot.

BAKED HAM WITH APRICOT-BOURBON GLAZE

MAKES 17 TO 26 SERVINGS

1 (12 to 13 lbs.) fully cooked smoked ham
1 cup apricot jam
2 tablespoons bourbon
5 drops green food coloring
Water
Candied citron, cut into thin strips

15 dried apricots, soaked briefly in ¾ cup warm water
3 whole Maraschino cherries, drained
Blanched whole almonds

1. Preheat oven to 325°F. Place ham fat side up in shallow foil-lined roasting pan. Insert meat thermometer so that tip is in center of thickest part of meat and does not touch bone or rest in fat. Do not add water. Do not cover.

2. Roast ham for approximately 3 hours 15 minutes, allowing 10 to 15 minutes per pound. Meat thermometer should read 130°F.

3. Forty-five minutes before end of baking time, remove ham from oven. Remove rind with sharp knife and kitchen shears.

4. In small bowl, combine apricot jam and bourbon. Set aside 2 tablespoons glaze for garnish.

5. Brush ham with apricot glaze; return to oven. Bake until done, brushing 3 or 4 times with glaze. When golden brown remove from oven and transfer to serving platter. Cover loosely with foil to keep warm.

6. Meanwhile, prepare garnish: While ham is baking, combine food coloring and water; soak citron in water for about 10 minutes to tint bright green.

7. To garnish: Form 3 apricot flowers on the ham. For each flower overlap 5 apricots in a circle, place cherry in center. Make stems from the strips of citron and leaves from almonds. Brush reserved glaze on apricots, cherries and almonds to make them glisten.

POTATO LATKES

MAKES ABOUT 4
DOZEN PANCAKES

4 medium potatoes
½ onion
2 eggs
3 tablespoons flour

1 teaspoon salt
⅛ teaspoon pepper
¼ cup salad oil
Applesauce

1. *Grater method*: Pare and coarsely grate potatoes and ½ onion.
2. Add eggs and mix well. Sprinkle with flour, salt and pepper; mix well.
3. Heat oil in a large skillet. Drop potato batter by heaping table-spoonfuls into skillet and cook, turning once, until latkes are well browned. Serve immediately with applesauce.

1. *Alternate Blender method*: Place eggs in container of electric blender.
2. Pare potatoes and cut into small chunks. Cut ½ onion into chunks. Add to blender container.
3. Sprinkle with flour, salt and pepper. Blend at low speed just until the potatoes are uniformly grated, but not until they are almost liquified.
4. Heat oil in a large skillet. Drop potato batter by heaping table-spoonfuls into skillet and cook, turning once, until latkes are well browned. Serve with applesauce.

TZIMMES

MAKES 4 TO
6 SERVINGS

1 lb. carrots, pared and cut into ½-inch slices
1 sweet potato, pared and cut into 1-inch chunks
1 white potato, pared and cut into 1-inch chunks

¼ cup margarine
½ cup honey
1 teaspoon grated lemon rind
2 tablespoons lemon juice
½ teaspoon salt
⅛ teaspoon nutmeg

1. Place carrots and potatoes in saucepan; add water to cover. Bring to a boil, cover and cook until tender, 10 to 15 minutes; drain.
2. In flameproof casserole, melt margarine and add honey, lemon rind, lemon juice, salt and nutmeg. Add carrots and potatoes, mix well. Bake uncovered in 350°F. oven for 30 to 35 minutes.

BAKED CURRIED FRUIT

MAKES 2½ QUARTS

1 can (1 lb. 14 ozs.) cling peach halves, drained
1 can (1 lb. 14 ozs.) pear halves, drained
1 can (1 lb. 13½ ozs.) sliced pineapple, drained
½ cup Maraschino cherries, drained
1 can (1 lb. 14 ozs.) apricot halves
½ cup syrup from apricots
⅓ cup butter or margarine
3 teaspoons curry powder
¾ cup packed light brown sugar

1. Preheat oven to 350°F. Drain all fruits, except apricots. Reserve ½ cup apricot syrup, then drain. Pat fruits lightly with paper towels.
2. Arrange fruits in a large shallow baking pan.
3. In small skillet combine apricot syrup, butter, curry powder and brown sugar. Heat to boiling, stirring until butter melts and sugar dissolves. Drizzle syrup mixture over fruit.
4. Bake 30 minutes. To serve: Gently spoon fruits into casserole, serving dish or chafing dish; serve hot.

Editor's Note: Can be made ahead through step 3. Refrigerate, covered. Bake just before serving. Can also be made using 1 lb. 1 oz. cans of fruit, ¼ cup Maraschino cherries and same amount of syrup-curry mixture. This will make 1¼ quarts.

WALNUT-HONEY CAKE

MAKES 8 TO 10 SERVINGS

2 cups unsifted all-purpose flour
¼ teaspoon salt
1 teaspoon baking powder
½ teaspoon baking soda
½ teaspoon ground cinnamon
¼ teaspoon ground ginger
¼ teaspoon ground nutmeg
¼ teaspoon ground cloves
¼ teaspoon ground allspice
3 eggs
½ cup sugar
2 tablespoons vegetable oil
2 cups honey
¼ cup strong cold coffee
1½ cups finely chopped walnuts

1. Preheat oven to 325°F. Grease a 9-inch spring form pan.
2. On large sheet of waxed paper mix flour, salt, baking powder, baking soda, cinnamon, ginger, nutmeg, cloves and allspice.
3. In large bowl, with electric mixer beat eggs until light and foamy. Gradually add sugar, beating until very thick, will take about 5 minutes.
4. Add oil, honey and coffee, beat well until combined.

5. At low speed, gradually add flour mixture, blend well. Stir in walnuts.

6. Pour batter into prepared pan. Bake 1 hour and 15 minutes to 1 hour and 25 minutes or until cake tester poked in center comes out clean.

7. Cool on rack 20 minutes. Loosen cake from side of pan and remove. Cut with serrated knife.

PLUM PUDDING

MAKES 10 TO 12 SERVINGS

4 slices bread, cut in ½-inch cubes
1 cup milk
1 cup unsifted all-purpose flour
1 teaspoon baking soda
½ teaspoon salt
1 teaspoon ground cinnamon
¼ teaspoon ground allspice
¼ teaspoon ground nutmeg
¼ teaspoon ground ginger
1 cup raisins
1 cup chopped dates

½ cup mixed chopped candied fruit
½ cup chopped walnuts
1 cup packed dark brown sugar
¼ cup orange juice
1 teaspoon pure vanilla extract
6 ozs. suet, finely chopped
2 eggs, beaten
½ cup brandy, warmed
Orange Hard Sauce (recipe below)

1. Soak bread cubes in milk. Sift together flour, soda, salt, cinnamon, allspice, nutmeg and ginger into large bowl. Add raisins, dates, candied fruit and walnuts to flour mixture, coating well.

2. Stir brown sugar, orange juice, vanilla extract and suet into eggs.

3. Stir soaked bread, and egg mixture into flour and fruit combination, until well mixed.

4. Spoon batter into well-greased 1½-qt. steamed pudding mold. Cover with greased lid.

5. Place mold on rack in deep kettle. Add boiling water to a depth halfway up side of mold. Cover and let boil 3½ to 4 hours. Add boiling water during steaming to maintain water level.

6. Remove mold from kettle, uncover and let cool 10 minutes. Invert on platter and unmold.

7. Stick a piece of holly into top. Pour brandy over all, ignite and bring to the table flaming. Serve with Orange Hard Sauce.

Editor's Note: Make steamed pudding several days ahead, refrigerate. Remold, cover and resteam about 1 hour for best flavor.

ORANGE HARD SAUCE

MAKES ¾ CUP

½ cup butter, softened
1 cup sifted confectioners'
    sugar

4 teaspoons grated orange
    rind
4 teaspoons orange juice

1. In medium bowl with electric mixer at low-medium speed, blend butter and confectioners' sugar. Beat in orange rind and orange juice.
2. Refrigerate until serving time.

EGGNOG CHIFFON PIE

MAKES 1 (9-INCH) PIE, 8 SERVINGS

Chocolate Pie Shell:
¾ cup semisweet chocolate
    morsels

2 teaspoons vegetable
    shortening
1 cup very finely chopped
    walnuts

1. Line a 9-inch pie plate with enough aluminum foil to extend about an inch over edge; keep foil smooth and even.
2. In top of double boiler, over hot, *not boiling*, water, melt chocolate and shortening. Remove from heat. Blend well. Stir in walnuts.
3. Working quickly with spatula or back of large spoon, press warm chocolate mixture evenly onto bottom and sides of foil-lined pie plate.
4. Chill in refrigerator about 30 minutes, or until firm.
5. Holding foil at edges, carefully lift firm shell out of pie plate. Gently peel off foil. Return shell to pie plate. Place in refrigerator.

Eggnog Filling:
2 envelopes unflavored
    gelatin
¼ cup cold water
2 eggs, separated
¼ teaspoon salt
¼ teaspoon ground nutmeg
2 cups canned eggnog

1 teaspoon pure vanilla
    extract
¼ cup light or golden rum
¼ cup sugar
1 cup (½ pt.) heavy cream,
    whipped, optional
Sweet cooking-chocolate
    curls, optional

1. Sprinkle gelatin over cold water; soften 5 minutes.

2. In top of double boiler combine lightly beaten egg yolks, salt, nutmeg and eggnog. Cook over hot, *not boiling*, water 12 to 15 minutes, stirring until mixture thickens slightly and lightly coats a spoon.

3. Stir in softened gelatin until completely dissolved. Blend in vanilla extract and rum. Chill over ice water, stirring frequently, until consistency of unbeaten egg white.

4. In medium bowl beat egg whites until soft peaks form. Gradually beat in sugar until stiff peaks form.

5. Fold beaten whites into eggnog mixture. Chill over ice water until mixture mounds slightly when dropped from a spoon.

6. Turn into chilled chocolate shell. Refrigerate 3 hours, or until filling is set.

7. If desired, garnish with whipped cream rosettes and chocolate curls or spread whipped cream on top of pie and lightly sprinkle with ground nutmeg.

Vegetable of the Month: Mushrooms

MUSHROOM-BARLEY SOUP

MAKES 2 QUARTS, 8 SERVINGS

1 lb. fresh mushrooms, rinsed and drained
4 tablespoons butter or margarine
1 cup finely chopped onion
1 clove garlic, finely chopped
2 cans (10¾-oz. size) condensed beef broth
5 soup cans water
3 tablespoons tomato paste or ketchup
¾ teaspoon salt

Few twists freshly ground black pepper
1 bay leaf
½ cup barley
¼ cup chopped parsley
1½ cups sliced celery and leaves
1½ cups sliced carrots
2 tablespoons butter or margarine
4 tablespoons dry sherry
1 pt. sour cream

1. Chop ½ lb. mushrooms. Slice remaining ½ lb. and set aside.
2. In large saucepan, melt 4 tablespoons butter. Add the chopped mushrooms along with onion and garlic; sauté 5 minutes.
3. Stir in broth, water, tomato paste, salt, black pepper and bay leaf. Heat to boiling. Stir in barley. Reduce heat; cover and simmer 1 hour.
4. Add parsley, celery and carrots; cook, covered, about 30 minutes longer, or until vegetables and barley are tender.
5. In medium skillet melt 2 tablespoons butter. Add the reserved sliced mushrooms and sauté 5 minutes. Add to soup along with sherry.
6. Ladle into large soup bowls and serve with a dollop of sour cream.

296

GOURMET MUSHROOM-VEGETABLE SOUP

MAKES ABOUT 6 CUPS, 8 SERVINGS

¼ lb. fresh mushrooms, rinsed and sliced, or 1 can (6 to 8 ozs.) sliced mushrooms
2 cans (10½ ozs.) chicken broth
2 soup cans water
½ cup thinly sliced carrot

¼ teaspoon ginger
¾ cup peeled and diced tomato (1 medium)
¼ lb. fresh spinach, coarsely chopped
1 teaspoon soy sauce, optional

1. In 3-qt. saucepan, combine mushroom liquid (if canned mushrooms are used), chicken broth, water, carrot and ginger. Bring to boiling, reduce heat, cover and simmer 10 minutes.
2. Add mushrooms, tomato and spinach. Cover and simmer 5 minutes longer. Stir in soy sauce, if desired.

SEAFOOD-STUFFED MUSHROOMS

MAKES 15 TO 20 MUSHROOM CAPS

¾ lb. medium-size fresh mushrooms, rinsed and dried
7 tablespoons butter or margarine, melted
1 can (7½ ozs.) crabmeat or tuna, drained and flaked
2 eggs, lightly beaten
4 tablespoons soft bread crumbs

2 tablespoons mayonnaise
2 tablespoons chopped chives, scallion or onion
1 teaspoon lemon juice
⅛ teaspoon ground white pepper
1 tablespoon butter or margarine, melted
2 tablespoons soft bread crumbs

1. Preheat oven to 375°F. Remove stems from mushrooms and chop finely; set aside.
2. Brush mushroom caps with 7 tablespoons butter; arrange on lightly greased baking pan.
3. In small bowl combine remaining ingredients except 1 tablespoon butter and 2 tablespoons bread crumbs.
4. Fill each cap with some of mixture. Combine reserved butter and bread crumbs. Sprinkle over stuffed mushrooms. Bake for 15 minutes.

MUSHROOMS MAGNIFIQUE

MAKES 12 STUFFED MUSHROOMS

12 large mushrooms	½ clove garlic, minced
Salt	¼ teaspoon salt
2 tablespoons softened	⅛ teaspoon thyme leaves
butter	½ cup heavy cream
½ cup finely chopped pecans	Triangles of thinly sliced
1½ tablespoons chopped	buttered toast
parsley	

1. Clean mushrooms; remove stems from caps and finely chop enough of the stems to make ¼ cup. Salt caps lightly.

2. Add to the butter the chopped mushroom stems, pecans, and next four ingredients and mix until thoroughly blended.

3. Heap filling into mushroom caps and place caps in a shallow baking pan. Pour cream over all.

4. Set in a 350°F. oven for 20 minutes, or until mushrooms are tender, basting once or twice with the cream. Garnish with toast triangles.

GOOD EARTH SALAD

MAKES 6 SERVINGS

1 teaspoon salt	1 lb. fresh mushrooms,
1 teaspoon sugar	sliced, or 2 cans (6- to 8-oz.
¼ teaspoon ground mustard	size) sliced mushrooms,
Few twists freshly ground	drained
black pepper	1½ qts. washed, chilled, torn
⅔ cup olive or vegetable oil	lettuce and spinach leaves
¼ cup lemon juice	6 slices crisp-cooked bacon,
1 hard-cooked egg, chopped	crumbled
1 tablespoon chopped	
parsley	

1. In large bowl make dressing: Combine salt, sugar, mustard and pepper. Add oil, lemon juice, egg and parsley. Stir to blend.

2. Toss mushrooms in dressing; allow to marinate 5 minutes.

3. Just before serving, add lettuce, spinach and bacon. Toss well.

Index